PRESS, POLITICS, AND PERSEVERANCE

EVERETT C. JOHNSON
AND
THE PRESS OF KELLS

"THE HISTORY OF TOMORROW WILL BE WRITTEN
FROM THE NEWSPAPER OF TODAY."

PRESS, POLITICS, AND PERSEVERANCE

EVERETT C. JOHNSON
AND
THE PRESS OF KELLS

ROBERT C. BARNES AND JUDITH M. PFEIFFER

OAK KNOLL PRESS

CEDAR TREE BOOKS

1999

First Edition

Published by

Oak Knoll Press
310 Delaware Street, New Castle, DE 19720

and

Cedar Tree Books
Nine Germany Drive, Wilmington, DE 19804

ISBN: 1-884718-82-5

Title: Press, Politics and Perserverance
Authors: Robert C. Barnes & Judith Pfeiffer
Typographer: Andrew Pfeiffer
Publication Director: J. Lewis von Hoelle
Cover Design: A. Pfeiffer & M. Hohne
Cover Portrait: Everett C. Johnson: Collection of Marjorie Tilghman
Copyright © 1999 Robert Barnes & Judith Pfeiffer

Library of Congress Cataloging-in-Publication Data
Barnes, Robert C. (Robert Charles)
Press, Politics and Perseverance: Everett C. Johnson and the
Press of Kells / Robert C. Barnes & Judith M. Pfeiffer, -- 1st.ed
p.   cm.
Includes bibliographical references and index
ISBN 1-884718-82-5
1. Johnson, Everett C., 1877-1926. 2. Publishers and publishing-
-Delaware--Biography. 3. Printers--Delaware--Newark--Biography.
4. Statesmen--Delaware--Biography. 5. Newspaper publishing-
-Delaware--Newark--History--20th Century. 6. Press of Kells-
-History. 7. Newark Post (Newark Del, : 1910)--History.
I. Pfeiffer, Judith M. II. Title.
Z473.J737B37 1998
070.5'092--oc21
[B]   98-31420 CIP

Printed in the United States of America on 60# archival, acid-free
paper by Quinn-Woodbine

We, the authors, are at a loss for words that could convey our Love and Gratitude to the only person who could make this book possible. She has become much more to us than just a friend. So to Marjorie J. Tilghman we dedicate this book.

Table of Contents

∽

PREFACE

∞

I first heard of Everett Johnson when I was an undergraduate at the University of Delaware in the early 1920's, and a speaker at assembly, Delaware's Secretary of State, extolled the memory of this man. His features, though not his name, were already familiar to me, for his unlabeled portrait by Stanley Arthurs hung in a prominent place in the lobby of Old College.

Years later, after I had returned to Delaware as a faculty member in 1942 and gave closer attention than before to the history of my university and my state I learned to appreciate the contribution of Everett Johnson to these two institutions. Indeed a course that was part of my teaching assignment, the History and Government of Delaware, was of his devising. And the Women's College, campus home of half of my students, was as much his creation as that of all but one or two others.

In just one term in the state legislature, from 1911 to 1913, Johnson may have done more for Delaware College (as the school was then named) than any other legislator at any date. The Delaware history course was prescribed in a Johnson motion creating a State of Delaware Chair of History, with an annual appropriation for its support. Another Johnson bill established an agricultural extension service, based at Delaware College, to bring useful science to farms and homes. A third bill provided an annual state contribution for the upkeep of the college campus, an innovation in this state. And a resolution, in lieu of a statute, put the legislature on record in support of higher education for women. In 1913, though no longer in the general assembly, Johnson helped secure passage of a bill incorporating a Women's College to be affiliated with Delaware College.

An opportunity soon came for Everett Johnson to make further contributions to the advancement of education and of women. In 1917 he became secretary of state to his old friend Governor John G. Townsend, Jr. Unofficially he was more than a secretary; he was the governor's speech-writer and his intellectual partner, linked to the governor in what Townsend's biographer called "one of the least known but most remarkable relationships in the political history of Delaware."

The Townsend administration (1917-1921), covering the years of the First World War, was the apogee of the progressive movement associated with Theodore Roosevelt in the Republican Party. Townsend, in fact, was elected on two tickets (products of the Republican schism of 1912), the regular Republicans and the Progressives.

The major struggles of this administration were waged over school reform and women's suffrage. In the first struggle, Townsend and Johnson were successful in procuring desperately needed school reform legislation in 1919 and 1920, magnificently supported by the benevolence of Pierre du Pont. In the second struggle, they sought to make Delaware the decisive state in adoption of the Nineteenth Amendment, granting women the right to vote. They lost the battle, narrowly, but their cause triumphed, for the amendment was ratified without Delaware's support.

After leaving office Johnson continued battling for the causes he believed in, for good roads and good schools, for instance, largely through the agency of the weekly paper, the Newark Post, which he had founded in 1910, but also through membership on various committees and councils and as a popular speaker to groups throughout the state. "The best orator I ever heard" was the comment of a veteran newspaperman I was interviewing. One of his triumphs was the success of a statewide campaign, of which he was general chairman, to raise funds for a new University library as a war memorial dedicated to those Delawareans who lost their lives in the armed forces in the World War. One of his defeats was a campaign, in which again he was chairman, to save the old Henlopen Light House from the advancing ocean currents.

While his newspaper has proved its success by its longevity his further ambitions as a printer were not realized. From his Press of Kells, named for the famous Irish seat of learning, he produced a variety of works, taking great pride in the workmanship (in the Arts and Crafts tradition), almost regardless of cost. His most ambitious project was the creation of a University of Delaware Press, with the support of Pierre S. du Pont and a du Pont-financed agency, the Service Citizens of Delaware. His untimely death dealt a finishing blow to this enterprise, which thereafter languished—except for rare fitful reappearances—for several decades. The publications of Johnson's press are listed in the appendix.

Inasmuch as it was Johnson's early ambition to be a teacher and a scholar, it is fitting that his major achievements were in the fields of education and publishing. The frail health that once forced him to abandon graduate studies in history and politics at Johns Hopkins dealt him further blows at various stages in his career, but never quenched the spirit of this erudite, enthusiastic, talented idealist. Robert Barnes and Judith Pfeiffer have explored his career in depth; their readers will come to know Johnson as the lively, attractive dreamer that he was. Like his hero, Lincoln, he moved from a rural background between the sand hills and cypress swamp of southeastern Sussex to a position of prominence and respect at the edge of a university campus. He never forgot his roots and never abandoned his interest in learning.

JOHN A. MUNROE
Professor Emeritus of History
University of Delaware
May 28, 1998

In Memory of

Cornelius A. Tilghman Sr.

ACKNOWLEDGMENTS

∞

We would like to extend heartfelt thanks to the following people who, during our three years of asking for assistance, never said "No".

John Munroe watched over us and on several occasions steered us in the right direction. He graciously took the time to write the preface.

Rebecca Johnson Melvin, Special Collections, University of Delaware Morris Library was an enthusiastic supporter who repeatedly provided us access to the previously un-cataloged Everett C. Johnson collection. Jean Brown and Betty Dunn, of the University of Delaware Archives gave generously of their time and talent in locating and making endless copies of fragile papers.

Elizabeth Wardrop retrieved Johnson's college transcript of 1889 which gave us valuable information concerning his school days and Barbara Morris's timely article in the alumni magazine, The Messenger, resulted in valuable feedback from readers and letters of encouragement.

The overall support of the University of Delaware was greatly appreciated, especially the posthumous induction of Everett C. Johnson to the Wall of Fame in May 1998 where he belatedly took his rightful place among other distinguished Alumni. The oversight was discovered during the research for this book.

Marjorie McNinch, and Barbara Hall at Hagley Archives, Hagley Museum and Library introduced us to the wealth of information available on early industries in Delaware as well as personal papers of Delaware's historical figures.

The Delaware Room, at the Wilmington Library was a major source of previously unknown Kells publications and the Delaware Public Archives Hall of Records, Dover, Delaware, provided information on Johnson's political career.

Barbara Benson of the Delaware Historical Society filled in genealogical facts and figures and Bob Thomas of the Newark Historical Society generously shared the only existing bound copies of the Newark Post from 1910 to 1935.

A special thank you to Jerry Shields who introduced us to Richard B. Carter. When we despaired of ever being able to prove the connection between Kells and Elbert Hubbard's Roycroft Press, Mr. Carter, author of a biography of Governor John G. Townsend, miraculously produced a taped interview with Louise Johnson from 1971. Her description of Everett's trip to the Roycrofters' and the lasting impression it made on him ended the debate forever.

Our interview with Elizabeth Taylor, the last person hired by Everett Johnson, provided us with the only first-hand impressions of the working atmosphere at Kells and an insight into what it was like to be a Kells employee.

One of the most enjoyable and rewarding parts of writing a book is meeting new friends. The following dealers of antique books showed interest in our project and often called with discoveries of elusive desired publications. They also took us seriously which was a great boost to our sometimes sagging morale, and were always willing to impart their knowledge of antique books.

Tom Dougherty of Baldwin's Book Barn, and Barbara and Marvin Balick of Barbara's Antiques & Books found many volumes. Glen Rude shared his extensive private collection of Delaware books and John Reid found books and wrote articles about the project in his newsletter, "Collecting Delaware Books." William Hutchison was also a valuable provider of Kells publications.

Martha Carothers, owner of the old "Newark Post" building on Thompson Lane, opened the old printshop so we could search for type which might have been used at Kells, and DuVal Cleaves provided an unforgettable moment when he handed us the original print-block of the Kells logo.

The YWCA staff allowed us to inspect the old stone building which had once been Kells, and Kip Crist opened her home to us, which was built by Everett and was his pride and joy.

Curtis Paper Mill, established in 1789 once provided fine paper used by Kells. Sadly, it ceased operation in 1998, but before its doors closed forever, Don King, Barry Pugh, and Roy Keys permitted us to see the old mill in operation, and the way it produced paper for Kells finest printing.

Special thanks go to Robert Fleck, the president of Oak Knoll Publications and to John von Hoelle who tucked two neophyte writers under his wing and kept us there until we hatched a book.

Thanks also to our families who remained patient during our long hours of seclusion in writing and researching this book. Joe spent many hours reading and editing while Evelyn and Paula were helpful in doing some of the typing. Bobbi Ann and Tamara were very tolerant, as were our friends and co-workers, of our incessant talking about our book.

Thanks to Andy Pfeiffer and Kathryn Hamill for designing and typesetting the book.

Of course there would be no book at all without Everett's daughter, Marjorie Tilghman and her husband Cornelius. From the very beginning they opened their home and their hearts to two people they had never met before, who appeared one day at their doorstep with an idea for a book. Family bibles, photos and books from Kells as well as personal belongings of Everett Johnson were shared without reserve. Some of the stories shared with us made us laugh and some brought a tear to our eye but they all gave us insight into the character of Everett C. Johnson.

Cornelius was a part of Kells, a Rhodes Scholar and journalist, he kept it together for a time after Everett's death. We will not get to see his smile, however, when the book is finally published. Regretfully, he left us in July of 1998, at the age of 96. To use his own words, "He has got underway to met the Editor of Eternity."

∞

Everett C. Johnson's portrait—an oil painting, by noted Delaware artist Stanley Arthurs—depicts a slender, serious man, whose intense blue eyes gaze out across a room in Old College, one of the few buildings in existence at the University of Delaware when he attended from 1895 to 1899. A plaque reveals his name but few people today are aware of who he was and what he contributed to his State and University.

An example of his printing craftsmanship, an exquisitely bound, handmade book, hand lettered on the finest of paper, studded with gold, rests under a glass case on a pedestal in Memorial Hall. It is often buried under students' coats and there are no clues whatsoever about

Oil painting by Stanley Arthurs that hangs in Old College at the University of Delaware.

This photo and all unattributed photos hereafter courtesy Collection of Marjorie Tilghman

the man who conceived it, lettered it, bound it, and presented it. It is "One of a Kind" and its meaning and value as a W.W. I Memorial are no longer fully appreciated.

The existence of an unusual, fortress–like stone building, near the southern end of the Main campus, piques the interest of many passersby but its connection to Everett C. Johnson is little known. It now houses the YWCA and the cheerful sounds of people swimming, exercising and enjoying leisure time have replaced the clattering of printing presses. The recognition that this was once the site of a print shop from which emanated not only fine books of the Arts and Crafts Movement, but also a spirited home town paper still in publication, is being lost as time passes.

There are very few people living who knew Everett C. Johnson personally. Stories change with the telling and with the passing of generations it becomes difficult to separate fact from fiction. An amusing aside is a persistent tale that Johnson, a frail, slightly built intellectual, cow-punched his way to Europe aboard a tramp steamer. In fact, he was part of a select tourist group from Newark aboard a passenger liner. [1]

Thus the time seems overdue to piece together into a biography the scattered accounts of the life and works of one of Delaware' most progressive citizens. A man who was born in a rural backwater town, he founded a newspaper and a print shop, championed women's rights, and served in the State Legislature. He eventually found himself rubbing elbows with some of the wealthiest and most influential leaders of his day. A brief biography containing the highlights of Johnson's life exists and a few academic pamphlets have been written, but none of these are readily available or tell the entire story. [2] There is no complete bibliography—and perhaps never will be—of the works of Everett C. Johnson and his Press of Kells, since many of his publications have no imprint.

As a result, Everett Johnson has remained a virtual unknown and has never taken his rightful place in Delaware history. A perfect example of Johnson' obscurity is an article in his own newspaper dated August 8, 1921, which he must have printed with a smile:

SIC TRANSIT GLORIA MUNDI (THUS FAME IS FLEETING)

The following news item, which appeared in Every
Evening yesterday, attracted no little attention:

"One month ago Harry C. Taylor, order clerk for New
Castle County, mailed a letter addressed to Everett C.
Johnson, former Secretary of State, who is publisher and
editor of the Newark Post. Mr. Taylor waited three
weeks for a reply. A few days ago the letter, which had
not been delivered, came back from Newark, with the
word "unknown" written on the envelope.

Truly, "A prophet is not without honor, save in his own
country." Think of the Hon. Everett C. Johnson, former
Secretary of State, who is publisher and editor of the
Newark Post, owner of the famous Kells printery,
Trustee of the University of Delaware, and a man who
has been termed the only real orator in the State, being
classed as an "unknown" by the postoffice in his old
home town!

Honor is chagrined; Glory weeps tears of mortification;
fame sends to the drug store to get some Paris green
with which to re-paint the laurel wreath. Unknown,
unknown! Thus is the fate of one of our Best Minds in
the Republican Party! - Every Evening.

The Evening Journal and the Delmarvia Star, with the latter
giving the following summation, wrote similar articles:

'Tis impossible that human intelligence could reach
such bottomless depths. 'S'death! Call out the guard!
'Tis a base conspiracy! Ruthless rival hands must have
engineered this blasting blight on a young man's fair
fame. Can it be - can it by any chance be possible that
Ed Davis, at the helm of the rival Ledger, concocted this
foul conspiracy to douse the gleam of the brightest star
in Newark's crown?

This were the unkindest cut of all.

In 1921 the postmaster didn't know his name. By November

3

sixth, 1935, the entire student body of his alma mater was having trouble identifying him. The following article appeared in the University of Delaware Review, a paper formerly printed by The Press of Kells.

UNNAMED PORTRAIT IN OLD COLLEGE THAT OF EVERETT C. JOHNSON, IMMORTAL DEL. CITIZEN

SCHOLAR, TEACHER, JOURNALIST, STATESMAN, AND LOYAL ALUMNUS

Our columnist who called attention to the unnamed portrait hanging in Old College was as much surprised as I was to discover the identity of the person whom it represents.

The man in that portrait was one of the most able citizens that Delaware has ever produced - Everett C. Johnson, scholar, teacher, journalist, statesman, orator, and loyal alumnus. A plate is being made for the portrait to identify this great personality...

The portrait attracting the attention was unveiled in 1927, as a tribute to Johnson's memory by the Delaware College alumni, and as mentioned, now hangs just inside the front entrance of Old College. Also hanging inside Old College, keeping Everett company, is a painting of Manlove Hayes who was a member of the Board of Trustees of Delaware College from June 1882 to October 1910.

As is often the case, clues to a man's life are frequently revealed after his passing. Therefore it is not inappropriate for a biography of Everett C. Johnson to begin at the end with a eulogy from his own newspaper written by Cornelius A. Tilghman, family friend, Rhodes Scholar, and later son-in-law.

UNDER WAY

Behold the endless sea!
Gaze not behind at the receding shore;
But perch thy soul on the ship's prow amid the
flying spray

And with a heart filled with courage inspired by
memories, watch "the emulous waves press forward".
Or if you WILL look back, turn thine eyes upon the trail of the
speeding ship
And see the shining curving waves and the sparkling foam that
marks the way already passed.

"The Old Man" at Kells took a book and left Saturday morning. He will not be back this week. Nor next. He has gone on a longer trip than he ever took before. His soul was too great for its house of flesh and he has got under way to a new home for it.

He lived a full life, a strenuous life, a life of service. He looked life in the face and laughed with understanding. He saw the trees in Winter with their bare limbs stretched dumbly toward Heaven and he never forgot that the Spring would come. He understood the language of flowers, of dogs, and of men. He knew the souls of all three and found them good.

He might not have left as soon as he did if he had been a selfish man or one who feared death. But he knew neither selfishness nor fear. He might have left sooner if he had been an unloving man. But he lived to love and loved living.

He lived life to its highest and fullest and could have followed no other course.

He found for others and for himself the "day full–blown and splendid—day of immense sun, action, ambition, laughter". And now he has found "the night" that "follows close with millions of suns, and sleep and restoring darkness".

"The Old Man" at Kells took a book and left Saturday morning. He will not be back this week. Nor next. He has got under way to meet the Editor of Eternity.

C.A.T.

The medical authorities of the day agreed Everett C. Johnson

5

would probably not survive his serious illnesses in 1903 and the flu epidemic of 1918; amazingly, he survived until February 20, 1926. During those years his accomplishments were remarkable and, as was his nature, were achieved without drawing attention to himself or his deeds. Johnson was a master at working behind the scenes while others enjoyed the limelight. Nevertheless, he gained a reputation as the district's foremost orator, held the post of lifetime trustee of The University of Delaware and President of the Alumni Association, and was President of the Chamber of Commerce of Newark (De.). In addition he served in The House of Representatives for Delaware, shouldered the burden of Secretary of State during the First World War and was offered the Chairmanship of the International Press Association. This is only a partial list of his achievements, all performed while those who knew him marveled that he was still among the living.

The business records from Johnson's printshop, 'Kells' have been lost over the years. Five old ledgers from the Curtis Paper Mill containing records of paper sales to Johnson's print shop reside in the Hagley Museum archives and provide some information concerning type of paper used for different jobs.[3] Luckily, Pierre S. du Pont kept a copy of nearly every transaction and personal bit of correspondence made during his lifetime, many of which shed light on conditions concerning Kells.[4] Because Johnson was both a graduate of the University of Delaware and a lifetime trustee, work done in affiliation with the college is fairly well documented.

It is therefore fortunate that Everett C. Johnson published his own newspaper. The weekly editorials, spanning the years 1910 to 1926, provide a running diary of his thoughts and concerns. His columns of more lighthearted writing, such as SQUIBS (a lampoon), SPARKETTS and SHOP TALK, reveal his sense of humor and ability to laugh at himself and the world around him.

Throwing in capital letters with wild abandon he would hammer home his point of view week after week on the printed page. If the citizens of Newark didn't have enough pride in their town to change things he would shame them into it and refuse to let up until the job was done. To rewrite Everett C. Johnson's story without quoting the *Newark Post* would be impossible. He told it originally, his way, in his newspaper.

In belated recognition Everett C. Johnson assumed his rightful place on May 15th, 1998, on the Delaware Alumni Wall of Fame with the other sons and daughters of the University who have made notable contributions to their Alma Mater and State.

CHRONOLOGY

∞

1877   Everett C. Johnson born in Sussex Co. De. September 8th.

1894   Works as a clerk in a general store and establishes a life long friendship with John G. Townsend Jr. (1871-1964)

1895   Enrolls at Delaware College in Newark, Delaware.

1899   Graduates from Delaware College.

1900   Enrolls at Johns Hopkins University in Baltimore, Maryland.

1901   Sails to Europe on a two-month tour.

1902   Marries Louise J. Staton (June 10) who was born in 1882.

1903   Starts teaching at Deichmann College in Baltimore, Md.

1903   Stricken with double pneumonia, the first of ongoing health problems.

1904   Mother dies in Philadelphia, Pa.

1904   Moves back to Newark, De., and buys 26-acre farm.

1907   Marjorie, the only child of Everett and Louise, is born August 4th.

1910   Starts the *Newark Post* (January 26th) on Main Street.

1910   Elected as State Representative.

1910   Elected to Newark Board of Health.

1911   Appointed lifetime trustee of the University of Delaware. President of Alumni Association.

1915   Moves the *Newark Post* to South College and West Park Place.

1916   The print shop is given the name The Press of Kells.

1917   Appointed as Secretary of State under Governor John G. Townsend Jr.

1918   Everett's father dies and the Newark farm is sold.

1918   Everett becomes seriously ill during flu epidemic.

1921   After four years as Secretary of State Everett again devotes full time to the *Newark Post* and the Press of Kells.

1925   Named chairman of Henlopen Lighthouse Preservation Committee.

1925   Board of Directors Newark Chamber of Commerce

1926   Elected member of The Grolier Club.
1926   Dies February 20th at the age of 48.

From the Swamps of Sussex

the Early Years

∞

While researching Everett Johnson and his ancestors, it became apparent he was not the only member of the Johnson family lacking recognition. Previous biographies identify his parents as Captain Isaac and Mrs. Johnson. The mother of the man who worked so tirelessly to enable women to vote and attend college in the state of Delaware deserves more.

Her maiden name was Belinda Aurena Williams of Williamsville, Sussex County and she called herself "Lena." The third of twelve children, she was born October 7, 1852 to Eleanor Isabel Miller and Ezekiel Clows Williams, who married January 12, 1848. Genealogical records show Belinda was just 21 years old when her mother and youngest twin siblings died in childbirth.[5] Family records describe the demise of Belinda's mother; "When Eleanor Isabel had twins on August 3, 1873, she departed this life. The Reverend Joseph Arters preached her funeral at Sound Church. She was buried with one of the twins in each arm."

Belinda's father, Ezekiel Clows Williams, was born June 22, 1823 in Sussex County. His occupations are listed as "farmer", "military", "church", in the Williams family papers. His cause of death was equally tragic; he was accidentally shot and killed when a loaded shotgun fell from a bolt of yard goods at a country store near his home.[6]

The few examples of Belinda's writings found, are in her Ebenezer Sunday school book. Along with a list of classmates is the inscription, 'Gave To Her by Miss Catherine May, October 25th, 1870'. It was a childhood parable titled Tuppy and it may well have been Everett's first book.[7] All extra pages are filled, not only with his mother's typically Victorian poetry, family names and funeral details, but also with his early attempts at penmanship and drawing. Belinda died only two years after Everett's marriage to Louise Staton. As a result, there are no family stories or recollections of her by her only grandchild, Marjorie Tilghman.

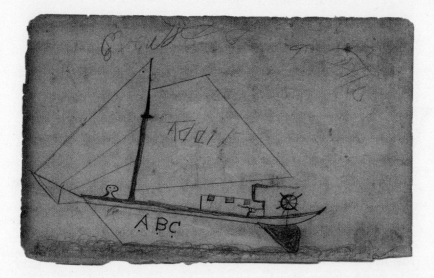

Everett's early artistic attempts at expressing his love of the sea.

A family bible records Lena's marriage to Captain Isaac Johnson in Philadelphia on November 12, 1876. They were to have only twenty-eight years together for Lena died in Philadelphia in 1904 of pneumonia, at the age of fifty-two. She rests next to her husband in the family plot at St. George's United Methodist Church in Clarksville, Delaware.

Everett's father, Captain Isaac R. Johnson, was born January 3, 1851. A colorful man in his own right, he was one of several children of Henry R. (who served in the Union Army throughout the Civil War), and Hattie Johnson. Choosing to "follow the water" at the age of nineteen, he was for many years master of a tugboat for The Standard Oil Company on the Delaware River and Bay.[8] The Johnsons lived in Philadelphia, and at Blackwater on the Indian River in Southern Delaware, where Everett was born September 8, 1877. Cemetery records show a second son, Harry F. was born June 20, 1884 and died in infancy twenty-six days later.

Isaac passed away suddenly, at the age of sixty-seven, on Friday September 20, 1918, "while hastening to catch a train near his home at Wilson Station (Newark, Delaware), in order to serve as a juror in the Court of General Sessions."

A vivid picture of Everett's rural birthplace, Blackwater, was portrayed by George Morgan, class of 1875, and Sunday editor of the Philadelphia Record, in his speech at the Midwinter Dinner and Reunion of the Alumni Association, February 19, 1927.[9] The occasion was the unveiling of Stanley M. Arthurs' portrait of Everett C. Johnson. It reads:

> "They were good substantial people—the Johnsons—and as for Blackwater, it dated from away back. The old Presbyterian Church was established at Blackwater the same year the Newark Academy was chartered (1769). From the branches of a white oak tree at Blackwater, Freeborn Garretson thundered forth some of the eloquence that must have remained in the air there that Everett must have absorbed when he was a bit of a lad. Blackwater too, was the home of the Tunnells; and Ebe Tunnell, fiftieth governor of Delaware was born there.

Left: Everett's grandfather, Captain Isaac Johnson
Right: The only existing portrait of Isaac and Belinda together.

Mark Twain speaks of his own birthplace as an 'invisible village'. Blackwater certainly is—at its best contained little more than a church, a school, a post office and a store, and now even these have vanished.

At Blackwater stood the first schoolhouse built in Baltimore Hundred and Everett may have learned the alphabet there but his parents moved to Selbyville when he was eight years old so that most of his primary training was with two teachers in the ungraded district school in that growing town".

The Selbyville school Johnson attended consisted of a seven room, two-story frame building on approximately two acres. Perhaps this is where he first learned to love books. *The General Report On School Buildings And Grounds Of Delaware*,[10] a book Johnson's press would publish in 1919, states: "This building is distinctive among Delaware schools in that it has a fairly decent library room and an unusually large collection of good books available for pupils, under conditions which are entirely acceptable."

A portent of things to come was a report card kept by his mother showing he had a course in elocution. Everett was to give many eloquent speeches during his lifetime and was considered one of the finest orators in the state of Delaware.

As a young man, he didn't have to travel far to find employment. Selbyville was home for many Johnson relatives and it was there, and in neighboring Bishopville, that he found part-time positions as a clerk. Dr. T. A. Holloway owned the drug store in Bishopville, Maryland; the stores in Selbyville were those of Henry J. Williams and Son and William R. and Caleb L. McCabe. The town was first settled by Matthew McCabe in the early nineteenth century and later named for Samson Selby who also opened a store there in 1842.[11] When Johnson left Selbyville for Delaware College, he would be in the company of sons from fine old Sussex families; two McCabes and two Tunnells would be listed among his classmates.

Sandy Branch, as Selbyville was first named, may have been bucolic but the town boasted many influential and stimulating residents. William R. McCabe was a member of the Democratic Party and served two terms as a representative in the Delaware State Legislature, being Speaker of the House during his second term.

Left: Everett in Victorian finery, about five years old.
Right: The young scholar, Everett, in grammar school.

In 1903 he founded the Selbyville Bank and served for four years as State Insurance and Banking Commissioner. [12]

Another person who would prove influential in Johnson's life was Isaiah J. Brasure, who was usually referred to as "Zare". He was a businessman interested in politics and he served as a leader to the young men in the town "carrying on long conversations and setting them to thinking about ideas larger than the confines of Baltimore Hundred and Sussex County". He won the senatorial election in 1898 running under the Union Republican Party ticket from the Fifth Senatorial District in southeastern Sussex. He received assistance with his campaign from John G. Townsend Jr., a businessman and entrepreneur who would lead Delaware through the tumultuous W.W.I years as one of its most progressive Republican governors. [13]

John Townsend had moved to Selbyville in December of 1896 in order to engage in the lumber and timber business. He later would become president of a canning company, several orchards, a highway engineering and construction company, The Baltimore Trust Company and director of the Farmers' Bank.

A member of the State Legislature from 1901 to 1903, he was a member of the staffs of three governors, Lea, Pennewill, and Miller, spanning the years 1905–1917.[14] When Townsend served as Governor of Delaware, from 1917 to 1921, he would appoint Everett C. Johnson, the young man he first met at McCabe's store, his Secretary of State.

In addition to his family and intellectually challenging friends, there were other factors at work that would influence Everett's life. As a youth he enjoyed the advantages of growing up surrounded by open fields, fresh air, and a slower pace of life commonly found in small towns in the late 1800s. But his little corner of the world boasted some very unique features.

Before the days of the railroads, Baltimore Hundred, located in the extreme Southeast corner of Delaware, was cut off from the rest of the state by inadequate roads. Muddy in Spring, dusty in Summer, the dirt roads were virtually impassable most of the year. Shipping was made difficult by the shallow, sandy nature of the Indian River and the coastline was peppered with treacherous shifting shoals. (A guiding light for sailors, the old Cape Henlopen Lighthouse, held a special place in Everett's heart; he would try valiantly in his lifetime to find a way to prevent it from sliding into the sea).

Religion played an important part in the daily life of isolated Sussex Countians. A history of the State of Delaware published in 1807 stated, "…the Methodists compose nearly one-half of the population of the counties of Kent and Sussex."[15] This was remarkable for Methodism did not make its appearance in Delaware until the last quarter of the eighteenth century. Everett was raised in the Methodist faith but as an adult was not a church-going man. He often took a good humored poke at ministers in his newspaper, however, he did admit to being very fond of Reverend Frank B. Herson of the Newark M. E. Church stating, 'He is a Man's Man as well as a Clergy-Man.'[16] It would appear he felt the latter were not usually the former.

The state of rural religion prevalent during Johnson's formative years is reflected in a story describing the founding of his Mother's church. Sound Methodist Church was started through the efforts of Freeborn Garrettson, the horseback riding missionary. According to tradition, Garrettson, while riding near the Cypress Swamp, was taken in for the night. The next morning he asked his host if he were acquainted with Jesus Christ. After mulling this over for a while, the man said, "Mister, Jesus Christ don't live around here 'cus I know everybody in these parts."[17]

The most unusual feature of Johnson's birthplace, was the Great Cypress Swamp. Older maps of Delaware show this as a large area stretching across the southern boundary of the state west of Selbyville. It included approximately 50,000 acres and the branches of four rivers radiated from it; the St. Martins and Indian Rivers drained toward the Atlantic, and the Nanticoke and Pocomoke Rivers flowed southwest to the Chesapeake Bay.

It was knee deep in sphagnum moss—a labyrinth of vines, dark water and cypress trees—the Northernmost site in the United States where these spectacular trees could be found. Some of them measured six feet in diameter and reached a height of one hundred and fifty feet. It was the site of whisky stills and the spawning ground of folk-tales and superstitions. Sections of it caught fire frequently and burned with a vengeance, the flames being fueled by peat moss and burning down to the underlying white sand. It effectively cut off any travel to the west and added greatly to the isolation of Selbyville.

The cypress swamp would be a sort of touch-stone for Everett; he would refer to it often in later years as if to assure the readers of his newspaper he had not forgotten his humble beginnings, or his old friends, now that he was politically active in the more prosperous, northern-most county of Delaware. He liked to refer to himself as "...the long haired farmer from the malarial districts of Cypress Swamp", and as being from, "...Sussex before the days of good crops." In his lifetime he would live in all three counties of the state, but New Castle County would be the site of his new home, alma mater and print shop. The love of nature, instilled in him in his youth in Southern Delaware would always be evident in the conduct of his life.

Evidence of this is a quotation from Robert Collyer often used in the heading of his paper, The Newark Post, "GOOD ROADS, FLOWERS, PARKS, BETTER SCHOOLS, TREES, PURE WATER, FRESH AIR, SUNSHINE AND WORK FOR EVERYBODY— THESE THINGS TO ME ARE RELIGION." Everett's two close friends, T. Coleman du Pont and Pierre S. du Pont would address the challenge of good roads and better schools. As for trees, some of the linden trees planted by Johnson still grace the old campus of the University of Delaware. His newspaper kept the public apprised of the town's progress in dealing with the issues of clean water and his modern print shop called Kells would be described by Johnson as providing fresh air, sunshine, green lawns, flowers and honest work for those willing to strive for excellence.

The College Years

Blue and Gold—Class of '99

∞

In the fall of 1895 Everett Johnson left Selbyville and headed north to enroll at Delaware College. There were twenty-one students listed in his Junior Class Yearbook in 1898. Three future professors of Delaware College were Johnson's classmates at various times during his four-year attendance. Wilbur Owen Sypherd '96, at first acting president and later president during 1944-46, was also head of the English Department. E. Laurence Smith '96 taught modern languages and was appointed the first Dean of Delaware College and Dean of Arts and Sciences, (1915-23) and Clarence A. Short '96 taught both mathematics and engineering from 1901 to 1920. Others who would achieve distinction were Hugh Martin Morris '98, appointed Judge of the District Court of the United States for Delaware in 1919 by President Wilson and Hugh Rodney Sharp '00, one of the University's most generous benefactors (the Sharp endowment investment grew to over fifty-eight million dollars). Another noted student of that time was George L. Medill '99, who became State Bank Commissioner, then president of the Delaware Trust Company. Many stately buildings on campus bear the names of these early graduates.

At the time of Johnson's enrollment in 1895, no entrance examination had been established for Delaware College and as the state had few High Schools or preparatory schools the standards for admittance were low. To offset the low entrance qualifications the faculty maintained strict criteria for graduation. In an effort to increase enrollment the policy of the college was to admit as many as possible and weed them out later. [18]

In 1899 there were only sixteen students in the senior class and a total enrollment of eighty. Thus a student so inclined could be a big fish in a small pond. Everett participated in many activities and clubs and seemed to be on the ruling committees of most of them. His fellow classmates had this to say of him in his class yearbook:

Old College, the first building of Delaware College, now the University of Delaware.

JOHNSON, EVERETT CLARENCE

One of the most important personages of the tribe of '99 is
Johnson, who by fate was blown by a strong Southeaster from
the sand swamps of old Sussex to the green terrace of Delaware
College. Johnson's highest ambition is to win military honor and
renown. He has a good class standing as a student. Takes well
with the girls and is well liked by all who know him. Though a
boyish youth with just enough fuzz on his face to make him
proud, he is always ready and willing and able to do his class a
good turn whenever an opportunity affords it. Johnson is a
student of languages taking Latin, French, German and Italian.
It was this man Johnson who was selected to manage Delaware's
first military promenade. It was Johnson who was selected to
edit the First College Annual the boys of old Delaware
published. It is Johnson who wears the military medal and holds
the highest military post in the Junior Class. It is Johnson who
by his deep sense of truth, honor, frankness, fearlessness and
sincerity has won the hearts of all his associates. We will leave
the further considerations of this young man's character to
readers of this book.

Classmates also wrote in the yearbook, "J-h-s-n: An admirer of
auburn hair.' (signed) Everybody," and added for good measure, "J is
for Johnson, our editor-in-chief, The way his work's done affords
us relief."

By his Junior year, Everett had attained the rank of First Sergeant
in the Corps of Cadets. He was Membership Chairman of the YMCA,
Tennis Manager of the Athletic Association, Treasurer of the
Shakespearean Club, President of the Delaware College Boarding
Club, and Inter-Collegiate Department Editor of the Delaware
College Review. One of three winners of the Declamation Contest
on June 14, 1897, he spoke on the subject "The New South".

He was also editor of the Delta Phi Literary Society's costly,
handwritten, biweekly paper, The Star, for which members paid
a princely five dollars per year. As only one copy of each edition
exists in the University Archives, it appears the paper circulated.
Additional copies could be purchased, but the fifty-cent price

Everett proudly wearing the Cadet Major uniform of Delaware College. The sword, owned by his daughter Marjorie, is engraved with his name and rank and only given to those voted worthy of the honor by fellow cadets.

probably discouraged buyers. In his freshman year he defended the reputation of his birthplace in an editorial entitled 'Sussex County'. It is reprinted here in its original form; his passion for the subject overriding his imperfect writing skills.

> This question of Sussex Co. has for some time been agitat-
> ing the minds of some of our worthy men from New Castle Co.
>
> Quite recently I heard one remark, Sussex Co. had never
> done anything for advancing the education in the State
> of Delaware.
>
> This is preposterous, and no man, who is well versed in
> the History of Education in Delaware would have made such
> a remark.
>
> Sussex can rank with the other counties in establishing the
> first schools in Delaware.
>
> New Castle has even gone so far as to call Delaware College
> her possession.

Ah! How badly she is deceived. In Sussex Co. by Sussex Co. men was the seed of Higher Education in Delaware planted, sprouted in New London, (Pa.) and is bearing fruit at Delaware College, (and glory be to those men, who set the Educational current in motion) a part of the fruit this tree is bearing is some of Sussex noble sons.

Again, Sussex can stand up and not only defy New Castle Co. but all America and say "It was in Sussex Co. and by Sussex Countians that the first institution for females was established."

Not only have we been working but are still at work. Sussex Co. has some of the best Public Schools in the State. Milford, Seaford, Georgetown, Milton, Laurel, Frankford being among the best.

A greater part of Delaware's great men are from Sussex Co.

So, My dear New Castle friends don't be jealous, but admit, as you should, that Sussex Co. has done as much for the advancement of Higher Education in Delaware as has her sister counties.

What a beautiful place is Down in Sussex Co., down in Little Delaware.

Johnson signed his article, J '99, signifying the class of 1899, but his additional signature is not so easily understood. He added, "The Man who got off at Buffalo," a phrase he may have borrowed from Elbert Hubbard who used it frequently and whose writing and printshop would have a great influence on Everett.

The first Delaware College yearbook was printed in 1898 with Everett as Editor-in-Chief. Called the *Aurora*, it glorified the goddess of the dawn. The inscription on page eleven reads:

Aurora, the golden hour, the dawn-was deified by the ancients, who pictured it as a goddess, She was arrayed in saffron-colored robes, with a star on her forehead and a zone of light around her waist. She was represented as breaking the bars of night and scattering brightness in her pathway.

May it be the mission of Delaware College, now in its dawning, to diffuse intellectual and moral light, and scatter health and gladness far and wide? Soon may she reach a high and glorious noon and long remain at the zenith of influence and blessing.

Let her loyal and faithful sons make our name a true prophecy of abiding good.

As early as his Junior year, Everett's patriotic tendencies were evident in the choice of a dedication for the yearbook. Next to a photo of the battleship 'Maine' is the inscription: "To the memory of those valiant heroes, whose lives were lost in the disaster of the good Battleship 'Maine," to the grieved fathers and mothers, to the sad and bereaved widows, to the loving sons and daughters, this book is solemnly dedicated. While others are erecting monuments to their honor, this oblation with like emotions is contributed by The Board to the same sacred shrine."

A contrast to these lofty words is the photograph of the Junior class. They are posed, irreverently seated on a giant American flag that covers the steps of Recitation Hall. Everett's feet are turned on edge as if to place as little as possible of his boot soles on Old Glory. Evidently the Seniors had other plans on picture taking day; the spot titled 'Senior Class' remained blank.

The Charles Elliot Company of Philadelphia and New York printed the *Aurora* and although the Junior Class challenged the following classes to continue the tradition, a second *Aurora* never materialized. The class of 1898 did their best to fling down the gauntlet by writing in the Delaware College Review: "we have not heard a word about the Aurora of '99. What shall we do? Give it up? Shame awaits at the door of the class that refrains from attempting to do something to keep up this publication which was first given us by the class of '98." The challenge was ignored, the specter of shame was insufficient motivation, and the next Delaware College yearbook was not printed until 1904 under the name *The Derelict*.

Like most students, Everett worked to help pay expenses. A bill paid to him by Delaware College, June 13, 1896, rewards twenty-five hours and twenty-seven minutes of laboratory work with a check for two dollars and fifty-five cents-a grand rate of ten cents per hour.

His course of study was 'Latin Scientific', which was composed mainly of the study of Languages, Mathematics, and Elocution. An anecdote concerning Johnson's college experiences has been repeated

The first yearbook ever printed at Delaware College; Everett was Editor in Chief.

so often it now has several versions. The story as written by Ethel Wilson, a close friend of Everett's, appeared in his eulogy in the *Newark Post*.[19] "When a freshman at the University of Delaware, he was one day in the library cataloguing books. He sat among the books with his hat tipped back on his head. Forgetful of everything, he worked and was unconscious that anyone had entered the room. He heard his name with a start, "Everett, I like your assurance, your self-importance, to sit here with your hat on in the presence of all these great men.' "I have never felt so humiliated in all my life,' he confessed. "I pulled off my hat sheepishly and stood to acknowledge Professor V's [Vallandigham] reproof and now I do not enter a library but I think of this incident."

The pattern he established in his college years of wholeheartedly taking on many difficult and challenging assignments would remain with him throughout his life. One can only wonder how much this dedicated man would have been able to accomplish had he not been plagued with illness.

Everett graduated with honors from Delaware College in 1899. In addition to a main speaker several students known for their

The Junior Class in 1898 irreverently seated on the American flag!
Everett is seated to the far left.

expertise in oratory were given the opportunity to share the stage at commencement. Everett felt very strongly that women were entitled to a college education. He was among those chosen to speak and despite a warning by Dr. Manning, one of his favorite language professors, who also advocated higher education for women, he addressed the controversial subject. Allowed to speak, his views were so well presented they inspired applause. This was fifteen years before the founding of the Women's College and forty-five years before the University of Delaware would embrace co-education. [20]

Eighteen years later, after having served a term in the State Legislature, Johnson wrote a highly critical article chastising the "College Man."[21] He accused the highly educated of hiding in their ivory towers and refusing to "mingle with the crowd and touch elbows with the masses in the struggle for better things," and with uncharacteristic harshness he penned, "As always the case with the student, they read as superior beings."

Using surprisingly strong words, Everett railed against the collegiate community as being "probably the last to enter into this spirit of taking part in the daily routine affairs of government." He continues in this vein accusing them of refusing "to face the ugliness of society in the making." His ire then focused on those who would scorn the political arena. The end of the article reads:

> In their aloofness, they are inclined to criticize those who take part in the actual mechanics of government. They see only tinsel honors or commercial gain as recompense for what they term 'dabbling in politics.'...The smirch of petty politics blinds them to any possibility of service...Their attitude today makes more serious the task of those working to hold true our institutions... The Nation, the State, the Community needs the College Men.... The aloofness held from the crowd makes for an ill-founded class. At least give cheer to those giving their best in keeping true the Democracy founded and nourished in the College Halls of the Revolution.

Unfortunately, with the passage of time, it becomes unlikely we will ever know what prompted such a sharp rebuke from a man who would devote his life to furthering the advancement of his Alma Mater and State.

Louise fondly described her husband as a romantic and related the story behind a silver-banded cane presented to him by the students.[22] Engraved, 1832-Delaware College-1902, it was made from one of the posts of the balustrade from the Old College staircase, which was being renovated. The gift was given in recognition of Johnson's devotion to the school.

These sentimental feelings almost got the best of him when the College became a University. April 13, 1921 the *Post* covered the historic event:

> Delaware College is a memory. The name passes into History. That which yesterday we called our Alma Mater has been, by onslaught of events, interpreted as Progress, transferred to the records of the past. By an act of the General Assembly, the College has passed out of existence. In its stead, the institution is now officially University of Delaware.
>
> And it is with a feeling of sadness that we record its action.

...Scholars of national recognition have taught within her walls and men have gone out from the Avenue of Lindens with training and inspiration that have builded strongly for the welfare of State and Nation. ...'From Delaware College? You studied under Professor _____, then we know your possibilities,' has been said to many a graduate in applying for a position.

...So the change of name marks the end of something that is intangible perhaps, but very dear to us. Our diploma reads Delaware College and the College no longer exists.

...Our ambition to make that little college down in Delaware, a leader in some phase of national life is never to be realized. A bit of foolish pride, perhaps a bit old fashioned, maybe, a dream, perchance, but we wanted to stand out, to be distinctive, As a University (which Delaware is not—'though by your smile you seem to say so'), she is just one of many. She has lost forever a certain individuality. The stranger does not appreciate this sentiment. Only the old student feels and understands. Webster would know at Dartmouth, Adams would know at Amherst. It is a very sacred thing to us.

But enough, Sadly we pass out under the Lindens into the world. Our Alma Mater is no more. Looking forward, however, we Hail the University of Delaware

After graduating from college, Everett began a teaching career at Deichmann College Preparatory School, in Baltimore, Maryland. It was founded in 1884 by Professor E. Deichmann and was originally called The Gymnasium School. Its first location was at 608 North Eutaw Street opposite Johns Hopkins University. The R. L. Polk and Co. Baltimore Directory lists the new name and location in 1900 as 847-851 North Howard Street.

The school was modeled after the German Gymnasium considered the "standard preparatory school of the world".[23] The following description was written in *The Book of its Board of Trade Baltimore City, Maryland*:

Its curriculum includes thorough collegiate instruction in Greek, Latin, modern languages, mathematics, the usual English branches, bookkeeping, and other commercial studies. It

has large, well-appointed class rooms, and one of the best-
equipped chemical and physical laboratories to be found in the
city...The graduates of this school have won the highest honors at
the Johns Hopkins University, Yale, Harvard, Princeton, Lehigh,
Washington and Lee, and the different theological seminaries.
During the last ten years more than one hundred of its graduates
have entered the Johns Hopkins University.[24]

While teaching at Deichmann Academy, Everett was also
enrolled at Johns Hopkins University where he was taking graduate
courses in history and political science. Unfortunately, ill health
would later prevent the completion of his studies.

In 1901, Everett fulfilled his wish to take a trip to Europe. A
group of nineteen departed for England with a tour arranged by
W. A. Johnson of 917 Madison Avenue, Baltimore.[25] The passenger
list identified him as Professor E. C. Johnson. Sailing from Liverpool,
on August 28th aboard the American Line's S. S. Westernland, they
also visited England, Holland, Germany, Italy, Switzerland, France,
and Scotland. The sixty-day tour cost three hundred dollars and a
selling point was the inclusion of the Passion Play at Oberammergau,
Bavaria. The party returned on the S. S. Belgenland.

Ireland was not on the itinerary, which would tend to debunk
the theory that the trip inspired him in later years to name his
printshop after the famous "Book of Kells" that resides in Trinity
College, Dublin, Ireland.

Marriage

From Purgatory to Heaven's Point

∞

In June 10, 1902, Everett C. Johnson and Louise J. Staton were married at the Welsh Tract Meeting House. They had originally met at Louise's mothers' house where he rented a room in 1898, (his Junior year at Delaware College). Newark was a small college town with a growing population. Housing was always in short supply for both students and professors and it was customary for widows to augment their income by taking in boarders. The list of people who stayed with Mrs. Staton includes many that would feature prominently in the growth and development of the University such as Rodney Sharp, Andrew Marvel, George Dutton, and George Medill. The house built by Mrs. Staton at 34 West Delaware Ave. is now owned by the University of Delaware and is next to the John Munroe History Complex.

Everett made a favorable impression on young Louise when he presented her with a gift of several of Shakespeare's plays, beautifully bound in leather, for her seventeenth birthday. In her memoirs she notes that the gift stood out among the more usual presents of handkerchiefs, candy, scarves and "the like."

In 1902 applications for marriage licenses were not taken lightly. Requiring the posting of a two hundred-dollar bond, to be rendered void and refunded upon completion of a lawful marriage, the license cost two dollars and fifty cents. One of the local newspapers would describe the wedding in great detail under the heading "Pretty Wedding." Elder Poulson, who performed the ceremony, had married the mother of the bride some twenty years earlier.

The twenty-two year old bride was described as "a beautiful young woman, gowned in Paris muslin, trimmed with lace and ribbon", while the groom wore "the conventional black." As they were receiving congratulations, a rainbow was noticed in the southeast, which was seen as a token of a bright and happy life.[26] The historic Welsh Tract Meeting House, dating to 1703, had been the site of

Louise Staton Johnson, probably her wedding photo..

only one previous wedding, which had occurred June sixteenth, 1814, eighty-eight years earlier.

On the carriage ride back to Newark, where the reception was to be held at the bride's mother's house, the couple passed professors Manning and Vallandigham walking to the wedding. Louise's comment, was, "They were a bit late!" [27]

The new Mr. and Mrs. Johnson then took the 10:30 train on the B. and O. Railroad for Baltimore where he was teaching and taking graduate courses.

The beginning of the next year, 1903, would be a turning point in Johnson's life. In January he was stricken with double pneumonia, followed by inflammatory rheumatism and shingles. Under the care of Dr. Dunott, a prominent physician living near by who took an interest in the young couple, he survived these serious illnesses but was strongly advised to give up his teaching career and graduate work.

Following their doctor's advice to leave the city of Baltimore, Everett and Louise moved to Mount Washington, a distance of six miles by trolley, where they leased a house for a year. During this time he suffered an attack of appendicitis, probably brought on by the diet of six raw eggs, four quarts of milk and beefsteak for dinner, which was prescribed by the doctor to counteract the effects of the previous medications used to combat his illnesses. [28]

While in the hospital for treatment he received a telegram from Philadelphia informing him of his mother's death from pneumonia. In true Johnson style he checked out, made the trip to attend the funeral, then returned to his hospital bed to continue his convalescence. His life would be a continuing struggle to prevent his infirmity from limiting his accomplishments.

Everett never fully recovered from his series of illnesses. He would often suffer from attacks of neuralgia characterized by headaches and severe facial pain. In later years he would take to his

The Welsh Tract Primitive Baptist Church where Louise and Everett were married in 1902. The church is still holding monthly services as it approaches its 300th year.

bed on Saturday afternoon after his Press closed and remain there for the rest of the weekend in order to conserve strength for the coming week.

Friends and co-workers often became worried as they watched

Johnson believed good books should be available to all.
It seems natural for him to have posed for a portrait with book in hand..

this frail man work himself into a state of exhaustion. Years later, in a letter written to Governor Townsend, during whose administration Everett served as Secretary of State, a family friend expressed concern:

My dear Mr. Townsend,

I have just made a little visit at Dover with Mr. and Mrs. Everett Johnson after not having seen them for five months.

You have seen them right along, and so may not have noticed what I did. That man is a sick man- and it came over me as a shock how very tired and sick he really is. I believe he is keeping up entirely on his will power and is trying to bluff us all into thinking he is well.

You are the only person in the world who can send him away for a rest of several weeks. I believe he would go if you insist.

The Governor, in his reply, acknowledged Johnson had been suffering from attacks of neuralgia and assured the writer of his intention to send him on vacation in the near future. [29]

Everett had always planned to return to Newark, not only to be closer to family and friends, but also to fulfill his dream of starting a newspaper that would serve the interest of the small university town. With further teaching and graduate studies out of the question the time seemed right to make such a move.

The Johnson's had built a house in Newark a few years earlier in anticipation of their return. It was however rented, which necessitated a search for a place to live. While Everett spent some time recuperating on the Delaware Bay aboard Captain Isaac's tugboat, Louise stayed with her mother and searched for a suitable home.

They settled in a small house outside of town. While living there, in his travels to and from Newark, Everett would have to pass by a farm which had at one time served as a parsonage for the Welsh Tract Primitive Baptist Church. The house had sentimental appeal because it was Louise's birthplace. One day Everett reported happily that a "For Sale" sign had appeared on the property. They were able to purchase the 26-acre farm on July 27, 1904 for $3,500 with help from his father who had retired and come to live with them. The farm was expanded in 1909 with the purchase of 22 additional acres for $2,500.

Their only child, Marjorie, was born at the former parsonage, August 4, 1907, in the same room in which her mother had been born and the same doctor, Dr. Henry, was in attendance. The parsonage was to be their home for the next twelve years.

Louise described the farm as Everett's retreat: "He did not like the name 'Purgatory' which had been given to the grove in our neighborhood where gypsies often camped. He straightaway named the crossroads at the corner of our apple orchards 'Heaven's Point.' He even used those words on some of his personal stationary after he established his print shop. The Farm itself was called "Crossways".

With the help of his father and a hired hand by the name of Bill Miller, Everett tried not to let his lack of agricultural expertise deter him from attempting to supplement their living by farming. He made many costly mistakes during the learning period but was always able to maintain his sense of humor. His lack of false pride and the ability to laugh at himself made him well liked among the small

Isaac and Marjorie in front of "The Crossways", the Johnson homestead that was for a time the Parsonage of the Primitive Baptist Church (Welsh Tract).

community of experienced farmers and he was often asked to use his gift of oratory at the local Grange Hall where he would recount amusing tales of his failures.

Everett, his father Isaac, and Bill Miller transported their produce to market in Wilmington, a thirty mile round trip, via a six-foot, two horse wagon, specially built for the purpose with "numerous shelves and boxes within and covered with heavy white canvas." The market on King Street was a lively place with few regulations governing sales. Everett tried to remedy the situation, first by exposing the problems in his paper and later by introducing a bill to try to improve this situation when he served in the House of Representatives (conflict of interest had not yet become an issue). The bill would exclude out-of-state fruit stands and "hucksters" from the curb market and when it was introduced, the Wilmington paper, Every Evening, went "up in the air." The representatives in Dover were told the affair was none of their business, Wilmington knew how to run things and would do it without any interference on the part of the Legislature.

The controversy revolved around non-farmers, sometimes

from neighboring states, buying their way into the market spaces. Everett had placed his name on a list for four years and was told there was never a vacancy on King Street. During that time he saw men secure stands who had never lived on a farm. "Crated eggs, cold storage chickens and produce of all kinds of inferior quality were sold to the residents of Wilmington as strictly fresh Delaware produce." Others traveled the country roads buying produce and later presented themselves as farmers. Johnson pointed out that not only was this a violation of the law but in the case of butter, eggs and poultry "Wilmington buyers were running grave risks."[30]

While Everett was struggling to sell produce and run a newspaper, Louise was afforded an unusual opportunity to gain a brief respite from farm chores to further her studies, something she had always expressed a desire to do. Dr. Sypherd, head of the English Department at Delaware College, had decided to offer two courses for girls and Louise eagerly enrolled.[31] She had harbored bitter feelings against an institution that excluded females, the group forming the majority of grade school teachers, from seeking a higher education. This situation would not be remedied until 1914, with the opening of The Women's College, in part a result of the relentless campaigning on the part of her husband for their inclusion.

In addition to establishing the *Newark Post*, described later, Everett was drafted as a Republican candidate for the Legislature in the fall of 1910. A favorite family anecdote concerning the election bears repeating. It illustrates Johnson's ability to out-fox the opposition by turning their attributes into liabilities. As Everett's daughter Marjorie recounts the tale, her father's Democratic opponent, Roseby McMullen was not only a fellow farmer but also one of Everett's close friends. Criticizing another candidate was not to his liking so Everett chose a different tack. Mr. McMullen was unexcelled at growing sweet potatoes while Johnson's shortcomings as a farmer were well known. Everett won the election by convincing the voters each candidate would best serve the public by doing that in which they excelled. Mr. McMullen went back to raising sweet potatoes and Everett C. Johnson took a seat in the Legislature.

November 1910, Everett was elected to the Legislature for a two-year term. As representative, he introduced a surprising number of bills. Since the Legislature was only in session from January through March every other year, issues not resolved during that time were shelved until after the following election year. Among his more important bills were:

(H. B., No. 333) An Act providing for the establishment of a Manual Training School for each of the Counties of this State.

(H. B., No. 334) An Act to re-incorporate the Trustees of Delaware College.

(H. B., No. 335) An act providing for the establishment and maintenance of a Chair of History at Delaware College. Passed as H. B., No. 355.

(H. B., No. 346) An act to provide for the establishment of a Division of Agricultural Extension at Delaware College and provide for the maintenance thereof.

A Joint Resolution (H.J.R. No. 24) entitled: Joint Resolution authorizing and directing the State Board of Education to take up and consider the higher education of women in this State....

(H. B., No. 390) An act to abolish the death penalty as a punishment for crime and to substitute life imprisonment in place thereof.

(H. B., No. 332) An act in relation to the Election Districts of Representative District Number 11 in New Castle County (Everett's district).

(H. J. R., No. 13) House Joint Resolution authorizing the Secretary of State to have printed the Constitution of the State of Delaware.

(H. B., No. 49 and 113) two bills appropriating a total of $121,710 to the Delaware State Hospital at Farnhurst.

Acts concerning roads, school meetings and the commission for the Blind.

At the very end of the session a resolution appropriating $5,000 annually for the erection, alteration, extension, repairs and general improvements of necessary buildings, and the grounds of the Delaware College and other expenses of the College.

Last but not least for this newspaperman, a motion that the House of Representatives formally thank the press! For all this effort,

Everett and the other Representatives received $300. [32]

The next election, November 6, 1912, resulted in Harry M. McCormick (R) of Iron Hill, Delaware, being sent to the House. Everett had declined the invitation to run for a second term. He did, however, lend his support to the bill for higher education for women by staying in Dover and presenting convincing arguments to the General Assembly during the 1913 session. [33]

This bill, #209, was finally passed on March 25, 1913, and paved the way for the establishment of the Women's College in Newark, Delaware.

WOMAN'S RIGHTS

A MAN AHEAD OF HIS TIME

∞

If man is a tyrant he has been so taught by his mother, and the sufferings of woman are the results of her own work. If the mother had exerted her full influence in the proper direction she most likely would have trained a race of men with a true feeling, and a keen sense of justice."

Everett Johnson's mother must have exerted her "full influence in the proper direction" to have produced a son so dedicated to ensuring women's rights. The preceding excerpt is from a lengthy article written by Everett in his Junior year, in the 1898 issue of the Delaware College Review. Titled "Woman's Social Position," it is a forceful diatribe against woman's acceptance of a subordinate position in society.

Before 1914, young white women from Delaware who desired a college degree were forced to leave the state. In an unusual reversal of discriminatory scholastic policies, Delaware State University, a school for black students that opened its doors in 1892, accepted both men and women. As a result of the lack of high schools for black students, it served as a preparatory school for the first years, but it never excluded women. Even the shameful existence of segregation was working against white female high school graduates.[34]

Everett's wife, Louise, was bitter at being refused entrance to Delaware College after finishing first in her class of 1897 at Newark High School. Presumably, he was drawn to his bride, not only by her beauty, but also by her interest in learning. While other suitors gifted her with frivolous trinkets, he appealed to her intellectual side with presents of books and won her hand. This may have been the first time Everett encountered the frustration of an intelligent woman denied a higher education. Since she was to become his wife, the issue now struck closer to home and her cause became his cause.

Whatever the motivation, Johnson used his literary skills in a campaign to establish the Woman's College and refused to let up until the dream was a reality. He began in the Delaware College

Review, November 1898, with a barrage of questions aimed at female readers. "O woman! Woman! Are you a woman? If so, why do you remain silent? Why do you bow without complaint to the will of your coarser sex? Why do you remain silent and let men, who are elected many times from corrupt classes, and almost all times by political trickery…make laws which shall govern you?" (He had no idea at the time he would become a politician himself!)

He continues, taking aim at the shallowness of a young woman's daily pursuits: "When I think of the time the young man is in college or studying elsewhere for a profession, which his sister is frittering away in showy dress, entertaining company, matching wool or making crazy work of some kind, I am surprised to find that there is as much companionship as there is between the sexes." This article, slightly rewritten, appeared again as one of four unsigned articles in Delaware College's first yearbook of which Johnson was Editor-in-Chief. The four authors wrote anonymously and all of them strongly advocated higher education for women.

The debate over co-education at Delaware College was intense. When the Women's College was finally established on nineteen acres of land nearly a half mile south of the main campus, one of the trustees bitterly opposed putting it in Newark, stating it should be in Dover or anywhere else, as long as it was far away. His wife must have disagreed, for she immediately enrolled and was graduated with the first class in 1918. [35]

Once the obstacles had been overcome and the last negative voice had been overruled, Everett's bill, first introduced in the House of Representatives in 1911, was approved by Governor Simeon Pennewill. It required the State Board of Education "to evolve a feasible plan for the higher education of women in Delaware." The bill was passed by the General Assembly in March 1913, and approved by Governor Charles R. Miller.[36]

When the college finally opened on October 10, 1914 Everett was chosen by his fellow Board of Trustees to accept the keys to the buildings. His description in the Post was emotional "the greatest day Delaware has ever known" followed by "Enthusiasm and faith in the possibilities of our little Commonwealth was the spirit of the day." By the time the college opened it was too late for Louise to take full advantage of the opportunity. With a farm and a seven-year-old

An aerial view of the Women's College (A),
showing its proximity to Kells, inset.
Memorial Hall (B) was the "dividing line"
between the Men's and Women's campuses.

child to care for, she was only able to take a few select courses. However, her daughter Marjorie, enrolled in 1924, and graduated with the
class of 1928, two years after her father's death. Had Everett lived to
see his daughter graduate near the top of her class he would have been
sorely disappointed to see how little the role of women had changed
since he wrote his article in 1898. Seventy years after her graduation,
during an interview for this book, Marjorie's blue eyes still flashed
with indignation as she recalled the following incident: "At the close
of the mid-year, students were expected to line up before Dean
Winifred Robinson for an evaluation. I had achieved excellent grades
and was looking forward to a favorable comment on my efforts. When
my turn came, imagine my disappointment when the only comment
I received was, "Marjorie, you must think about learning to sew like
your mother."

A scholarship of $200.00 was named in Everett's honor in
1928, and Katherine Rinard, chairman of the scholarship committee

honored him as "one of the originators of the idea of a college for women in the State of Delaware, and one of the best friends which Delaware College, his alma mater, and the Women's College have ever had." [37]

Ruskin, Morris, Hubbard, and Johnson

the Arts and Crafts Movement

∞

That there actually was a press in the conservative town of Newark, Delaware endeavoring to carry on the philosophy espoused by the Arts and Crafts Movement, having its origins in Europe, is unusual. That it was the result of one man's dream is not so surprising. The Arts and Crafts Movement was led by a handful of men pursuing the belief that art and industry could be unified. (1819–1900).

The English writer and artist John Ruskin is credited with the philosophy of the movement. He blamed the Industrial Revolution for isolating artists from the rest of society which led to mass-produced manufactured goods devoid of any redeeming aesthetic qualities. He believed beautiful things did not have to justify their existence; they were valuable and useful simply because they were made with "head, heart and hand".

Book design was one of the casualties of the Industrial Revolution and it wasn't until late in the nineteenth century when another Englishman, William Morris (1834–1896) led the way by treating the book as an art form, that things began to improve. Calling for a return to skilled craftsmanship, he believed art and craft should be apparent in the manufacture of everyday goods. He preached against the squalid conditions prevalent in cities and advocated the creation of a workplace atmosphere conducive to the health and well-being of the workers. Originally a designer of textiles, Morris later turned his attentions to graphic design and printmaking. His Kelmscott Press established in London, became famous for meticulous hand-printing, handmade paper, handcut woodblocks and intricate initials and borders.

Morris designed three typefaces. Troy was a black letter typeface easily read with wider rounder characters than previous gothic types. Chaucer was a smaller version of Troy and Golden was based on Venetian Roman faces designed by the printer Nicolas Jenson between 1470 and 1476. Morris F. Benton, (1872–1948) head of typeface development for the American Typeface Founders Company, later re-designed Jenson's type and renamed it the Cloister family.[38] The Jenson initials would be the choice of Everett Johnson for use in his finest books from the Press of Kells. The philosophy of William Morris may have been to improve the quality of life for the common worker but, in fact, only the very wealthy could afford the household furnishings of Morris and Company or the exquisite books from the Kelmscott Press.

The person who brought the Arts and Crafts movement to America offered his products to the common people. Elbert Hubbard began his career as a salesman for the Larkin Soap Company, which he established with his brother-in-law in Buffalo, New York. His flair for salesmanship quickly resulted in great profits for the company and in 1893 at the age of thirty-seven he sold his share in the mail-order soap business, receiving enough money to enable him to pursue his new avocation of writing. During a trip to England in 1894 he met William Morris and visited the famous Kelmscott Press.

Inspired, he returned to East Aurora and established the controversial Roycroft Press the following year. The Roycroft books were in many ways imitations of the Kelmscott books but they were not aimed at the socially elite. Within a few years more buildings were added and more than 500 people, most of them locals who were trained by Hubbard, were producing furniture, copperwork, metalwork, leather goods and stained glass as well as books. He was criticized by many as being a huckster who lowered the lofty philosophical standards of the Arts and Crafts Movement. In reality he brought finely crafted products into the lives of ordinary citizens and instilled a love of reading in the many people he reached through his mail order books.

The Creed, a copy of which was mailed to new members of the Roycroft Fraternity was borrowed from Ruskin: "A belief in working with the Head, Hand and Heart and mixing enough Play with the Work so that every task is pleasurable and makes for Health and Happiness."[39]

One of the buildings in the Roycroft community was the Roycroft Inn. A 1905 advertisement in one of Hubbard's popular series of Little Journeys in booklet form, (single copies 25 cents, by the year, $3.00), lists the amenities with typical Hubbard wit:

Out-of-Door Sleeping-Rooms with In Door
Dressing-Rooms attached, Electric lights, Steam heat,
Turkish baths, Running water, Art Gallery, Chapel,
Camp-in woods, Library, Music Room, Ballroom,
Garden and Wood Pile. By understanding of the local
W. C. T. U. (Women's Christian Temperance Union)
we supply chaser only. Parties without baggage will
receive special attention from Ali Baba (the handyman).
Hammers for Knockers without extra charge.

Everett Johnson, the man who would bring the Arts and Crafts
Movement to Newark, Delaware, visited Elbert Hubbard's
community in July of 1911. As Hubbard caught the printing fever
from Morris, Everett caught it from the Roycrofters. The desire to
publish limited edition books, using the finest type available on the
best paper he could afford, was a goal he set for himself as a result of
that visit. Unlike Morris and Hubbard, he did not have a personal
fortune to invest in his dream and the Press of Kells was frequently
in debt.

Johnson also imitated Hubbard's use of Mottoes and Creeds and
was not adverse to using some caustic humor in his newspaper.

Whereas the Roycroft Creed advocated mixing play with the
work, The Press of Kells was advertised as "The Shop down on Welsh
Lane where we mix a little brains with our ink." The ads for his press
usually ended with, "Kells—where Master Craftsmen study and work
at the Art of Printing."

Johnson constantly struggled to educate his prospective
customers concerning the difference between printing well done and
cheap, shoddy jobs run off quickly just for profit. At times it must
have seemed like a lost cause as he seldom earned enough to justify
the care put into his work. The fine, limited-edition books he hoped
would make the Press famous never caught on, and he was forced to
job printing to pay the bills. Even so, he made sure his customers
knew they were getting a lot for their money.

The May 31st, 1916 issue of the *Post* explained his idea of the
way printing should be done.

Kells Where Master Craftsmen study and work at the Art of Printing
Welsh Lane ~ Newark, Delaware

The Kells letterhead.

KELLS, WHERE MASTER CRAFTSMEN STUDY AND WORK AT PRINTING

A good piece of Printing requires a study of the proper kind of stock, the style and arrangement of type, the selection of ink with eye to color. All this must be thought out before the work is begun. Then the mechanical skill, in composition, and in press work. A love of the work must be there too.

Added to this must be an equipment in type, labor saving devices, presses, folding machines.
Added again to this, must be light, air, sunshine, pleasing surroundings.

With these must be an attention to management, giving business efficiency toward purchases of materials, wastes, overhead charges and efficient deliveries. Then, if there be a co-operation between the several departments, you may expect a good piece of Printing. And this is the policy at Kells.

Every job coming to this Shop is planned with a certain amount of study before the mechanical work is commenced. Study enters into our Printing. Mechanical skill enters into it. The best equipment, labor saving devices, love of work, surroundings approaching Ideal. A Printer's Heaven said a guest last week.

This Imprint of the Head, Heart and Hand Triangle is our Ideal toward which our work is tending always. Nor think all these ambitions tend to raise the price. Rather, just the opposite. These things just mentioned make this plant give value received. "Everything in its place and a place for Everything" is far cheaper than, where is this, that and the other thing entering into the job. If these words are not convincing—try our work—It never fails. Have your work done at Kells where Master Craftsmen study and work at the Art of Printing.

Everett Johnson and Elbert Hubbard both believed in their work but used completely different methods of conducting business. In addition, experiences with higher education left each man with a totally different outlook on life.

According to his wife, Everett was always scholarly. "And he was, well I've heard people say this to please me, he was the smartest man in Newark. But he didn't give that impression that he was trying to be smart...he was interested in the right things." [40]

Like Morris, Johnson did not wish to reinvent the Arts and Crafts Movement, he only desired to perpetuate excellent craftsmanship. College transcripts show he excelled at Delaware College, graduating with honors and achieving the highest rank possible in the Cadet Corps, that of Cadet Major. Only illness prevented him from achieving a graduate degree from Johns Hopkins. Unable to continue teaching, his press substituted as a vehicle to help his readers understand current affairs. Whatever he thought would be beneficial for Newark would be "boosted" in the *Post*. In 1917, in an attempt to encourage reading, Johnson departed from his policy of "all home print". *The Man Without A Country*, by Edward Everett Hale, had been chosen by the Newark High School Alumni Association as a second book for the year's reading. After becoming concerned over a shortage of available copies, Everett, as a service to the community, published the entire text in the May ninth and May sixteenth issues of the *Post*.

Hubbard, on the other hand, aspired to be a college man and failed - twice. He went to Harvard with a chip on his shoulder, determined to obtain a degree seemingly not for the sake of learning as much as to make his writing more acceptable to the intelligentsia. Unable to fit in, he summed up the entire experience as a waste of time stating "College is a make-believe, and every college student knows it." [41] Hubbard did, however, have a real talent for business and a way of writing that appealed to the populace. In spite of their differences, Johnson admired Elbert Hubbard, and the early issues of the *Post* contained many articles written in the Roycroft style. As Johnson became more experienced in dealing with the public and more knowledgeable in the world of politics, he abandoned Hubbard's theatrical style of writing in favor of a more erudite approach.

Instead of adopting the Roycroft style Everett should have studied Hubbard's talent for making money. The Roycroft Press was not known for printing without turning a profit. The Press of Kells, however, constantly ran in the red due to its owner's generosity. The profit margin was low to begin with compared to other print shops and jobs for his Alma Mater, Delaware College, were often done for little or no profit. In some cases, such as Professor Vallandigham's 153 page book, *Fifty Years of Delaware College,* published for the college's golden anniversary, he did the work gratis. [42]

THE NEWARK POST

PRINT ALL THE TRUTH YOU DARE

∞

By 1910 the town of Newark had two newspapers, *The Newark Post* and the *Delaware Ledger*. Records for 1928 show the cost of a year's subscription to the *Post* had risen from the original $1.00 to $1.50, with a single copy costing 4 cents. It was mailed to 630 customers and the newsstand on Main Street had a fixed order for 200 copies at 3 cents each. All of these were usually sold and frequently more had to be ordered to fulfill the demand.

The dealer's standing order with the Ledger was for 15 copies of which he seldom sold as many as ten. The paper claimed a circulation of 1,900 including Newark and lower Delaware, but it was common knowledge that most of them were mailed for free. The motto for the *Ledger* was; "We cover Delaware like the dew" which was interpreted by skeptics as "They're all wet". The advertising rate of the paper was alleged to be 40 cents per column inch, (as opposed to 25 cents for the *Post*), but it was also no secret that it was being subsidized and many ads were run gratis or repeated after the contracts with the advertisers had expired. [43]

The *Ledger*, founded in 1876, was the older of the two Newark newspapers. It changed names five times, the last two being the *Newark Ledger* and finally, under F. A. G. Handy, the *Delaware Ledger*. The Bowen brothers purchased it in 1883 and during their ownership relations between Johnson and the *Ledger* were cordial as evidenced by a December 23, 1914 entry in the Post. "We wish to express appreciation to our friends, the Bowen Brothers of the *Delaware Ledger*, for their gift of the First Volume of the *Newark Post*. The beginnings of the *Newark Post* make interesting reading-at least to us. The full year's publication is given us complete in a good state of preservation."

The friendly relationship ended when The Ledger came under the control of Alfred I. du Pont, who used it for political purposes. A letter from Joseph H. Odell to Pierre S. du Pont pointed out that the paper had been detrimental to the advancement of the best things in the State, particularly educational progress, and unscrupulous in its attacks upon members of the Du Pont family, excepting Alfred I., whose personal fortune kept it in business. In his opinion, "My feeling is that if Alfred I. Du Pont really knew the facts he would not sanction its continuance because it is losing at least $1000 a month and I am certain that E. M. Davis, (the publisher), is not paying this deficit out of his own pocket."

As long as Johnson was living the *Post* flourished. His personal creed was, "Print all the Truth you dare and dare a little more every week." After his death, Ed Davis, who reportedly had "a wholesome fear and consequent dislike of Mr. Johnson," tried his best to undermine his competition. Obvious economic pressure was being applied to prevent advertisers from using the *Post*, as evidenced in a letter from J. Spencer Brock to Charles H. Bowden, two men involved in trying to save the Press of Kells from bankruptcy in later years. "A number of Wilmington advertisers have expressed themselves as preferring the *Post* as a business medium but are coerced into using the *Ledger* by pressure with which you are familiar. Not content with getting an ad for the *Ledger*; he has frequently adopted measures to prevent the advertiser from using the *Post*"[44]

It was well known that Everett Johnson's opinions could not be bought, and this earned him the esteem of the community. In describing the advertising policy of the Post he wrote: "Our price is fixed. No favors, no special rates, no special discounts—no return business agreement. Our space is for sale at a fixed rate—and we do the fixing."[45] People who purchased the Wilmington and Philadelphia dailies read the *Post* for the local and personal news. The *Ledger*, printed on Fridays, often used articles from the Wednesday *Post* and ran them without credit or re-writing. As a result of all these practices, when anyone spoke of the "Paper" in Newark, they meant the *Post*.

In a comparison of similar booklets printed in 1916 by the Ledger and by Kells, it is easy to distinguish between quality printing and job printing. The paper used by the *Ledger* is similar in appearance to that used by Kells, but the *Ledger* paper is coarse and does not have the same feeling of quality. The pages of both are tied with silk, but the Kells binding consisted of weaving the cord through three holes as opposed to only two in the *Ledger's* booklet, which was the larger of the publications. That seemingly insignificant attention to detail often made the difference between a publication that survived handling and one that fell apart.

The quality of the printing also shows a difference in attitude towards the total appearance of the end product. Both have pleasing large margins but the *Ledger's* printing is too small to be easily read and is executed in an uninspiring type face—nothing here to catch the imagination or please the eye. The first page of the *Ledger* even has smears left by the paper being placed together before the ink had time to dry.

Everett Johnson may have had a personal vision of how a truly well run newspaper should look but in the beginning he lacked organization and experience. He received assistance with both problems from a fellow printer in a nearby town. The first issue of the *Newark Post* came off the press Wednesday, January twenty-sixth, 1910 with a little help from a friend. A description of the informal contract with Frank E. Williams, editor of the Cecil Whig in Elkton, Maryland, where the paper was printed in its first year, is found in his obituary written by Johnson in 1920. The two editors were close friends and, interestingly enough some of the words Everett chose to describe Williams applied equally to Johnson. He wrote:

> Frank E. Williams dead! We can't quite realize it. We can't write. We knew him as a citizen, a plain, honest, outspoken fighting citizen...Some ten years ago, with our first batch of Personals and Here and There News, we went to him and *The Cecil Whig*. We told him our ambitions, asked for his confidence and credit, challenged his advice-and he laughed. 'Ideals and youth, how foolish but I love them. Where's your editorial? 'Upon being told we had none, he gave us our first lecture on the County Newspaper. And we took his advice and accepted his credit. Without a contract, and payments conspicuous by their irregularity, *The Post* was printed in that office for over a year, brought over to Newark on the 4.29 and mailed

…Frank Williams accepted our enthusiasm as bona
fide. He was our friend, He trusted, and we would go
far and fight hard to protect the Ideals that were his.
The Head, Heart and Hand found in our Imprint was
to him typical of our youth, but he urged us on. So
that's why we can't write-but his memory will always
urge us on.

With the help of Frank E. Williams and the Cecil Whig,
the Newark Post went from a dream to a reality. Everett took
Williams' advice and wrote his first editorial January 26, 1910:

The name of this paper is *The Newark Post*. It is to
be published weekly. My reason for starting this paper
is: I have always had a desire for this kind of work. Not
that I have any editorial ink to spread, not that I have
any friends in favor, not that I have any enemies to
score. I just wanted to do it—to have a paper as a
medium for other people, and to try to do something
really worth while for the town and country. And a
paper can do that, if the right man is at the back of it.
Whether I am the right man is to be proven. I hope so.
I do not expect to do great things, but there are some
little things we can do if you will help me.

If this paper can, by your help, pluck one thorn
and plant one rose, as Lincoln tried and succeeded in
doing, then I shall be glad; if this paper can be your
help, be the means of suggesting and bringing about
Good Roads, Flowers, Parks, Better Schools, Trees,
Pure Water, Fresh Air and Sunshine for somebody and
Work for everybody, then I shall have won—I shall
have led a fairly religious life.

Another thing, besides what little benefit I hope
this paper to be, I want it to be a financial success. It
must be to be of any use. Nothing is truly worth while
that does not pay its way. A newspaper that is run to
further some cause or some individual's interest seldom
wields much influence for the public good.

I have no special cause to further, no theories to explode. I simply want to have some fun, make some money and make good. I expect to do this, with the help of my friends. You can not expect much real help from your enemies. I want "To do my work and be kind."

I am more or less of a stranger to you. I am a product of Sussex county, before the days of good crops. I was for four years (1905-1909)* somewhat of a student at the college (I hope you will not hold the Faculty responsible for my English) and have been around here more or less all these years. I am not ashamed of being from Sussex County. I was when I came to college, though I never told it. But not now. Things have changed. Sussex has forged to the front since then. I have been around a bit and know of no better place to be born than in Sussex County.

And New Castle is a very good place to live in. The sun shines very brightly on these hills of White Clay and Pencader to us who live here. And so I ask to be one of you. If there is anything I can do, set the task.

I an interested in the town, her churches and schools, her businessmen and industries, her social organizations and government. She has possibilities that I do not believe we realize. We need more industries—not so many that it will prove a detriment as a place to live. Some have said that more manufacturers would spoil the educational atmosphere. They urge keeping Newark the educational center of the State.

Factories will not do that. The smokestack has its place in making Newark a better place to live as well as the steeple or the college dome. And the factory whistle is calling at six o 'clock just as good men to their work as they who dress hastily to answer the call to their studies at nine o 'clock. The boy on the farm who is up and has his cows milked before the boy at college is up, is not any better, but just as good as the college boy who has not seen the sun rise during the college year.

No, factories and more honest working-men would be an advantage to our educational atmosphere. Let Newark be the center of learning in the State and also let it be a place where good work is well done.

I am interested in the traditions of Newark—they are noble—but not to the extent of retarding progress. We must give the future some traditions to represent what we have done. We can't live on our ancestors, altogether, Napoleon, on being asked who his ancestors were, replied—"I am an Ancestor."

Do not think this paper expects to accomplish all this. It hopes only to be the medium in which you may discuss publicly, the ways and means of making a better Newark and to give the news of its progress.

The columns of this paper are open to you to say what you will. I hope you will use it.

Personally, I shall try to keep as quiet as possible. The days of editorials by country editors on the ways and means of saving the State and Nation are over. I do ask, however, that you give me the same privilege as I accorded you—to let me say my say, realizing and asking you to recognize that it is only one man's opinion.

I shall try to be consistent in each issue. Further than that, I cannot say. I shall try to take the advice of Emerson, and speak—"what I think today, in words as hard as cannon balls, and tomorrow speak—what tomorrow thinks in hard words again," though they contradict every word I said today. Let me record day by day my honest thoughts without prospect or retrospect. And for this I ask no apology. The policy of this paper is dictated by no man, class, sect, institution, party or creed. But it is open to all.

When in doubt, I shall try to mind my own business.

I shall fail many times but want to conduct this paper according to the ideal and hope "to so live that when I die they who knew me best will say: 'He planted a rose and plucked a thorn wherever he thought a rose would grow.' "

Everett C. Johnson

Note:Hereafter I suppose this page will assume and be
conducted by the Editorial "We."

(*):The original editorial had incorrect dates for Everett's college attendence. It was corrected
in reprints to read (1895–1899).

The office of the Post was first located in an old brick
building on the corner of Main Street and South College Avenue. It
was a homely structure, which had originally served as a hotel and
tavern with an adjoining livery stable and "comfort station."
(The ladies of the New Century Club, located next door, would
adamantly insist on the removal of this edifice in time for an
important meeting in their new building!) The name of the hotel was
The Delaware House and the most complete description of the
building was written by Everett himself on the occasion of its razing,
February seventeenth, 1925.

The article gives us a glimpse of old Newark, and as the
building no longer exists, and much misinformation describing it
does, it may serve to fill in some historical blanks.

> Walls that housed great men from this and nearby
> states, walls which have looked down on Edgar Allan
> Poe, while he stopped in Newark, fell with a crash
> yesterday forenoon.
>
> The last recognizable trace of the Old College
> Library at Main and South College Avenues, passed
> into oblivion with that crash. To old residents, to lovers
> of history and The Post, it was a tragedy; to the up and
> going world of today, it was merely "another old
> eyesore gone."
>
> We will not argue the point. It was both.
>
> Men and women of Newark long since dead, their
> names but memories to even the oldest of our present
> citizens, once sat around the jovial board of the
> "Delaware House" in the good old days. Weary
> travelers stepped from lurching stagecoaches into the

Photo courtesy University of Delaware Archives

The old print shop on the corner of South College Ave. and Main Street Newark.
Originally the Delaware House Hotel it was the first home of the Newark Post in 1910.

coolness of its porch and parlor. It was a hotel in those days-a center, a common meeting place, an institution.

FOUR TAVERNS HERE

There are only a few left today who distinctly remember the time when Newark held three flourishing hostelries. Hundreds perhaps do not know that the present Fraternal Hall on East Main Street at Choate was once "The Choate Hotel"; that its owner, John Choate, owned about all the land there was to own in that section. Then there was the Washington House, and further up the street The Deer Park. The latter two buildings have withstood the varying fortunes of time and are mute sentinels to a generation that is gone.

According to the version of Nate Motherall, who

perhaps is as familiar with Old Newark as any man in the community, one Philip Marvel was the first owner of the Delaware House he could remember as a boy back in the early (18)60's, he remembers well the old place. How far beyond that, the old hotel was active he could not say.

There is a well founded story, however, that during Dr. William Purnell's undergraduate days, long before the Civil War, Edgar Allan Poe stopped at the old inn while in Newark. He came here to address the students of Delaware College. There is also a supplementary story of how he slipped while getting out of the hack at the corner of Main and South College Avenue and about ruined his suit in the mud.

CHANGED HANDS OFTEN

From the time Landlord Marvel left Newark, the old tavern changed hands several times.

Bayard Widdoes, grandfather of Ott Widdoes, Newark Councilman, took the reins and ran the business for some years. Following him came Henry Boyd and later John Lemmon.

Lemmon, according to Mr. Motherall, took charge about 1877, failed to have his license renewed and finally was forced to vacate.

It may be stated here for the benefit of the younger generation that the old inns were in a large degree dependent on the annual liquor retail license. At that time Delaware College frowned upon, individually and collectively, the tavern across the street. From Mr. Motherall's version, it is evident that college influence helped keep that license away.

James Morrison and William Currinder both tried to revive "The Delaware House," but to no avail.

In the meantime Frank Griffith started and maintained for several years a prosperous livery stable.

Troubles came aplenty to Currinder late in the eighties, and the property passed into the hands of George Evans, father of Charles B. Evans, the former holding a mortgage on the place.

Mr. Evans rented the building in parts to various enterprises from that time on, among the more prominent lessees being the late Leonard Lovett, who conducted a flourishing furniture business there.

The plot of ground just in rear of the building was famous in these days. While the community center was not known as such in those days, certainly no place ever flourished in civic and commercial manner as did this spot under the old willow and near the old town pump. The publisher of this paper recalls his first view of this spot, and it was years back in 1895 he arrived in Newark from Sussex County to enter Delaware College.

On this particular day the Finals of a contest of some three months playing was being played out. The contest was between Pop Lovett and Father Hart, remembered as the genial funeral director. The game was not quoits nor even "quates," but hoss shoes. Some thirty men were gathered about, watching attentively, and we learned afterward that they represented the elect of a cross-section of this community; it was generally admitted-they admitted it themselves. The spot was the scene, too, of Mr. Lovett who, a few years before, had been the star baseball pitcher of the big eastern leagues of that day, warming himself up and training other stars. Newark 's fame in baseball probably dates from this spot and with that wonderfully interesting character as the inspiration.

Charles and George Strahorn then started business in the livery stable, providing teams for the elite of the community.

NEWARK POST STARTS

Events rapidly brings our story to 1910, and the founding of *The Newark Post* by Everett C. Johnson.

The Post at that time, it will be remembered, was started in the parlor of the residence part of the house, the paper being printed at the Cecil Whig, Elkton, Maryland, for the first year, Mr. Johnson renting the rear section to the Strahorn Brothers and store room to Rankin Armstrong. In 1911 a wing was built, extending to the Samuel Donnell 's property, then known as Newark 's Senate, the House of Representatives being Bill Barton 's feed store. Possession rather than ownership was the legal title of *The Post* at that time. The door, 5 ft. in width in the new wing-just a door-created a sensation that was discussed amusingly and seriously, not only in the aforesaid Community Congress, but at all social functions, then known as Thimble Parties, Prayer Meetings and with an occasional dance—The Blue Danube Waltz, if you please. In 1912 another wing was built on South College Avenue and *The Post* grew.

THE COLLEGE LIBRARY

In 1915 it became the property of The Delaware College, being taken over in the Pierre duPont development and the building became the heart of the University—the Library.

An interesting career, ill-conceived and awkward in architectural features. If its story could be told from the days of the old Inn, then the days of the Tavern, down through its commercial career, then as the beginning of a country newspaper and then as the library of an old college and coming university, it is interesting indeed.

Buildings, like men, serve their day and generation. We regret to see it go-that 's sentiment; we are glad it is gone-that is a fact.

According to Everett's daughter, Marjorie, Dr. Hullihen, who was president of the University in 1920-44, did not always see eye to eye with her father on issues concerning the college. He was undoubtedly pleased to see the historic, albeit unattractive, building razed as he considered it an "eye sore" and one of the few obstacles remaining preventing him from enjoying an unobstructed view of the campus as he left his office in Recitation Hall. Forty-six properties were purchased during the expansion of the College in 1915 funded by Pierre S. du Pont. The corner lot on which the print shop was located was a prime location and Everett had received $21,000, the highest amount awarded for all the lots. The sale occurred at an opportune time, as he was not only running out of space he also held three mortgages totaling $7,000. [46]

All that remains of the print shop is the wall at the Main Street end of the College Mall, which was built with the old bricks from the building.[47] As the paper gained popularity, Johnson gained the courage to speak his mind and dictate the policies that would guide it throughout his lifetime.

FEBRUARY 4, 1925

The Newark Post is a Country Weekly, published every Wednesday after noon, at the Shop called Kells, at Newark, Delaware. It is a country paper, neither pretending nor aping anything else. In fact it is proud to be known and read as such.

OUR NEWS

We feature news of Newark, surrounding country and neighboring towns. We advertise our town, tell its story and try to reflect the spirit of this good country side and the good folk living here. Along with the news, we write occasionally a story of yesterday and those heroes sleeping at our foot-hills. Every organization, society or individual with an idea that would seem to help the town has our support. This policy is ours always, whether public or private. Whether we agree personally or not makes no difference in our news columns. Every one is welcome to tell his story and to use our columns to exploit his idea.

THE EDITOR'S COLUMN

In our Editorial Column, we are, or, at least, try to be, economical with our opinion and comment. When expressed, however, it is personal, ours-and, we hope, honest. We reserve this right-to speak in commendation or condemnation of any man or men in their public words or deeds. We may be right or wrong as our point of view may direct. But this right we reserve or rather take. This is granted by every real American-others don't count except as enemies of ours and free speech.

Speaking of enemies-we are proud of them. An active citizen, unafraid and trying to do his bit in life has them. They inspire us. "Give us this day an enemy," the Persian prayer makes an interesting slogan for civic doers and newspaper men.

So we take only what we give. Any citizen, man or woman, can write for our columns on any question of Public interest-if he signs his name. Others cannot. There are no cowards on our Staff.

OUR ADVERTISERS

The Post carries the largest amount of local advertising of any rural paper in Delaware. We make this statement advisedly. No rural paper in Delaware, according to the population of its territory, carries so much space of local advertisers as the Post.

We appreciate this confidence. But then it is not all confidence-it is business return based on experience. And pertinent too, the space used last month, the last

Photo courtesy University of Delaware Archives

The wall at the North end of the Mall; the old print shop bricks were used in its construction.

six months, the last year, is more than at any time in its history.

Our prices are fixed. No favors, no special rates, no special discounts-no return business agreement. So This is to say That the news in the Post is controlled by events—neither colored nor suppressed. Our editorials are our own—neither suggested, dictated nor written by anyone else. Our advertisers do business with us—on business principles, not for friendship nor for favors.

The Post is an Independent Paper printed in the Country, for the Country, by those who live and make a living in the Country.

"Print all the Truth you dare—and dare a little more every week" is a personal creed. Our Faith in Newark led us here and that Faith abides, still.

We offer our Time, Thought, Energy to this day and our country. "To spend and be spent" appeals to us

as the Great American Game. To voice the life of this
community, to be the medium of exchange for opinions, to record the deeds worthy, is the mission of the
Post. To be lenient and honest, to be generous, and
worth-while is our ambition. The Post is a part of
Newark—its columns are yours. Use them.

The first employee of the fledgling newspaper, The Newark
Post, was Edna Chalmers, "a local girl who knew everyone in town
and was willing to do any job that needed to be done, even if that
were washing the windows." Etta J. Wilson, a woman who would
contribute greatly to the fields of education and journalism, later
joined her.

In January of 1911, in an effort to reach new subscribers, The
Post enlisted the help of the local school children. A piano from the
Lindeman and Sons Piano company of New York was offered to the
school whose pupils secured the greatest number of new yearly subscribers. In addition, the pupil responsible for obtaining the most
new customers received a cash prize of fifteen dollars, with second and
third place winners receiving ten and five dollars respectively. Everett
appeared to be slightly defensive in his disclaimer: "We have
heretofore made no campaign for subscriptions. Nor is this to be so
considered." The piano was won by the Newark Grammar School and
the contest was defended as being,"…a modest but genuine offer that
will be of mutual benefit…a way in which the pupils may by a little
work add to the happiness of all and at the same time make a little
pin money." The piano probably outlived its donor and
hopefully is still being played.

THE PRESS OF KELLS BUILDING

THE STONEMASONS SANG OPERA

∞

The old *Newark Post* building of 1910 was cramped and not suited for Everett's needs. With actual floor space of 288 square feet it was nothing more than a glorified office. By October 1911 he had expanded to 1,476 square feet and begun printing the newspaper himself; the Post was now a hometown publication in all respects. As more equipment was purchased, floor space was increased—to 2,386 square feet in September 1912 and to 3,226 square feet by August 1914. [48]

In anticipation of the need for expansion of the newspaper, Everett had purchased a large lot on the corner of Depot Road (South College Avenue) and West Park Place. The adjoining lot, later the site of their new home, was purchased by Louise with money inherited from her mother. The land was less than a mile from Main Street, but far enough from town to be taxed only by the county. Fortunately, The University of Delaware was actively trying to purchase the old print shop, considered an eyesore in the middle of an expanding campus. Negotiations with Mr. Charles B. Evans, representing the purchasing committee funded by Pierre S. duPont, became strained at times. Johnson's building was the last of forty-six properties to be purchased and he definitely held the upper hand. Holding out for the highest possible settlement, Everett raised the price from the $18,000 initially offered, to $20,000 plus, "losses incidental to moving, such as loss of time and work, and increased cost of new plant over capital represented in present quarters." He seemed to be aware of the committee's desire to take advantage of his sentimental feelings for his Alma Mater by offering a below market value price for the property. He countered with a letter stating, "While interested in the College and ready always to do what I can for its advance and development, force of circumstances compel me to consider this merely in the light of a business proposition." The matter was settled, June 23rd, 1915, with Everett retaining the use of the building rent free until January 25th, 1916, and paying fifty dollars a month after that time until he vacated the building. [49]

Everett had told his wife that he wanted to "go big" and with the money in hand from the sale of the old shop, the time seemed right. After visiting the Roycroft Shop owned by Elbert Hubbard in East Aurora, New York, he returned to Newark inspired and determined to reproduce it on a smaller scale. The design for the new print shop was so clear to him, he did not feel the necessity to hire an architect. Instead, he created a cardboard model to guide the builders. [50] Previous accounts of the construction of the print shop have stated that the inspiration for its monastery-like appearance stemmed from Everett's travels abroad and his memories of stone castles in Ireland where the Book of Kells was created. This is unlikely since during his time abroad he had no premonition that his goal to be a teacher would be thwarted by ill health and he would eventually be head of a print shop.

His new plant was built and opened January 19, 1916, with 6,298 square feet of useable space. Using fieldstone from nearby farms the building had a fortress-like, medieval appearance, with central tower, crenellations, high ceilings, wide heavy doors, and

A very early photo of Kells before the stone pillars were built on either side of the driveway.

deep-set windows. The outside walls were made of stone twenty inches thick.

The main entrance to the building, facing east, led into the two-story crenellated tower. The doorway was inset with small windows on each side of the recessed area. Down the entrance hall and to the left was the office area twenty-three feet wide and forty feet long with a curved area in one corner of the room plainly visible from the outside. The inside of this semi-circular wall faced a stone fireplace and the walls were finished with raised wooden panels. A long room twenty-one by thirty-five feet called the Whim was on the right. This was used as a lounge and meeting place and featured a large stone fireplace with a rough-cut cedar mantel. The upstairs of the tower measured twenty-five feet by twenty-five feet and was used as a storage area and a secured, private area for printing special jobs. The entrance hall led into a large print shop thirty-nine feet by eighty-seven feet. It was outfitted with the most up to date equipment; some of which Everett boasted were one of a kind in Delaware. Large high windows on all sides of the print shop allowed for good ventilation and a well-lighted work area while the open-rafters of the shop made for a pleasant and airy workroom. The outside grounds were just as elaborate-on each side of the driveway was a large stone pillar with the distinctive Kells triangle. The landscaping consisted of well placed trees, shrubs and flowers that further gave the appearance of a Library or College building.

Everett still must not have been satisfied for, just prior to his death, construction was nearly completed on an addition that would increase the floor space from 6,298 square feet to 10,788 square feet. At the west side of the existing building an even larger crenellated tower was built with a smaller tower to the south, all completed shortly after Everett's death.

That Everett would go to such expense to build a massive stone print shop when the same work could just as well have been accomplished in a traditional manufacturing facility of the time is revealing. A building of this sort would be a luxury, even for a well established and financially secure business. Kells had earned a reputation for quality work but because of Everett's generosity, low prices, and poor sales of the Sesqui-Centennial edition of the Declaration of Independence in Philadelphia, the elaborate shop put

Kells in debt. Johnson knew he was not going to enjoy a long life; the Press of Kells would outlive him and bear testimony to the way he thought things should be done. Underneath a picture of one of the towers he quoted the English writer and sociologist, John Ruskin (1819-1900) "When we build, let us think we build forever. Let it not be for present delight nor present use alone. Let it be such work as our descendants will thank us for…"

Everett wrote several articles for the *Post* explaining that his Shop was not an extravagant waste of space, and that its design actually promoted a feeling of well being by providing a pleasant work environment. People working in such an atmosphere were more efficient and motivated and this led to greater profits in the long run. Such an article from the *Post* printed April 20, 1921 follows:

PRINTING COSTS AT KELLS

A recent visitor at Kells made the observation that our "building was palatial for a country job office." I crossed my fingers and thanked him for the compliment. Glancing at him, I wondered what he meant to say. There was a long _____ in his expression. So I have been thinking. In the language of University Circles, he said a mouthful. At first it did not seem to be much but the blank line insert was the thought. He had hidden it by what he thought would flatter. But it didn't. He did not sense us nor the place. His expression contains two errors, one reflection and one very pertinent question.

First the building is not "palatial." The word smacks of aristocracy and royalty in the gilded sense. And Kells—the building nor the Idea are not thus conceived. There is nothing of palatial royalty here.

Second, this is not a "country job office." It is a Plant. The country job office as generally and correctly understood is a smell of oil, ink, litter and dirt--unfit and unfitted for any expression of one's work. The engine and boiler room of the ordinary factory far surpass it. Neither light nor sunshine are welcome. But at Kells--a plant where Master Craftsmen study and work at the art of printing, it is different. Here is a Shop open on all four sides, light, air, sunshine, a place where boys and girls laugh and work, play and express the best that's in them. Kells, a palatial building, and job office are but faintly associated with one another. Yes, we are in the country and proud of it. The idea of printing being done only in the city is out of date. In some quarters by the unknowing it prevails, but not among those used to the best in either artistic or commercial printing. All the way back to the Monastery of Kells itself in the Seventh Century, the best in printing has been done in the country.

The visitor meant to inquire our costs of printing but a social training reared upon a false basis, prevented the business inquiry. Such a building with such spaces, with expressions of interests in the workmen's welfare, meant to him increased costs. This is pertinent and is deserving of a reply. There are printing places and in cities nearby of ten times our machinery and capacity with less floor space than here. Down town on some close side street, half a hundred men work at press and machine by fly specked electric bulb, all day long. They eat their lunch leaning up against the roller rack. The idea of color of walls that is restful, a flower in the window ledge that cheers, a lawn to enjoy are all unknown to them. Then surely printing could he done cheaply there. But wait. Electric lights cost money, rents are high and enter into costs. Insurance costs, dull headaches from lack of air add to the time card.

At Kells, sunlight, air and cheer of the open are all free. No lights are necessary. Insurance rates on Kells are reduced to minimum. Taxes are out-in-the-country taxes. Our overhead is such that city printers dream of. Rent costs are insignificant. Our building upkeep and all that goes into overhead do not compare with the smallest "job office" of the city.

But how about equipment and labor-saving

machinery, you say? All right. The lay out and arrangement at Kells has been copied and blue-prints made by one of the largest Type Foundries in the country. It is considered a model. Our machinery is the most approved in the craft.

So at Kells, you will find our overhead charges very low. Our men? They are the kind that the City is constantly trying to get. They are efficient and love their work.

Our building and lawn, our little touches of color and art are not only lovely things to have but are labor saving, cost cutting devices.

Our Ideals are all well founded and practical. Printing here cost less rather than more than in the city shop. That is--for the Kind of Printing we do and the service we render.

So here endeth the lesson on "palatial," "country job office," and printing cost.

The Old Man at Kells

The new building needed a name to match its impressive architecture. The name Press of Kells was chosen, not by its founder, but by an itinerant linotype operator named John Shultz who appeared fortuitously just when the growing business required the addition of that piece of equipment. Louise Johnson recounted the events leading to the adoption of the new name: "It followed that Everett gave John Shultz the mission of finding a name for what, until then, had been called the Print Shop. It happened that the young man during his printing career had heard of the famous Book of Kells, and he looked up its history in the University library. He found that the beautiful book, now a priceless illuminated volume, was the work of a monk during Ireland's Golden Age, in the seventh century AD. The Print Shop became the Press of Kells." Later that year the Johnson's received a copy of the Book of Kells, sent to them by Mr. and Mrs. Lee Cooch of Cooch's Bridge, Delaware. It had come by ship from London during the submarine warfare just prior to the United States' involvement in W.W.I.

In fact, the most obvious inspiration for Kells came from

Everett's admiration of Elbert Hubbard and his Roycroft print shop located in East Aurora, New York. That he admired Hubbard and his press is recalled by those who knew Johnson and is substantiated not only by his frequent quoting of The Fra's (as Elbert called himself) rhetoric but by the set of books entitled *Little Journeys* which still reside in Marjorie's library.

One of these books, bound in stamped leather, bears the imprint, "This copy of the Memorial edition for Marjorie L. Johnson known as 'Boots'." (Boots was Marjorie's nickname given to her by her father.) It is described inside as a 'manuscript edition' of *Little Journeys To The Homes Of Good Men And Great*, dated 1916. Marjorie also recalled her father frequently expressing a desire to visit Hubbard's shop.

Everett did indeed make the trip to East Aurora in the summer of 1911. His wife, in a 1977 taped interview, described the visit and her husband's resulting determination to build a print shop similar to that of the Roycrofters. She was speaking to Richard Carter who at the time was researching the life of Governor John G. Townsend Jr.

> He started that himself (*The Post*) down there and he wasn't satisfied 'till he got this building. And he went up that summer to Elbert Hubbard, did you ever hear of him? He went up there and it just turned his head. He wanted to do things the way Elbert Hubbard did ...well he didn't have the money to do it. Of course he had to borrow the money, and the help increased, and he just got badly in debt. It would have been greater, or better, if he had got a barn and had his press in there. He would have, in fact, made just as much. But, anyway, that was his way of doing. And he had an idea of how things should be." [51]

A souvenir of Everett's trip is a small, paperback edition of Hubbard's, Letter To Garcia, which bears this inscription across the cover in Everett's unmistakable handwriting: Everett C. Johnson, East Aurora, July 3rd, 1911.

Part of the furnishings of Kells consisted of a heavy bench, now owned by his daughter, which came from the Roycroft Studios. Called an "Ali Baba" bench, it still retains the bark on the underside and is clearly stamped "Roycroft". The products of the Roycrofters were sold mostly by mail order through their catalog. The bench was listed as #046, was made of oak and ash, and cost $10.00. [52]

Hubbard's ploy of convincing the local farmers of East Aurora he was doing them a favor by allowing them to donate unwanted stone from their fields to build the Roycroft shop did not go unnoticed by Everett. The stone for Kells came from the neighboring fields of Iron Hill and the farmers were "so glad to be rid of it that they charged only for their labor and the hauling. The stones were placed and pointed by two Italians who sang Italian opera as they worked, to the delight of E.C.J.!" [53]

The similarities between the Roycroft and Kells print shops are striking. Both were constructed of local stone and featured curved towers. Portions of the flat rooflines were crenellated which lent each a castle-like appearance (as well as an unfortunate propensity to leak) and square, stone pillars at the entrances led through sweeping lawns to massive front doors. The final effect was certainly something other than an ordinary place of business.

Johnson and Hubbard also shared a love of fresh air, sunshine and hard useful work as a means to achieve a happy and healthy life. Sunshine was allowed entrance into the building by way of large windows on all sides. This was a radical break from the usual sweatshop approach to a printing plant. Johnson often had to defend himself to provincial townsfolk who were unfamiliar with his dream and more than a little startled to see a small castle suddenly appear in old Newark. To his critics he retorted:

> "The lines of the building, the subject of comment (smiling and sarcastic) are strange to stay-at-homes, but every angle was designed for a specific use. There is a method in our madness. Everyone who visits us admits that this is the ideal place to do ideal printing. Even Curious Critics become our patrons when they visit us." [54]

Calling his neighbors 'stay-at-homes' probably did not endear him to the locals but he always seemed to have the bravado to back his beliefs. He built Kells with an eye to the future allowing for more space than was necessary at the time. Some of his thoughts on design follow:

> This new Shop was designed with a foot rule, a No. 2 Faber and what wit the owner possesses. There's method in his madness. The main shop is lighted on all four sides, the office on three sides. Other rooms have their lighting features. Open air, sunshine, space dominate the place. In construction, rugged stone, straight lines, tile walls - all have their reason. Simplicity dominates. No 'fille de lieus', no false walls, nothing bizarre, it is a simple building selected for work, a place where a man, a boy or girl can do his best. [55]

One large room in the new building was given a name which harks back to Everett's teaching days. Before his illness forced them to leave their home in Mt. Washington, Louise surprised him one day by fixing a room at the top of the stairs into a study to house his growing collection of books. She had been reading Emerson's essay on Self-Reliance and remembered these lines: "I shun father and mother and wife and brother when my genius calls me. I would write on the lintels of the door-post WHIM. I hope it is somewhat better than whim at last, but we cannot spend the day in explanation." Louise named that first study WHIM and when Kells was built Everett planned for a new Whim complete with a large stone fireplace.[56]

The Head, Heart and Hand imprint designed by him was prominently displayed above the rough-hewn mantle. Both Johnson and Elbert Hubbard borrowed it from John Ruskin who wrote: "Fine art is that in which the hand, the head, and the heart, of man go together. Recollect this triple group; it will help you to solve many difficult problems." The imprint was composed of three elongated H's enclosing a letter K; this became the imprint for the Press of Kells. The only other imprint previously used by Johnson was a stylized signpost bearing the words, "Printed at the Shop of the Newark Post," with a printer's inkball below the sign.

A comparison of the Press of Kells printshop (top), with the Roycroft Inn (bottom), shows the similarities in their design and construction.

In an interview with Elizabeth Taylor, the last person to be hired by Everett, she recalled the Whim as a place of refuge for the exhausted editor when he needed rest. "It was a special room for small parties and literary gatherings and early Christmas Eve, after all the presses were silenced, Everett would call everyone together for a little bit of holiday sharing before they all left for their own celebrations."

This special room was also the site of a wedding, when on September fifteenth, 1932, Everett and Louise's daughter Marjorie was married to her former history professor, Francis H. Squire of Westfield, Massachusetts. She had first met Mr. Squire in the same way that her mother had met her father-both suitors had met their brides while boarding at their future mother-in-laws' houses.

On Friday, August 17, 1917, correspondents for *The Newark Post* were entertained at Kells. Miss Etta J. Wilson, in the absence of Everett, entertained the guests, one of whom wrote the following detailed description of the interior:

> ...the guests, who passing through the reception hall, were made acquainted and spent awhile socially in the north room, called The Whim, with its massive chimney made from Iron Hill boulders. Later, all were invited to examine the artistic and beautiful work done at Kells,-dainty and original Christmas cards, wedding stationery, post cards, books of exquisite design, Governor Townsend's recent war message to the citizens of Delaware, Channing's "Symphony', enlarged copies in suitable coloring of the tents of Company E, First Delaware Infantry, photographed on "The Border" last year by a member of the Company, patriotic quotations surmounted by "Old Glory", beautifully colored and embossed, and many other attractive specimens.
>
> Conspicuous upon the wall was "The Newark Post" motto: "Good Roads, Flowers, Parks, Better Schools, Trees, Fresh Air, Sunshine, and Work for Everybody," with original lettering in gold upon a background of purple leather. Fine drawings and other works of art; an American battle flag, and quantities of golden-glow blossoms, added to an impression that

shall not be forgotten.[57]

Both Hubbard and Johnson were fond of using the then popular words "knock" and "boost". "Every knock is a boost!" turned up first on the Roycroft motto cards and later in the pages of the Post. Everett also liked to "boom" things. Mimicking his critics he repeated the accusation "He is said to be booming Newark to boom himself " and then playfully added, "Part or perhaps all of which is true-just according to the way you look at it. Anyhow, all this makes the paper worth a dollar-whether you agree with it or not."

Evidently, when the unusual building with the unusual name of Kells was taking shape there was a lot more knocking than booming and boosting taking place among the skeptics. It was labeled The Tower of Failure and Newark's Monument to Folly. "Six months will wind it up," was the comment of the local "knocker and loafer" back in 1910 when the paper made its debut. He obviously underestimated the man, the building, and the newspaper. Kells still stands today; as the site of the YWCA it continues to serve the town of Newark. As for the Post, at the time of this writing it is celebrating its ninetieth year.

John Shultz who gave Kells its name wrote the most accurate description of the building and its ambiance in an anonymous booklet titled the Vagabond Printer.

KELLS-THE STORY OF THE VISIT OF A VAGABOND PRINTER TO THE SHOP WHERE MASTER CRAFTSMEN STUDY AND WORK AT THE ART OF PRINTING

"ART IS THE BEAUTIFUL WAY OF DOING THINGS,"

"JUST A WORD BY WAY OF INTRODUCTION "

A kind, good friend whom The Old Man met out
in the work-a-day world came to see us one fine day
last spring. When he went home, he wrote this story
and sent it back to us. Naturally we are a bit proud. He

says some very good things, all of which are either true or it is our ambition so to make them.

We have other friends who have never been to see us and our Shop-but just hope to come some day. That they may catch a glimpse of the place, we are printing this story by our good friend.

He calls himself a Vagabond Printer. If like him, they are not so bad as the term is sometimes interpreted. He is a philosopher, a man of world experience, a printer, a writer and lover of Truth-and a friend.

He and our other friends are welcome, always. It is they that make Kells.

Kells is Friendship put into type.

The Craftsmen at Kells.

The room called the "Whim", the heart of the print shop; it's fireplace still welcomes visitors today.

While Vagabonding trough Delaware I dropped into Newark. Being in Newark, I dropped into Kells. I had heard of Kells; had seen on some of its out-put its distinctive triangular mark of identification. To me, it stood for a printing plant. That's what I expected to find,-greeted at the threshold by the smell of ink and the peculiar odor of old, close paper flavored with benzene, making that combination of neither aroma nor stench, which has become intimately associated in the human nostril with all print shops. I expected to see the regulation "office" separated from the "shop" by a dwarfed wooden picket fence; a desk piled high with letters, bills and proofs; in the background, the cases, the stones, the printers, the rhythmically clattering linotypes and a couple of Gordon jobbers; from some back room I expected the salutation of a Cottrell or Miehle.

I experienced a sensation of surprise and began to feel that everything was not orthodox when the village bus driver stopped in front of what I thought was either a church, the public library or one of the buildings of Delaware State College and said "Here it is," in

Left: The Kells logo composed of Head, Heart and Hand with a letter K in the center. Right: The earliest imprint of the Newark Post in use until the name "Kells" was adopted.

response to my previous request to "put me off at Kells." But before I had time to card index my sensations, I was across the lawn (who ever heard of a print shop having a lawn!) and into the door. Then it was useless to attempt any card indexing of my sensations. All my previous experience with print shops out of which I had draw material for picturing Kells, all of my stand-pat ideas as to what constituted a print shop, collapsed. It was not a wreck; it was a cataclysm; there was nothing to salvage. There weren't even any landmarks left by which I could guide myself back to the more or less familiar world of print shops. I was standing in what might have been the ante-room of an art exhibit, looking through a broad doorway into an unusually large, well-lighted, open raftered room that might have been the home of some artist's private library.

But all of this is material whose description and narration belong to those who know and can describe interior finishings and furniture. Besides, unusual and attractive though they were, I felt they were only the symbol, the outward sign of Kells. I knew they were not a print shop; I began to feel they must represent an institution, an idea and an ideal and that this institution was christened Kells, where, so I had somewhere read, "the art of printing is studied and practiced." And it was that which I wanted to see.

I went into the "business office." A safe, a file cabinet and a typewriter probably justified its being called a business office where folks did routine work and people came in and paid bills and got estimates and all that sort of commercial thing. Otherwise it was in harmony with the two other rooms.

Then somebody came up and asked if I wanted to see the "Shop." I did. He (it was the owner and proprietor himself) acted as guide. It was a genuine print shop, minus all the disorder and dirt and dinginess that are considered the bosom companions of print shops. It was a genuine print shop as machinery and equipment, plus high ceilings, many broad windows on four sides, lots of fresh air and cleanliness. It was a genuine print shot, [sic] -plus personality, plus esprit de corps. There, that is what I have been trying to say! You could see it and feel it the minute you entered the shop.

I knew then I had come upon the secret of the place. Here was the tangible thing of which Ruskin and Morris and Browning wrote; the performance of work, not from a sordid commercial viewpoint but from the viewpoint of turning out a product that is a credit to the workman; that finds its justification not in its cost tag but in its honesty and perfection and artistry; that reflects not merely technique, but also temperament; something that is not only handicraft, but also soulcraft into which the workers have put something of themselves. Raphael, when asked how he obtained his wonderful tones and matchless expressions, replied, "I mix my paints with my tears and I paint with my soul rather than with a brush." If Raphael had been a printer, he would have worked in a

Johnson often borrowed slogans from Elbert Hubbard's Roycroft Press; one of his favorites was "Every Knock is a Boost."

Every Knock is a Boost

shop like Kells.

The masterpieces of fiction have been written, the masterpieces of art have been painted, the most exquisite harmony has been composed by those who thought of the work rather than the reward; who strove to transfer and translate into material form the truth and beauty that was within them. They looked upon their work as an opportunity rather than a necessity, as something to be endured.

"The man most man, with tenderest human hands works best for men, as God in Nazareth."

Christ worked-to what end? To establish a political kingdom, to make himself rich, to gain power? None of these! He worked to do good, to make mankind happy! He worked for men! So, too, have the greatest men of all ages. And by so doing they have been blest with that which has been denied those who have worked for gain. Not a school child but can tell of some great man or woman who did great whole-hearted, burning-souled work, who are remembered not for what they got from their work, but for its character and quality.

How much did Columbus get for discovering America? The price Shakespeare received for running the scale of human emotions and dropping the plummet into every depth of the human soul would be rejected by a newspaper sporting editor of to-day. Michael Angelo didn't receive the compensation for painting the Sistine Chapel that a member of the painter's union would receive today for painting a house; yet when men look upon that great work, they fall upon their knees and worship God.

What did Harvey get for discovering that blood circulates; or Jenner for discovering the virtues of vaccination; or Lister for giving humanity the theory and practice of antiseptics or Gorgas and his band of medical students who lived in a hell of yellow fever to prove it was not contagious but was carried by a certain family of mosquitoes?

What did Eads get for building the first great jetties into the very maw of the ocean? What did Goethals get for constructing the Panama canal-in comparison with the achievement and the world benefit?

How many rich men of the past ages can you now recall-men who did what they did because of the money that was in it? Time has washed their names from the memory of man as a rude scrawl from a schoolboy's slate. But the men who toiled with human hands and human sympathies for men; the men who worked at their task for the love of it have their memories carved on tablets of stone and indelibly written in human hearts. Those who starved in garrets while they wrote of human love, who fought the wolf from the door while they wrote of human wrongs, who mixed their paints with tears while they limned the beauties of God and nature-these men's names are today all that is left out of yesterday's multitude.

Who was the wealthiest contemporary of "Bobbie" Burns or Thomas Hood? What did he do? You cannot tell; yet the world is familiar with the "Song of a Shirt" and "The Cotter's Saturday Night," written not for money nor fame but because the men who wrote loved their work for its sake, because they had a message in their hearts they wanted to give to the world. The very reason their work lives behind them and glorifies their memory is because they gloried their work and did not debase it for lust of gold or the bauble of reputation.

On the other hand, the men who work and sweat and cringe and fawn and lie and sell their souls in order to acquire wealth and fame are cheated. They are cheated out of the life they are living here and the life to come. Living, they are cheated out of the respect and the love of their fellowmen; dead, they are denied the grateful memory of their posterity.

The spirit of service and fellowship is at Kells. Those who are on the payroll do not work for the proprietor; they are his associates, who work with him. They both work for one thing-the reputation of Kells as a place which does good and honest work that represents an ideal rather than a cost plus system. Work is not a drudgery here. Those associated with the proprietor and the proprietor, himself, conquer their work, dominate it, breathe into it the breath of creative genius and make it distinctive.

Only the spirit of the place could do this. In one corner of the proprietor's office, I saw a card, printed in two or three colors, captioned, "A Tribute to the Old Man of Kells." It was a reprint of an editorial from a paper which praised some service the proprietor had rendered the public. At the bottom of the card was the line "Done by the Kids without the Old Man's Authority." The "Old Man" is the proprietor. "The Kids" are those in the "shop." Both terms originated in the "shop." No such comradeship is possible where commercialism prevails, where the plant is divided into capital and labor, where things are on a cash basis-the employer, thinking of profits and the employee, think- ing of the scale; where the "help" tiptoe into the front office to appear before the "boss" and the "boss" struts through the shop to impress his "help"; where when the whistle blows all intercourse between the two must cease because of the decrees of Social Position and Money.

No Snobocracy at Kells! "The Kids" gave the "Old Man" an electric grill and chafing dish; then one day, in his absence, borrowed the chafing dish because they needed something in a hurry in which to boil some glue! Imagine that happening with one of our "Captains of Industry"! But that is the misfortune of the "Captains of Industry." Think what they are missing! Think what they are becoming,-callous, hard-hearted, taskmasters in search of dividends and surpluses and subsidiary corporations. To them work is measured by the accumulation of money rather than by the good it does, the men it gives honest and self-respecting employment, the homes it makes possible and contented, the opportunity it affords creative genius and the joy the created product gives to the lover of a thing well and beautifully done.

And when in the winter of their years, they find the fruits of life turning to ashes on their lips, they will probably realize, if they candidly review their motives, they made their mistake in working to acquire gold rather than to accomplish good for their fellow-man and lift the world a little higher. They turned the fires of their genius and zeal upon selfish gain rather than upon the problems of human service and so they were self-consumed. Of them it was once written "What shall it profit a man if he gain the whole world and lose his own soul."

They are not gaining the whole world at Kells. But they are making a small portion of it in their immediate vicinity well worth living in and they are keeping their souls free from the curse of Midas and their work free from the dollar sign. When you see the finished product you say not "How much is that worth?" but "What a fine piece of work!" It speaks to you not of profits but of men and women.

And so I came away from Kells with a feeling that I had spent a day in an institution instead of a print shop and I had witnessed master craftsmen who lived their work and loved it and wrought honestly, patiently and beautifully not that the unthinking rabble in the market place might admire and purchase, but that "the gods who see everything" might approve and the work might live and speak its own message of sincerity and beauty.

The Vagabond Printer

Employees

"Success is in choosing someone to do well, what you in your dreams would like to be able to do yourself." Everett was proud of his employees and appreciative of their skills in printing. He understood quality printing and was able to attract people with the ability to produce the kind of work he considered worthy of this imprint. Everett fully realized that his dreams for Kells relied upon others being willing to "work and play at the art of printing." In order to keep abreast of new techniques or develop skills required for a new job, Everett would send one of his craftsmen to a print shop in Baltimore or Philadelphia for training. He was the office manager who kept the plant operating and he earned his title of "Master Craftsmen" by doing much more than overseeing the printing.

The feelings of the employees were poignantly described in Everett's eulogy written by Ted Dantz. It was titled "30", which was the printers "mystic signal" at the end of a proof sheet, signifying 'The End.'

"30"

Everett C. Johnson, founder and owner of this newspaper, the Master Craftsman at Kells, has passed on. He was buried yesterday at the foot of old Iron Hill, in the little church yard he loved.

The news of his death reached us early Saturday morning. As a candle's flare is snuffed out, so vanished the gay chatter and laughter in the shop and office. The bright light of morning seemed to suddenly pale. Presses idled to a dead stop. Around the time-honored "stone" where he used to call us, five words were spoken:

"The Old Man is dead."

The State and her people may claim him, but we at Kells know where his heart lay. We know because we have seen him cruelly punish an already frail body for us; we know because we have felt Inspiration that no man could give to a cause unless he lived for it; we know because we have watched him, as the late afternoon sun threw fantastic shadows across the shop, standing quietly at a window—planning for us. Behind him, linotypes clattered and the presses rumbled on. He never seemed to hear them. We knew then he was dreaming of a finer Kells. Today, as if in answer to the dream, his favorite window opens into the New Shop.

The "Old Man" looked ahead through distances our eyes could not bridge, yet he was patient with us. Of his time, his brain, his marvelous energy, he gave unstintingly—was sometimes sad for want of more to give. He loved every one of us. His brave heart beat for Kells.

And so today The Post goes to press with the saddest story it has ever told. In sixteen years, it has never missed an issue. He would not want it to miss today. Never again will his "copy" go out to the machines. In a little time now the presses start. Perhaps he will hear their rumble and be glad. Perhaps, too, the shadows of late afternoon will again come creeping across the floor, and search among the corners.

T.R.D.

With a few exceptions, little can be found about the employees of Kells. Regretfully, only a name and fragments of employment dates are available for others. Everett treated all his staff with equal respect, from the tradesman to the grounds keeper and handyman. The following is a partial list of "Craftsmen at Kells" and what little information was available.

∞

Edna Chalmers was the first person hired by Everett at a time when the *Cecil Whig* did the actual printing of the Post and the print shop was not yet established. She was a local girl who knew everyone in town and was willing to do any job that needed to be done, even washing the windows. She married J. Harvey Dickey August 7, 1920. Despite her husband's success with the Atlas Powder Company she continued to work for the *Post* and was listed as Circulation Manager in 1934.

∞

Harry Cleaves, was born July 31, 1893 and he started in the printing trade at the age of thirteen working for the *Elkton Appeal* in Elkton, Maryland. When the *Appeal* was sold to the *Cecil Whig* Publishing Company in 1907, Harry finished his apprenticeship with the *Cecil Whig* and left the trade in 1911. For a short time he attended auto school in Philadelphia, but the printers ink was still in his blood so he found work in West Chester, Pa. building and designing special printing machinery. Following a disagreement with the company, Harry left and after a brief rest decided to re-enter the newspaper world. Able to choose between two offers, *The Evening Journal* and the *Newark Post*, Cleaves chose the latter. With the addition of Harry Cleaves to the staff of two, the Post started doing its own printing and Harry, at age eighteen, was its first printer. Harry remained with the Post for fourteen years as foreman and superintendent and was remembered for always bringing in fresh flowers that he had grown in his own garden.

In August 1925, Harry Cleaves left Kells and the *Newark Post* to start his own print shop in Elkton. The new shop was opened with all new equipment in a building also occupied by the Victory Sparkler Company. In July 1926 a fire in the Sparkler and firecracker section of the building totally destroyed the print shop. Harry Cleaves returned to Kells sometime in 1930 as foreman and Business Manager of the Post. When the Press of Kells ceased operation in 1940 Harry returned to Elkton and formed a partnership under the name of C&L Printing Company. In 1944 Harry bought out his partner and acquired the Cecil Democrat in 1945. In December 1947 the Cecil Democrat was sold but C&L maintained a modern printing plant for commercial work. At one time, they had received an order for 30,000,000 individual pieces of printing, considered to be the largest order in the State of Maryland.[58]

In an article titled "English vs. Slang" in the *Post* April 13,

1921 Everett tells a story about Harry and an English Professor who went to Kells to place a printing order:

> ...So with a bit of the Stand in his attitude, he called for the Foreman. Now Kells is not the ordinary Printing Plant but "Foreman" is a title unused here except in documents, violently official. He asked for the Foreman and Harry (Cleaves) came. For that he is-- and a good one. But he doesn't exploit it. He's a Master Craftsman and real Craftsmen do not know nor recognize Foreman. Harry has an ancestry, too. He draws a College man's salary, called "so-much-a-week." He's a mechanical genius--porn that way. He knows Printing- -the how, when and why. He may not know Chaucer but he knows old English. He is unacquainted with Architectural History but he knows his Gothic Types. He may not know his Shakespeare, but he can beat any Professor in seven states in a Spelling Bee. He learned it at the case and proof stone. He's an American--looks it, acts it, lives it and talks it.

When the area surrounding Kells began to be populated, Cleaves built a home a short distance away and named the road Kells Avenue. It was the first house built on that street and, like Kells, it was made of stone. Often referred to as an "Elkton boy", Cleaves started a campaign in 1921 for a Memorial honoring Cecil County boys who died in the War. The Memorial was unveiled on Armistice Day 1921 in the town of Elkton. Harry Cleaves' son DuVal worked for his father in the printing trade. DuVal and his wife Eileen continue to live in Newark, and during an interview he provided the authors with what we consider to be one of the most valuable pieces of Kells memorabilia remaining, a printing block of the Kells logo. Items of interest "Printed by The Cleaves Printing Co., Elkton, Md., U.S.A." are half tone post cards of local scenes, "Published by Frank Mackey and Company, Newark, Delaware.

∞

John (Jack) R. Shultz (Craftsman-at-Large) stopped in at Kells one day in 1914 and introduced himself as a wandering printer from Boston who was seeing the country by traveling from print shop to print shop, working awhile and then moving on. He wondered if Everett might need an additional linotype operator. According to Louise, "this young man had made a favorable impression on my husband." (He was selected to attend the Delmarvia Press Association in Ocean City in July 1914.)

When he arrived in Newark, Johnson's building was called simply 'The Print Shop." After being hired to run the new linotype, he was given living quarters in an unfurnished part of the second floor of the Kells building. It was his intention to try, through his journeys, to improve his education since he had never attended college. He asked for suggestions, as there were no extension courses at the College at that time and he did not wish to interrupt his daytime duties.

Everett's suggestions were: "that he buy a dictionary and a Victrola, and some records of classical music. He should study a certain number of words each day and use them either in writing or speech. He could do all of this in the evenings. The success of this project was amazing even if, in speaking, some odd pronunciation of words resulted. But they could be corrected." [59]

He left Kells in 1917 and entered typothetae work in Philadelphia. Shultz honored Delaware by enlisting and serving under her colors during the war (WWI). He volunteered and enlisted as a private in the Delaware Regiment (Newark's Company "E"), serving first under General Wickersham in Staff Headquarters, who recommended him to a Corporalcy. Later he was made first Sergeant. He was with the Regiment at Anniston, Camp Dix and overseas. Under Major LeFevre, of Dover, he was in the thick of things. He came back with his Lieutenancy and loud praises from his superior officers and men. At the close of the war he became secretary of the Boston Typothetae and Printers' Board of Trade. He would visit Kells when he was able as he did in September 1921. [60]

After the death of Everett, John Shultz returned to Kells as shop Manager. "He does not come here to take the Old Man's place. No one could do that. He comes, rather, to join the Craftsmen in perpetuating the ideals that for so many years were held high by the

Master Craftsman of Kells."[61]

SHOP TALK

The "Craftsman-at-Large" Returns. John R. Shultz, who studied and worked with the Old Man when Kells was very young, has returned to the shop. We welcomed him yesterday as an old friend.

"Craftsman-at-large" is the title that has clung to him since the day back in 1917 when he left to gain added training and knowledge in his chosen profession. In the years that followed, "Jack" Shultz was even at heart a craftsman of Kells. He comes back to us, then, not as a stranger but still one of the "kids."

Shultz has created for himself an enviable record in the printing trades. Upon his departure from Newark, he entered typothetae work in Philadelphia. At the close of the war, which he entered as a member of Newark's Company "E," he went to Boston, where he has since attained prominence in trade association activities. Always a student of the graphic arts, he has gained a technical training of great value both to himself and to his old love—Kells.

He does not come here to take the Old Man's place. No one could do that. He comes, rather, to join the Craftsmen in perpetuating the ideals, that for so many, were held high by the Master Craftsman of Kells. We bespeak for "Jack" Shultz, as manager of our shop, the close co-operation of every member of the staff and, we hope, the good will of a Community.

Shultz again left Kells June 2, 1926 to work for Stephen Greene Co. of Philadelphia.

∞

Ted Dantz graduated from the University of Delaware in 1922, with a BS and was a member of the K. A. fraternity. While attending the University he was class preside,nt was involved with varsity baseball, varsity club, Wolf chemical club and glee club. In the *Post* Everett wrote; "…He is rated not only as a sportsman on the field, a good fellow among associates, but a man among men on the street. He is sized up as more than a College man; he is a healthy, human, life-loving American boy—out in the world to do his bit and make good." Dantz was hired as the News man for the *Newark Post* after he graduated.

Theodore Roosevelt Dantz was named after his fathers "near neighbor and close friend" President Roosevelt. His father established the Middle Butte Quarter Circle Diamond Ranch in the badlands of North Dakota.

After four years of faithful service at the *Post* and The Press of Kells, he left September 1, 1926 to become associate editor of the DuPont Magazine. In November 1927 he advanced his position with the DuPont Company and was appointed advertising manager for the rayon division of the DuPont Rayon Company, with headquarters in New York City.

Harry Cleaves, foreman at Kells for fourteen years.

Photo courtesy DuVal Cleaves

*Top: The employees of Kells assembled in front
of the print shop in 1923.*

*Inset: Frank Balling and Edna Chalmers outside
Kells in 1923*

William J. Lovett was born on December 5, 1871, in Trenton, New Jersey and received his education at the New London Academy in Chester County, Pennsylvania. His father L. W. (Pop) Lovett moved the family to Newark, Delaware where he opened a furniture business on the South East corner of Main Street and South College Ave. This site later became the home of the *Newark Post* in 1910. "Pop" Lovett later became the Justice of the Peace and held the office under four governors until his death in 1922. He was also the Alderman of Newark.

While the family was residing in New Jersey, William Lovett entered under an apprenticeship with John P. Murphy, a job printer. After his apprenticeship he joined and worked for twenty-five years with Craig, Finley & Company, a lithographing and printing concern of Philadelphia. In 1917 he joined the *Newark Post* as a compositor. While working for the *Post*, Lovett became interested in development work. In 1924 he developed a tract of land which he owned south of Delaware Ave. On Lovett Avenue he had thirteen houses built, on Academy Street three houses, and on Haines Street another three houses. After the land was surveyed it was included within the limits of the town. In May 1927, Lovett was sworn in as a Newark Councilman and served until April 1936. Lovett was also a member of the Newark Chamber of Commerce, Knights of the Golden Eagle, and Senior Order United American Mechanics. [61]

∞

Frank Balling came from Riverside Press, starting at Kells April 1916. In December 10, 1919, as Head Pressman at Kells, he spoke before the Benevolent Pioneer Literary Society of Wilmington. The subject was "Printing from the standpoint of the Pressman." He left Kells in April 1918 after entering the service and went overseas with the 87th or Acorn Division. Returning February 19, 1919 he resumed his former position after the Armistice was signed.

A group photo taken in front of the Kells building in 1923 has the following Kells employees: from left (top row) Frank Balling, John Sparkling, Everett C. Johnson, John E. Frazer and Ted Dantz; (second row) Samuel Cole, Joseph Crockett, (unknown man), William Lovett, John Kauffman, Harry Cleaves, William Gerthie; (bottom row) Miss Edith McCall, Miss Alice Fell, Mrs. Alta Gregg, Miss Ona Singles, Mrs. Edna Chalmers Dickey, Miss Charlotte Mahaffy.

∞

John E. Frazer worked as grounds keeper for U of D then became grounds keeper for Kells in 1921. "In charge of grounds and other work." He died on October 11, 1927.

∞

Miss Charlotte Mahaffy started with Kells in 1919 and became such a close and trusted friend of the Johnsons she was listed along with Louise as Administratrices to the estate of Everett. Mrs. Elizabeth Lindell Taylor was the last person hired by Everett Johnson and continued to work for Post after it moved to Thompson Lane.

Etta J. Wilson started with the Post around 1911 as secretary. In 1919 she joined Dr. Odell in Wilmington, where her work was mostly on educational programs in 1919. In her affiliation with the Service Citizens she went on to promote better education in Delaware and is honored with an elementary school named after her in the Newark area.

∞

Miss Mary L. Powers (Post February 9, 1921) "News editor of the Post has accepted a position as Instructor at the Rehabilitation School at Delaware College. Miss Powers will continue her work as representative of the Post, being relieved only of the office duties."

∞

Norris "Lefty" Smith was hired on April 12, 1916 as a sub on the Colt printing press and Wallace Evans started at Kells in April 1916 as Printers Devil.

Other employees that worked at the Press of Kells and the Newark Post after the death of Everett can be found under the Chapter heading "The End of Kells"

∞

THE END PRODUCT

PAPER, TYPE AND BINDING

∞

The *Newark Post* was strictly a home town paper just as Everett wanted. The Press of Kells, however, reached beyond the town limits due to Everett Johnson's popularity and his far-reaching contacts. The lack of records makes most of the out of town and out of state printing elusive. Because of the close proximity of Kells and the ties Everett had with the University, the items printed locally constituted most of the items found. In fact more items printed at Kells were for the University than for any other customers. Of the one hundred and nine items listed in the Bibliography of Kells printing, forty-five are directly tied to the University. The remaining publications fall into five categories. Twelve items were strictly Kells creations, nine were for the State of Delaware, seven were for Service Citizens, five were for the du Ponts, aside from those under University of Delaware Press, and the rest were individual jobs.

Among the most elusive items from Johnson's press are the Christmas cards. Advertised as, "Attractive, artistic Christmas cards, beautifully printed on Japan paper, are now on sale at Kells. Each card has a bit of color, done by hand. The prices run from five to thirty cents."

Only one example was found, a woodcut by Miss Jane B. West, of Perry Point , Maryland. Titled , "The Carol Singer," the design won first prize in a competition at the Philadelphia School of Design in 1925 and was printed at Kells.

Probably the most widely circulated items printed by Kells were those for the University of Delaware Press. The weekly newspaper, called the *Review*, also had a large circulation, beginning in 1882 and continuing today as the University newspaper. First printed by The Star Printing Co., it was taken over by the *Newark Post* in 1913. The items printed for the university by Kells always showed the finest paper and craftsmanship.

The earliest books printed at the Press of Kells are examples of the quality of work Johnson was striving for. He admired the works of

Miss Jane B. West's Christmas card printed by Kells

the Caxton Society in Massachusetts, Thomas Mosher's Press in Maine, The Roycrofters in New York and James Grifis's Golden Press in California.[63] Had he been a wealthy man there would have been more of the fine, limited editions for bibliophiles to collect. As it was, Everett quickly faced the facts—in order to maintain his dream of running Kells, job printing was a necessity.

In choosing paper he often selected from the many high quality rag papers produced at the Curtis Paper Mill. Established in Newark in 1789 the historic mill was famous for its specialty papers. Business ledgers spanning the years 1914-1935 show many orders from Kells and all the paper used by the University of Delaware Press bearing their watermarks was produced by Curtis.[64] The best example of the fame and desirability of the paper made at Curtis was a job done "quickly and secretly towards the end of 1946." It was chosen to furnish rag vellum paper for peace treaties between the Allies and Italy, Bulgaria, Hungary, Romania, and Finland. [65]

Whenever possible, Everett would try to use the best paper. His customers did not always understand or appreciate his effort. The frustration of a printer asked to use inferior paper is revealed in an article he wrote for the *Post* in 1924 titled, "Modern Professional vs. Craftsman". It describes the reaction he received from a group of professional men at a luncheon who had asked him to print an address given by a distinguished member of the bar. After being asked to preserve it for following generations Everett took them at their word, designed the pamphlet and quoted a price from Kells. "Shades of Tea Pot Dome: Such a price:" was the way Everett described the reaction."...Then rose a young'un saying, "We want the meat of the address not a display of it-anything so we can read it as cheaply as can be gotten out. Kells will do good work, I know, but this is for information, not preservation."

Disheartened by the lack of appreciation for quality materials Johnson replied, "...Lots of important printing in Delaware, legal and documentary, today will not last over 30 years. No comment is necessary. Sane men recognize it. "If it's worth doing it's worth doing well" is old copy book stuff but is very practical in the printing of worth while things. It's an age of speed and jazz, tawdry and cheap, but let us hope it does not attack the beautiful that crops out from time to time. That let us honor and preserve for tomorrow's review by those who follow. Certainly the professional who thinks will aid the Craftsman who works to preserve that thinking."

Some of the papers with or without watermarks made by Curtis and used by Kells are: Double Antique, Enfield India, Utopian, 100 percent Curtis Rag, Antique, Nonantum Double Antique, Nonantum Wove, Curtis Super, Curbro, Curtis Vellum, London White Kid, Velvet Finish, Wedding Antique Bristol, Linweave Text and University of Delaware Press. Other papers used with watermarks that may or may not have been from Curtis are: Old Stratford, Alexandra, Bay Path Book, Strathmore Courier, Duchess, Warren's Old Style, Kingsley, Broadcloth and Fabriano Duca D'Este.

The most innovative material used by Kells for binding material was "Du Pont Fabrikoid", Du Pont having bought the patents from the Fabrikoid Company of Newburgh, New York in 1910. "Fabrikoid" was a waterproof fabric made by treating cotton cloth with successive coatings of pliable nitrocellulose lacquer and was designed and used as a replacement for leather. In addition to bookbindings, the material was used for luggage and tops for cars. The lacquered fabric came in a wide variety of colors and finishes

Top: Aerial photo of Cutris Paper Mill.

Right "Little Joe Curtis" a symbol of the Curtis Paper Company introduced in the 1950's.

simulating leather but resistant to deterioration. It was tough, pliable and resistant to grease, oil, perspiration, and mildew. Customers could choose from a variety of colors and weights. The surface grain came in Baby Alligator, Box Calf, Pigskin, Seal and Morocco. Fabrikoid looks and feels so much like real leather it is difficult to determine the difference without scraping the surface. Looking through a magnifying glass however reveals Fabrikoid's glistening surface. The material was sold at a fraction of the price of leather and was found to be more durable than leather and easily cleaned. Kells first started using the Fabrikoid for bookbinding in 1917 and the examples found by the authors show less deterioration than leather bound editions. In 1919 the *Collier's New Encyclopedia* was bound in Fabrikoid as were *The Harvard Classics* and *Junior Classics*.[66] Many informative articles on Fabrikoid can be found in early issues of *The Du Pont Magazine*. The Kells Bibliography lists those books that were bound in Fabrikoid.

The type used at the Press of Kells was purchased from the American Type Founders (est. in 1891), the favorites being Caxton, Caslon, Jenson, Gothic and Cheltenham. Johnson's feelings on the use of classic type were clearly stated in his column "SHOP TALK", February 2,1916:

> Types designed by these Masters represent the best in printing today. Type foundries are constantly making new designs to catch the eye for the bizarre, but the truly great pieces of printing are with these old designs."

"In our new equipment, we are not adding any of the new fan-gled types, but going back to the designs of the Masters of the Art. Ornaments and borders can be bought by the pound, but in order that our printing may be distinctive, we have them made, according to our own sketches. A few of our customers have designs to be used on their work alone, just to give it a touch of originality."

Other major purchases from ATF were the "American Cut Cost" cabinets. These were designed to place everything within easy reach of the composer and increase profits by saving time. The ads promoting them boasted, "One user in ordering additions to his Cut-Cost Composing Room wrote that we had 'made each alley a miniature

Divinity

Thou that art! Ecclesiastes calls Thee Omnipotence; the Maccabees call Thee Creator; the Epistle to the Ephesians calls Thee Liberty; Baruch calls Thee Immensity; the Psalms call Thee Wisdom & Truth; St. John calls Thee Light; the Book of Kings calls Thee Lord; Exodus calls Thee Providence; Leviticus, Holiness; Esdras, Justice; Creation calls Thee God; man calls Thee Father; but Solomon calls Thee Mercy, & that is the fairest of *all* Thy names.
—*Hugo*

Example of Motto Card

composing room.' That was the object of the designers: to concentrate within arm's reach of a compositor, in liberal quantities (in addition to the type faces), all the materials ordinarily used in commercial compositions..."[67] The lay out and arrangement at Kells was copied by ATF and blueprints were made as it was considered a model print shop. Everett purchased so much from ATF that by December 1921 the company owned a percentage of the Kells mortgage.

Post 2/1916: Shop Talk

There may be Printing Plants that are better equipped than ours, but just at this moment, we couldn't tell you where they are. Our plant represents the best in Printing Efficiency. It is a matter of pride with us that the lay-out of our work room has been requested by an Efficiency man of one of the leading Type Foundries of the country.

Light streaming in on all four sides of the room, makes an ideal work room. Arrangement of machinery according to cut-cost methods; Machinery the last word in Printing Mechanics; a set of kids with an interest in their work—all make this place interesting.

The lines of the building, the subject of comment, (smiling and sarcastic) are strange to stay-at-homes, but every angle was designed for a specific use. There is method in our madness. Everyone who visits us admits that this is the ideal place to do ideal printing. Even Curious Critics become our patrons when they visit us. They see just how easy it is to do good work with place, the equipment and love for the work—all of which we have.

The Newark Post started off with one chair, one table, stove, scuttle, 1/4 ton of coal, but no shovel for the first three months.[68] By October 1911 it had acquired a Babcock press with the best type face that could be purchased and a Chandler & Price jobber, folder. In September 1912 a power stitching machine and a Colts Armory press, built for heavy embossing, was added to the shop.

In October 1912 a Linotype was added to the shop. It came equipped with three magazines of type giving the operator 540 characters at his immediate control. The machine was delivered direct from the factory and there was only one other machine of its model in the state at the time. [69]

In April 1913 Everett had attended the National Printing, Publishing, Advertising and Allied Trade's Exposition held at the New Grand Central Palace in New York. He was so impressed with the Dexter Book and Catalogue Folding Machine on display that he had it delivered to his shop. Everett made the following comment about the Dexter; "You are invited to stop in some fine day and see the Blooming thing work." "It is Wonderful." "For speed, accuracy, and delicacy of operation." "It is almost weird in its action." "Not a human thing of course but by pressing a button, it will do what

Johnson purchased most of his type from the American Type Founders Company
and took great pride in the new style of type cabinets, called Cut Cost Cabinets.

human cannot do-and do it quicker." "By the way of tooting our own horn, we have in the shop 2,703,00 pages for it to fold." [70]

In a 3/4 page spread in the Post on March 4, 1914 two cuts were displayed of pieces of equipment also described in the article as follows:

OUR SHOP

Perhaps the greatest invention of recent years for Printing Industry is the Linotype. It gives speed, accuracy and new type for every job. This insures a neat job providing the Press is right.

The 4 roller—two revolution Miehle Press is absolutely the last word in Printing Machinery. The finest grade of Color Work exhibited in the Country is done on a Miehle Press.

These two machines—NEW, of the very latest models are the Pride of our Shop. The Size of other

Photo courtesy of Roanoke Press Museum of Printing

Kells boasted two Linotypes. Invented by Otto Mergenthaler in 1886 their addition enabled Johnson to print his own paper.

shops may exceed this one—but better models of machines, cannot be had—Ask any printer. He will acknowledge it.

These machines with our Dexter Book Folder make up a part of our equipment which is especially adapted to Book and Catalogue work, where quality enters into the job.

You are invited to inspect our plant, New customers have consistently brought us Duplicate orders and new customers.

Shop of the Newark Post. Where printing is considered an art and not a job.

SECRETARY OF STATE

∞

From 1904 to 1918 the Johnson family living on the farm called Crossways consisted of Everett, Louise, their daughter Marjorie, and Everett's father, Captain Isaac, who had been widowed in 1903. The years on the farm were pleasant even though the work was hard and Everett and Isaac were constantly learning from their mistakes. It was a time for Marjorie, an only child, to enjoy the company of cows and calves, chickens, horses and colts, a dog and thirteen black cats. She had her own Hackney pony named "Chum", and at the age of ten she temporarily filled in for the hired man, Bill Miller, proving her worth by milking two cows in the time it took her grandfather to milk one.

Everett had been advised to sleep outside on the porch in order to strengthen his lungs, a common practice in the days when tuberculosis was prevalent. His little daughter joined him during the summer and the two of them slept there, rain or shine, enjoying even the wild beauty of the lightning during thunderstorms.[71] *Harper's Magazine* printed a spoof of the sleeping porch craze in 1912:

> Move out my cot to the next vacant lot,
> For this "Sleep-in -the -Open" Fad I have got!
> Mitts on my fingers and socks on my toes,
> But long before morning I'm perfectly froze!

Louise supplemented their income by selling fertilized eggs for hatching. She advertised in the *Newark Post* and the phone number given for requests was simply 93. They also sold timothy hay, "clean and finely cured", "Johnson County White Corn" and seed rye. Frail as he was, Everett made a brave attempt at farming, even to the extent of taking a total loss trying to raise strawberries. His newspaper and print shop were, however, becoming more and more important to him. His interest in politics, and the challenge of influencing the growth of a small college town by employing the

Top: The farm called "Crossways"
offered fifty acres for Marjorie to explore.

Left: Marjorie, age six.

power of the printed page were leading him closer to assuming a role more suited to a man of his ilk than that of farmer. The name he would eventually give himself was "Master of Kells". The name affectionately given to him by his employees, though never spoken to his face, was " The Old Man of Kells."

1917 to 1918 proved to be difficult years for Johnson because his political appointment by Governor Townsend made it necessary for him to travel to the state capitol where he boarded during the week, returning home only on the weekends. A staunch supporter of the Regular Republican Party, Everett had spent a great deal of time promoting his close friend John G. Townsend Jr. An article in the *Post* October 25, 1916, gave this glowing description of him:

> In Sussex and Kent counties and the city of
> Wilmington, John G. Townsend knows more people
> than probably any man in the State. Further than that
> he knows them sympathetically. He appreciates their
> needs, sees their point of view, speaks as he said
> recently, their language. He understands their position
> because he has been there himself. As a farmer, a timber
> man in the woods, a lumber dealer, manufacturer,
> business man, banker, he has lived a life teeming with

83

interest. He knows labor-he has labored. He knows farming; he is one. He knows business as a manufacturer, as a producer. ...A strong fighter, smiles when he fights and forgets when the fight is over. Among his staunchest friends you will find an old enemy since befriended.

Townsend meanwhile, had been sizing up Everett; his integrity, perseverance and popularity with people from all walks of life had not escaped his notice. John Townsend was elected Governor of Delaware in 1916 and appointed Johnson as his Secretary of State. Everett did not want to uproot his family and sell the farm with all its equipment and animals. Instead, he chose to take the train from nearby Wilson Station to Dover on Mondays, returning on Fridays to spend the weekend on the farm. The train suited him much better than a car as it afforded him an opportunity to gain a much-needed rest while catching up on his reading. As long as Captain Isaac was alive this arrangement was productive since they could continue farming.

Governor John G. Townsend Jr., under whom Everett C. Johnson served as Secretary of State, 1917-1921.

In 1918, a turn of events made it necessary for the family to move to Dover. Everett's father had enjoyed serving as a juror in Wilmington, which offered him a respite from being the only man on the farm all week. Louise Johnson related the details of his last day in her diary:

> One morning, after eating a hearty breakfast, he went to his room to prepare to take the train at Wilson Station to go to Wilmington. Marjorie had geared up her pony to the cart and I took her to the Welsh Tract School.
>
> On my way back, Mrs. Wilson came from her front door to stop me to report "Captain Johnson is dead." He dropped on the platform at the station. Men lifted him to the baggage car and the train took him to the depot at Newark. He was now at the undertaker's. All this in such a short time!

Governor Townsend offered his support and the use of his Packard, which unfortunately became mired in the mud at the end of the farm lane. Leaving his car and driver behind to help the family

Marjorie awaitng her father's return.

the Governor took the train back to Dover. The big Packard was used to transport Everett, Louise and Marjorie to Sussex County, where Captain Isaac was laid to rest in St. Georges' Cemetery, near Clarksville, Delaware.

Just a few weeks later the Spanish Influenza epidemic claimed so many victims in Newark the College sent the students home on October 1st and did not re-open until October 28th. Two of the buildings on campus, Harter Hall and Purnell Hall, served as hospitals[72] for the community operated, with the exception of one paid nurse, strictly by volunteers.[73] In the United States it is estimated that 700,000 people died from the Influenza in 1918.

One day, as Louise and Marjorie were preparing to drive into town to buy feed, they heard the train whistle blow to signal a stop at Wilson Station. Louise described the following scene:

> Soon we saw a tired figure of a man dragging himself up the road. It was Everett and I feared the worst, but when he reached the house, he said: 'I think I am catching a cold. Please fill a tub with hot, salt water, and go on with your errand.' That was practically the same greeting he had given in Baltimore when he was stricken with pneumonia. [74]

His "cold" turned out to be a serious case of influenza. There followed a long, exhausting struggle for recovery, not only for Everett, but also for Louise and the doctors. Dr. Blake came daily as Everett fought the high fever. As the days passed, Dr. Steele relieved Dr. Blake who was on the verge of collapsing himself. Medicine was administered every hour, around the clock. Neighbors helped by leaving wood and provisions on the porch since no one was allowed in the house.

After two weeks, Louise herself was on the verge of becoming ill. She was rescued by Mary Rich, the head of the Department of Education at the Women's College, who moved in and managed things so Louise could finally get some sleep. Governor Townsend called twice a day to check on his friend and Secretary of State. It was Louise's belief that "no one thought Everett would recover from that illness."[75]

Everett did recover, but in his weakened condition, and with his father no longer on the farm to be with Louise and Marjorie during the week, the decision was made to move to Dover. Everett was reluctant to sell the farm, so it was rented to a nephew until it was sold in 1919 to Hettie and Samuel C. Stroud for $10,000.

In consideration for Marjorie's youthful attachment to the farm animals, Everett sought to find a suitable house with a barn in Dover. Unable to find one for rent, he and Louise finally purchased one at the north end of State Street. Marjorie was then able to take with her one horse, one cow, one dog and one of their thirteen black cats. Everett named this favorite feline "Booker" in honor of Booker T. Washington and he traveled to Dover on the train in a basket.

One of the first tasks of the new Secretary of State was the composing of Townsend's Inaugural Address. His writing skills and ability to help the governor refine his thoughts resulted in many fine speeches. The Inaugural Address contained a list of impressive goals most of which appeared to have been accomplished. The highway improvements, School Code and Women's Suffrage are but a few of the most progressive achievements of the administration.

Everett, as Secretary of State was required to keep the Executive Register, which is a journal of the official acts of the Governor. This journal is now in the State Archives and is written in Everett's longhand. The writing, which in the beginning is flawless, is an excellent indicator of Everett's health. As the four year term progressed his handwriting deteriorated noticeably. The last page, however, is signed with an oversized "Everett C. Johnson" signature complete with flourishes and his private joke of crossing a non-existent letter "T". The impression left with the reader is a job well done.

The Secretary of State serves at the pleasure of the Governor and is keeper of the Great Seal to be affixed to such documents as the law authorized. When "a commission is granted by the Governor", the document is registered and made out by the Secretary of State who attaches the Great Seal. He issues licenses in blank form to the various state officials who are empowered by law to grant them. The job comes with memberships to the State Board of Education and State Board of Pardons, and Ex-Officio duties with the Board of State Supplies, Commission to invest the Railroad and Railway, Guarantee

Deposit Fund, State Board of Forestry and member of the Boulevard Commission just to list a few. The Secretary of State also performed the duties relative to the registration and licensing of motor vehicles and operators, and the licenses of the time bear Johnson's signature. Everett never needed one himself for he never owned a car. "One time an automobile company wanted to make him a gift-a blanket for his car. Everett told them it would not be necessary since his only vehicle was a wheelbarrow!" [76]

One situation that could easily have led to a conflict of interest was that of contract printing for the State. It was also the Secretary of State's duty to direct the printing, binding and distribution of Law Books. All of this work was open for bids. The authors were unable to locate any printing done for the State of Delaware with the Kells logo while Everett served as Secretary of State. Kells did some printing during this time that was indirectly connected to the State but it was not done at state expense. Even so many of those items did not bear the Kells logo and have to be identified by other sources.

While serving as Secretary of State, Johnson evidently gave more than his time and energy-he failed to seek reimbursement for

The Johnsons house in Dover

personal funds spent for State programs.

> ...Secretary of State Everett C. Johnson also retired
> today, after a term in this office marked by conspicuous
> and creditable success. His highest compliment is that
> the new governor earnestly desired him to continue in
> the office, and that his retirement is in no sense
> compulsory. No man ever filled the office with greater
> efficiency, or with more economy, his regard for the
> latter element leading him to spend much of his pri-
> vate means in furthering the service of the State; in
> plain words, of personally meeting expenses that should
> have been paid for out of the contingent fund of the
> office. It would be only an act of justice, and not mere
> courtesy, for the Legislature to take steps to accurately
> ascertain the amount of money thus spent by Mr.
> Johnson during his term of office, and remunerate him
> to the last dollar. The salary of the position is not of
> ample proportions, and it will be a reflection on the
> State to permit so good an official as Mr. Johnson has
> been to suffer a single dollar of personal loss in this
> manner.[77]

Johnson served Governor Townsend with great loyalty and distinction during the difficult years of W.W.I. The Selective Service was established during this period and was under Everett's direction. The two most important changes made in the State of Delaware during the Townsend administration reflected the influence of the duPont family.

The first great change was to the school system and was financed by Pierre du Pont. The acceptance of the new School Code would raise Delaware's standards of education. The second major undertaking was the improvement of the state's roadways, financed by T.Coleman du Pont, who said he wanted to make a monument one hundred miles high and lay it on the ground.[78] In effect, this is exactly what he did, creating the du Pont Highway which traversed the entire state.

Both of these improvements, of which Delawarians are still

benefitting, drew considerable opposition and criticism from citizens who believed the Du Pont family was running the state. Despite Everett's close ties with the du Pont family, he was well aware of the animosity of those who felt threatened by the vast fortunes being spent in the tiny state. From his vantage point as a politician, he realized the worthiness of the causes, but would occasionally joke about the situation.

"Everett Johnson of Newark, as Secretary of State epigrammatist in ordinary to the Governor, once said to Coleman du Pont that Delaware had two capitols, one on Dover Green, the other the Du Pont building, and perhaps at the moment there was more truth in this than in most epigrams, as there was in Johnson's postscript, to the effect that he could not always tell in which capitol resided the government of the state."[79]

Townsend's greatest speeches are credited to his friend Everett who worked quietly, behind the scenes. After he respectfully declined to serve a subsequent term under the next Governor, announcing his desire to return instead to Newark and his printshop. The Sunday Star ran the following article on January 16, 1921:

There is state wide regret that Delaware is to be deprived of the continued services of Secretary of State Johnson, who retires from his post on Tuesday, with the outgoing governor, after four years of splendid service to his chief and to the people of the entire commonwealth. It is indeed, not immoderate praise to say at this time that Delaware has never had a more efficient Secretary of State, nor perhaps has the State ever had any other official who has filled a post more acceptably and ably, and with such high regard for the welfare of all our people.

Although never robust in health Mr. Johnson found himself at the head of the administration's advisers at the time when the duties of the office had been multiplied manyfold, and it is violating no confidences, to set it down here that he gave unsparingly of his strength, of his time and of his substance to those problems brought to us by the World War. He took the initiative in Delaware and among all the States in responding to the call for men to go to the battlefields, and from the first moment that we joined issue to save the world from Teutonic domination he found almost every moment of his waking hours occupied in the direction of the registration of our man-power and later with the draft. He was summoned to Washington frequently for conferences in the big task the nation had set for herself, and there his advice and counsel was solicited and followed.

Mr. Johnson's sense of duty to the young men who marched under the flag kept him ever alert to further their interests and comfort, and from the memorable moment when the call for troops came flashing to Delaware until the beaten Kaiser was put to flight, he was constant in his attention to not only his obvious duties, but to the great sense of responsibility that he felt reposed in him as Secretary of State. He spoke and addressed bodies and directed many of the notable war activities here to raise money, to emphasize the high ideals of our people, or to inspire the young men who marched away to a realization of their mighty duty to the world that they had been called on to undertake.

Mr. Johnson gave his whole time to the service of the State without regard to the strain upon him physically, nor to the outlay demanded from his personal means, and if he has decided that he must withdraw from the public service to return to his business we find ourselves in his debt financially as well as for his splendid service to Delaware.

His employees, who liked to call themselves 'The Kids from Kells', looking forward to his return, added:

"We bespeak for the retiring Secretary of State the thanks and gratitude of the people of Delaware for his notable service and for his part in giving Delaware a conspicuously successful administration."

"Printed by the Kids without his authorization"

Everett not only declined to serve an additional term as Secretary of State, he also refused to consider nomination for the Governorship of Delaware.

EDITORIAL
TYPE OF MAN FOR GOVERNOR

The State Sentinel, in answer to the Sunday Star's suggestion, has set a standard of what it thinks the requisites for an ideal Governor for Delaware. The standard is a high one, but certainly not too high for a State whose attainments, since we broke away from the British yoke, have been second to no other State in the Union. True, we haven't always been such that an intellectual successor in office would be proud to follow in his footsteps. True, we have allowed the grade and standard of our chief executives to be somewhat depreciated, but in this enlightened age, when we have concluded that it isn't wise to longer remain thirty-third in education, wouldn't it be doubly unwise to revert to the ninety-ninth degree of illiteracy in picking our chief administrator of our laws?

The diagnosing of a disease, without suggesting a remedy, however, is not only unwise but foolish, and the remedy we suggest is the nomination of Everett C. Johnson, a man of brains and intellect. A man of education-a thinker-a man who can put those thoughts into words, and who can put those words into deeds. No man's slave and no man's slavemaster. Oh, but you say, he has been too closely affiliated with John G. Townsend's administration, and Townsend's administration hasn't been a howling success. Our answer to that is: Mr. Johnson's capacity with the Townsend administration was the capacity of employee and employer, which called for and received absolute loyalty to the latter on the part of the former. Mr. Johnson probably didn't agree with many of the steps taken by the Governor. The employee is not responsible for the acts of the employer; still, we think if conditions are investigated, the searching public eye will perceive that no mean part of the brains of the administration of John G. Townsend will be found in the head of his Secretary of State, Everett C. Johnson.

Without, in any way, knowing whether Mr. Johnson would, for one moment, consider the gubernatorial nomination on the Republican ticket, we submit his name for approval of the Republican voters of the State, and we are sure when the spotlight is turned on, this little man with the big intellect will measure up to the ideals of all free thinking, liberty loving Delawareans who hold manhood, pride of State and efficiency in office above low-brow party boss servitude.

The Sunday Star, as representing the great populous and industrial centre of Wilmington, has the right to demand that Wilmington see and hear the candidates who present themselves for nomination and election. Wilmingtonians have the right to know what those candidates stand for, and we suggest that the Young Men's Republican Club of that city invite the candidates, who are spoken of for nomination on the Republican ticket, to speak to them and present to them their views and the platform they would care to run on, if nominated. Wilmington would then see for itself, hear for itself, and could judge for itself. Our one request, however, would be that Everett C. Johnson, the man, be invited to that meeting. [80]

It was not only an issue of time and energy that caused Everett to decline further political nominations. His wife Louise recalled:

"He came in laughing one day to tell me that a group in Dover had spoken to him of running for U.S. Senator. When I asked him why he was laughing, he

answered: "You don't know that it would cost me
$10,000 to run that campaign. I could buy the Knoll
or Jack Armstrong's property, the house and most of
the land, for that much money." [81]

The next two years did not provide the rest that Everett so
needed. As the end of his term as Secretary of State was in January,
midway through Marjorie's school year, provisions had to made for
her to remain in Dover with Louise. Everett rented a house in
Wilmington where he lived alone until spring when the house was
sold. Louise recounts in her diary that both the farm and the Dover
house were sold at a loss, "Everett lost one year of his Dover salary in
these two transactions."

"After our move to Wilmington, Everett was at a
low point physically and he found the commuting to
Newark hard work. Dr. Hullihen told him of a brick
house on South College Avenue that he was holding

Everett and Louise's house built on property adjoining Kells.

until September for Dr. Crooks who was coming to join the faculty. We took the house for that short period and then we moved to a bungalow almost opposite Wells. When we moved into our own house, which was being built, we had moved four times in two years!"

During this period, Everett was also occupied with building their new home next to Kells, on land Louise had purchased with money left to her by her mother. Again deciding he had no use for an architect, he made his own plans and a cardboard model. His romantic side manifested itself with the addition of four fireplaces, one in the bedroom and one with a stone mantel. The outside doors were of walnut from a Christiana drugstore counter and the bedroom doors were of Sussex County cypress.

"Our cedar mantel in the living room on West Park Place was a conversation piece. Everett had secured an amateur wood carver to depict the Henlopen Lighthouse and the receding shoreline. The preservation of the Henlopen Lighthouse was to become one of his passions in the next few years. He later became chairman of a committee for that purpose.

He was anxious to move into the house before Christmas and he did so, but there were only dangling light bulbs and no fixtures; no kitchen cupboards, and the stone had yet to be pointed."

The Johnsons lived in the house at 29 West Park Place until Everett's sudden death in 1926. The touches that had made the house so special had also made it very expensive to build. Unable to pay the debt, Louise put the house up for sale in 1927 but had no buyers as it was considered to be too far out of town. Again, taking in borders seemed to be the only way a widow could survive financially and rooms in the magnificent house were rented.

In 1936 the house was sold to Phi Kappa Tau Fraternity, which was unable to pay the mortgage and ownership reverted back to Louise after one year. The house was finally sold in 1938 and Louise and Marjorie took up residence in the Kells building which had been partially converted into apartments. The Press of Kells and the Newark Post had previously been sold, leaving only the sale of the building itself as a means to alleviate the debts incurred over the years the Craftsmen of Kells had struggled to bring quality printing to Newark.

This lighthouse still stands. Complete with a built-in light, it was hand carved into the cedar mantle of the living room fireplace.

the Service Citizens of Delaware

the Universtity of Delaware Press

∞

During World War I, Everett Johnson, then Secretary of State for Governor John G. Townsend, was appointed Director of the State Council of Defense. This Council found itself the recipient of files that had been compiled by another group, known as the General Service Board, whose self-appointed task was to research and document civic and social conditions in Delaware beginning in 1914. Part of their program emphasized the need for improvement in educational opportunities, which became the task, of a Woman's Committee under the leadership of Mrs. Charles R. Miller and Miss Jeannette Eckman. The country was caught up in a wave of patriotism with the feeling that while American boys were fighting and dying overseas, "…there were possibilities in Democracy which we ourselves had never enjoyed, there were also forces in our own nation which threatened to strangle the very ideals which we were making such a heroic effort to save on distant battlefields." [82]

On July 23, 1918, all this patriotic fervor came to a head at a meeting in Wilmington attended by Johnson and numerous civic-minded citizens. They organized themselves for action on the home front and called themselves The Service Citizens. Their purpose was to do all they could to make Delaware an ideal state in the areas of public health, education, Americanization and community development. Their organizational charter was for a period of five years, later extended to nine. Pierre S. du Pont, at that time president of E. I. DuPont de Nemours and Co. and chairman of the Board of Directors of the General Motors Corporation, was elected president. His first act was to establish a working fund of $90,000 (interest from $1.5 million trust fund) fortune, for the building of schools, an amount that would escalate to nearly six million dollars. [83]

In addition to improving Delaware schools, one of the goals undertaken by the organization was the Americanization of "unassimilated aliens." Everett poked fun at the average citizen's lack of knowledge concerning the Constitution in an article in the

Post in 1919:

THOSE IGNORANT FOREIGNERS

"You want to become American citizens?" he said. "Good" You will pass the examination for naturalization papers I am sure. Giuseppe Palavicini, what clause of the Constitution is still in force?"

"No tella judge. Not know."

"You don't know, eh! Well neither do I. You, Aristarchos Papadopoulidus, were the efforts of the founders of this republic to achieve our independence of Great Britain successful?"

"Don't know."

"Nor does anybody else. I'll admit you both to citizenship for you're just as ignorant as if you were native Americans."

The Delaware State Council of Defense, of which Everett Johnson was Director General during his term as Secretary of State, engaged Esther E. Lape to research the problems confronting immigrants who wished to become citizens. Considered an expert on the subject, her resulting report was printed by Kells under the title, Americanization in Delaware and formed the foundation upon which all of the work in the State was based. Like all of the printing done for the Service Citizens it does not bear the Kells imprint. It does, however, make use of the Bookman Oldstyle typeface with its distinctive swash characters.

Johnson executed a unique bit of printing for a very special occasion. The money to train a corps of teachers to instruct the foreign born was provided by Pierre S. duPont. These dedicated individuals often gave home schooling to housebound mothers with small children. A "Thank You" letter straight from the heart was assembled at Kells with ninety-eight photographs of some of the children of foreign born mothers receiving home schooling. (There were 3,840 children of home class mothers.) Printed on heavy rag paper, the publication is embossed with the University of Delaware seal and bound with blue and gold satin ribbons. It begins with a hand written letter dedicated to Pierre from two of the grateful mothers who were helped by the program. An inscription on the third page reads: " We could not go to school because of our many small children. Then, Mr. du Pont, you sent a teacher to us." [84]

The publication thanking Pierre was printed by Kells and bore the imprint of The University of Delaware Press which was established under Dr. Hullihen's presidency.

> "Nothing perhaps excepting always sound scholarship and adequate equipment for instruction, redounds more to the credit of an educational institution or adds more to its prestige than a Press bearing its name, wisely administered, and issuing only books andjournals of acknowledged and permanent value which carry to other institutions of learning and to, educated men in all parts of the world the name of the institutions, with books which indicate the breadth of its interests and the character of work for which it stands." [85]

With this laborious endorsement, Dr. Hullihen recommended to the Board of Trustees of the University that a Press bearing Delaware's name be established in the spring of 1922. The idea had been presented to the President of the University by Dr. Joseph Odell, Director of The Service Citizens.

The Service Citizens, in turn, provided working capital necessary to establish the University of Delaware Press, which was closely affiliated with the Press of Kells. A ledger titled Service Citizens of Delaware, Journal and Cashbook, covering the years 1918 to December 29, 1926, shows more than $45,000 for various printings for Service Citizens and $16,500 for the University of Delaware Press. The ledger shows that Kells printed numerous pamphlets for the Summer School held at the University for the certification of teachers, Americanization in Delaware, the PTA and community organizations. None of these bear any imprint or identifying marks. Printing under the heading of "publicity" included the bulletins for the Service Citizens.[86]

General plans for the incorporation of a press were outlined at an

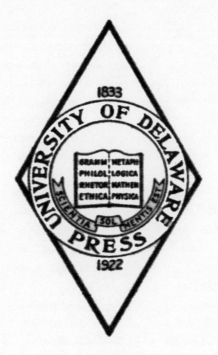

The imprint of the University of Delaware Press.
A similar watermark was made by Curtis Paper and used exclusively by the Press of Kells.

informal meeting at the Hotel du Pont with the following members in attendance: Dr. Joseph H. Odell, Pierre S. du Pont, Henry P. Scott, Dean Winifred F. Robinson, Dr. Finley M. K. Foster, Judge Hugh M. Morris, George B. Morgan, Dr. Walter Hullihen and Everett Johnson. The first informal meeting adjourned to meet again when the appointed committee made up of Hullihen, Morris and Johnson secured a charter for the corporation. [87]

Control of the University Press was to be exercised by a Board consisting of three members from each of four different areas of interest with Dr. Hullihen as President. Twenty-six shares of stock with no par value were to be issued with two shares for each member at one dollar per share. Any profit accruing from the business was to revert to the treasury of the Press. The actual composition of the Board shows:

President
Walter Hullihen

Board Pres.
Pres. U.of D.

University Trustees
Henry P. Scott

VP of Service Citizens

Henry Ridgely

VP of Service Citizens

H. Rodney Sharp

Secretary of Service Citizens
Sec. Tres. U.of D. Press

University Faculty
Winifred J. Robinson

Dean of Women's College

Wilson Lloyd Bevan

History Department

Finley M. K. Foster

English Department
Manager U.of D. Press

University Alumni
George Morgan

Class of 1875

Judge Hugh M. Morris

Class of 1898

Edward Vallandigham

Class of 1873

Delaware citizens
Pierre S. du Pont

President of Service Citizens

Christopher Ward

Author and Lawyer

Joseph H. Odell

Director of Service Citizens
VP U.of D. Press

As is evident, actual control of the Press resided with a group with cross if not conflicting interest, dominated by the Service Citizens and their behind-the-scene benefactor Pierre S. du Pont.

The charter of the Service Citizens did not permit them to engage in any form of business for profit, so all rights to the books printed were reverted to the University Press. Service Citizens was also to pay all expenses of printing, advertising, and distribution of its publications, which relieved the University of any financial obligation. After selection of a manuscript by the Board, it would be submitted for review to experts in the field who would give recommendations as to whether or not it would be suitable for publication. If accepted, the manuscript would be sent to the Press of

Kells for type setting, printing and binding of a prototype copy. The prototype would then be presented to the Board for approval or recommendations on changes. Upon final approval Kells would complete the full press run with specific instructions for packing, shipping, and distribution. With Pierre and his brother-in-law H. Rodney Sharp on the Finance Committee of Service Citizens, no one was overly concerned about fund raising for start-up. The initial $12,000 appropriated to launch the project was obtained from the funds previously earmarked by Pierre for educational projects in Delaware, and the first ten lectures by Professor of History, Glenn Frank were underwritten by Pierre personally for an additional $5,000. Frank's lectures, which were collected into one volume titled *An American Looks at His World*, and all subsequent Service Citizens publications from the University of Delaware Press were to be printed at Everett Johnson's Press of Kells.

The overall guidelines for choosing the subject matter for publications produced by the new Press, beyond those from Service

Four color fromtispiece from
Life of Eleuthere Irenee duPont, from Contemporary Correspondence 1772–1834

Citizens, were admirable but too erudite to appeal to other than scholarly readers. Scoffing at some of the popular writers of the day, such as Zane Gray and Rex Beach, they aimed instead for "that more lasting fame of a Spencer, a Meredith, a Macaullay, a Pasteur, a Rousseau..." [88]

Joseph Odell, Director of Service Citizens, was trying to choose subject matter that would compel readers to think.

> "Education as a mere process of absorption is a failure, and a waste of effort, time, and money. Young men and women must be taught to think for themselves and anyone who can lure or lash another into independent thought is doing something greater than Promethius did."[89]

If the Press had adhered to these lofty goals they might at least have captured the attention of the scholars with a careful choice of subjects. The dilemma was how to avoid becoming a specialty publication without turning into a popular press. They elected to choose a wide variety of subjects, many of which were of limited appeal.

The initial two publications to be printed shared a common, benefactor's thread—the du Pont family. The first, *National Education in the United States of America,* by du Pont de Nemours was written in French by Pierre Samuel du Pont de Nemours (1739–1817) in 1800, at the request of Thomas Jefferson. An un-translated second French edition of 1812, found in the basement of the old Wilmington library at Eighth and Market Streets, was translated by Bessie Gardner du Pont, and offered for publication and printing by the Press of Kells, with financing of the 2,000 copy run by Irenee du Pont, as interest to students of Education. The second publication consisted of eleven volumes entitled *Life of Eleuthere Irenee du Pont, from Contemporary Correspondence 1772–1834*, and was paid for by Pierre du Pont, prefaced with this cryptic inscription: "Two hundred and fifty copies only of this book have been printed for private distribution."

The remaining seven known publications printed by Kells and sponsored by Service Citizens adhered more closely to the original guidelines established by the University of Delaware Press. *Negro School Attendance in Delaware*, and *The One Teacher School in Delaware*, both by Richard Watson Cooper and Hermann Cooper, brought the inadequate state of the public schools to the attention of Delawareans with irrefutable evidence supported by charts and photographs. *An American Looks at His World*, by Glenn Frank, was an analysis of the problems faced by Americans during the post World War I years. *The English Bible, Revised Edition*, by Wilbur Owen Sypherd, Professor of English, was used in many college courses as a literary approach to the study of the King James Version. *Lectures on History and Government*, was a compilation of presentations by H. M. Morris, Willard Saulsbury, R. H. Richards, Henry Ridgely and V. P. Neilds.

Unlike Service Citizens publications, Delaware Notes, a series of scholarly works, was open for general bids. The 5th and 6th editions of Delaware Notes (1928 and 1930) bear the University Press watermark indicating Kells printed them. Others, without identification, may have come from Kells since they are similar in many respects except the choice of paper. The contents of the books clearly illustrate an attempt to reach a diversified group of readers through articles by professors of different educational disciplines. The purpose of the Delaware Notes is clearly stated in a letter of July 3, 1923 from President Hullihen to Henry Thompson: "...Perhaps I ought to add that the publication of Delaware Notes has no connection with the University of Delaware Press. It is not of the kind suitable for the purpose of the Press. Its purpose is to encourage and stimulate activity and research among the members of our teaching staff."[90]

A suggestion by Everett Johnson that, at the end of each year, four pamphlets from different departments be printed and bound together in one volume substantiates the theory that all printing of *Delaware Notes* was done by Kells. A different format was eventually chosen but there is never any mention of an alternate source for printing in any of the correspondence found by the authors. Only one unusual book has been found with an out of state printer credited along with The University Of Delaware copyright. Entitled *Jephthah*, it is a sixteenth–century Greek drama by John Christopherson, printed by the University of Chicago Press, with an introduction by Wilbur Owen Sypherd. The best explanation is that the book is

printed in Greek on one page and translated in English on the oppos-
ing page. Obtaining the required Greek type would have made the
cost of publication prohibitively high for Kells.

The offerings of the University Press may have been extremely
varied in content, but the printing quality of the Press of Kells was
consistently in keeping with the high standards set by Everett
Johnson. In a report to University Press stockholders and Board of
Directors, Manager Finley M. K. Foster, gave the craftsmen of Kells
high praise:

> "I wish to take this opportunity to call attention to
> the high grade of workmanship displayed by the crafts-
> men at Kells in the work which they have done for the
> University of Delaware Press. "*An American Looks at His
> World*" is a beautiful piece of printing and binding, and
> "*Negro School Attendance*" is a splendid composition of
> what at some point in the work looked like a hopeless
> jigsaw puzzle. I have yet to see finer printing of
> statistical tables than is to be found in this book."[91]

Similarly from the Managers' report of 1923.

> "...Kells has had to be patient with us while we
> made up our minds about many things and has always
> been ready to change to suit our opinions. I wish par-
> ticularly to speak of "Negro School Attendance in
> Delaware. This book by reason of its complicated
> tables, charts, and text, has been one of the most diffi-
> cult books any publisher would ever have to undertake.
> I am sure you will agree with me, as you glance over
> the advance copy before you, that Kells has done a very
> fine piece of work. We are indeed fortunate in having
> Kells so conveniently situated for the Press and in
> having so good a printer as Kells."[92]

It is evident from the records of these years, that Dr. Hullihen had a
vision for the Press and its importance to the future of the University
beyond Service Citizens:

"In respect to the value of the University Press, the advertising power of such an institution cannot be overestimated in comparison with other means of giving the public an idea of what attractions the Newark institution holds. The books, novels, educational works, studies in scientific research, anthologies, collections, or whatever may come forth from its type will represent the best that is being produced by Delaware's alumni, faculty and friends. Recently there has been considerable activity in the publication field by some of Delaware's alumni. Under the seal of the University Press the double value of such works must attract the attention of the thinking world."[93]

To promote the books, as well as the Press and University, advertisements were placed in *Century Magazine, New York Evening Post Literary Review, New York Times Book Review* and *American Mercury.* Thousands of letters were sent to booksellers, College Presidents and Professors, City and College Libraries, County Superintendents of Education in thirteen States, and to residents of Newark. Advertisements also came with each book, on the back inside of the dust jacket in the form of a brief description of current or upcoming publications. *National Education in the United States of America* for example, calls the readers attention to *An American Looks at His World* and *Negro School Attendance in Delaware*, while T*he English Bible* advertises *Poems To Ianthe* by Walter Savage Landor, *The Gospel According to Saint John as Found in the King James Version*, and *Story of the Unknown Church* by William Morris.

In compiling a bibliography of books from the Press of Kells, researchers will encounter a frustrating inconsistency in work printed for the University Press. The founders had a specific agenda, with publications reinforcing their views of the dismal state of Delaware's public school system. Since they were a non profit group, it was fortunate that a benefactor and a local printer, not only believed in the cause but were willing to provide money and services. Pierre S. du Pont had the money, Everett C. Johnson had the print shop and both believed strongly in the need to improve Delaware's educational system.

The earliest books, paid for by du Pont family members or the Service Citizens, are examples of the quality of work worthy of the "Craftsmen of Kells" and are imprinted with one or more of the shop's logos. Fine paper from the Curtis Paper Mill in Newark was used, some with a custom made watermark for the University of Delaware Press. Everett was given the freedom to choose the binding, covers and typeface, and the layout was left to his skilled staff.

After the organization of the University Press, the President of the University, Dr. Walter Hullihen, perceived it as a vehicle to encourage and stimulate his faculty's literary output by offering the best of their writings, handsomely printed and bound under the title Delaware Notes. These were generally used for exchange with other universities enabling Delaware Notes to find their way into many scholarly libraries. This venture also depended on benefactors; trustees pledged subscriptions of between one hundred to one hundred and twenty–five dollars again realizing no profits. This limited amount of funding was insufficient to maintain the standards that had been set by the earlier publications funded by the Service Citizens, the quality of materials decreased and Kells was forced to use cheaper paper and bindings. This may have caused Johnson to withhold his logo.

Whatever the reasons for the lack of printer's marks, it is highly unlikely that any print shop other than Kells would have done the work. The only printer with sufficient interest in the venture, and willing to donate his services on a break–even basis, would have been Johnson, himself an alumnus and life–time Trustee of the University. The second print shop in town was The Ledger, source of a little read newspaper that often plagiarized articles from Johnson's Post and resorted to offering free advertising in an effort to attract customers. It was not involved with the University in any way and it is highly unlikely they would have printed anything non–profitable.

If Johnson had placed the Press of Kells logo on all of his publications identifying his work would be as simple as turning a page. Unfortunately, for those seeking indisputable proof of a Kells product, he often chose not to do so. While Secretary of State he carefully avoided lucrative government printing jobs to avoid a conflict of interest, long before such a charge was of concern to the public. Very few bids are found in the business records of the

Townsend administration from Kells and even if the contract was won fairly the logo is very often missing from the product. No such obvious reason has been found for the sporadic use of the imprint in University publications. Everett may have been avoiding the appearance of making a profit from his Alma Mater, believing the presence of his imprint would have implied Kells was benefiting from his association to the College as an alumnus. Whatever his reasons might have been, Everett left us to ponder over watermarks, bindings and typefaces for clues.

PRINTED IN U OF D ALUMNI NEWS SEPTEMBER 1922
THE UNIVERSITY OF DELAWARE PRESS

The establishment of a University Press marks another milestone in the pathway of progress at the Alma Mater. The press has already begun operations for the publication of some of the seven works of literature, dealing with literary, educational, and scientific subjects which led to its creation. The supervision of the work has been delegated to three members of the Board of Trustees, three members of the Faculty, three members of the alumni, and three members not belonging to any of these groups under whose direction it is expected to become one of the well known presses, similar in its activities to those maintained at Harvard, Oxford, and other educational centers.

In respect to the value of the University Press, the advertising power of such an institution cannot be overestimated in comparison with other means of giving the public an idea of what attractions the Newark institution holds. The books, novels, educational works, studies in scientific research, anthologies, collections, or whatever may come forth from its type will represent the best that is being produced by Delaware's alumni, faculty and friends. Recently there has been considerable activity in the publication field by some of Delaware's alumni. Under the seal of the University Press the double value of such works must attract the attention of the thinking world.

J.P. Truss '21

The following report of the Manager to the Stockholders and the Board of Directors, July 11, 1923, details the operation of the University of Delaware Press.

Gentleman:

The work of the University of Delaware Press for the year 1922–1923 can best be considered under the following headline: "Finance". In the fall of 1922 the Service Citizens of Delaware voted $12,000 to the University of Delaware Press "to be used by the Trustees of the Press in carrying on the work." This money has been used by the Press to purchase a stock of paper, to pay current bills on books for which the Press will later be paid, and to pay the expenses of the Manager's Office.

The financial arrangements for the book now in hand are as follows:

"National Education in the United States of America" by DuPont de Nemours.

The Press has advanced all money spent on the manufacture and distribution of this book. When this transaction is complete, the Press will submit a bill to Mr. Irene du Pont for the whole amount. Under the terms of the agreement the Press has five hundred copies of this book for sale. From these copies whatever profits the Press may make will come.

"Negro School Attendance in Delaware" by Richard Watson Cooper and Hermann Cooper

The Press is printing 1,200 copies of this book of which the Service Citizens has ordered 1,000 copies. The Press has assumed all the bills of this book until its manufacture and distribution are completed. The bill for the 1000 copies will cover the cost of the whole edition of 1200. This will leave the Press with 200 copies, which it may sell at $5.00 a copy, on which to realize a profit.

"An American Looks at His World" by Glenn Frank.

On this book the Press is assuming the whole financial risk. The possibility of making a large profit on this book is very slight. Because we are a very small publishing house, we must depend on Baker and Taylor and other distributing houses in the United States for the marketing of a large part of these books. Baker and Taylor charge a discount of forty–six per cent. This is a very large discount; but when one considers that they must give the bookseller a discount of one-third, Baker and Taylor are not making a very large profit on the transaction. The size of the book, 372 pages, will necessitate a price, which may not make it a best seller. However, I am hopeful that judicious advertising will bring us a fair sale for the book.

Accounts: Attached to his report is a financial statement by the Treasurer. "Books Under Consideration."

Your Executive Committee has considered and rejected the following books:

"Jamaican Negro Songs" by H. H. Roberts

"From Cosmos to Man" by Edmund Noble

"American Pronunciation" by John S. Kenyon

"How People Should Live Together" by Alice Krackowizer

Your Executive Committee has under advisement the following books:

"The English Bible" by W. O. Sypherd (a second edition)

"The Revolt of the New Immigrants" by M. G. Hindus

"A History of the English Language in America" by C. P. Krapp.

Your Executive Committee has accepted the plan of Dr. Odell for Dr. Otis Caldwell to deliver a series of lectures in the Summer School of the UD, which will later be published by the Press in book form. Inasmuch as the book has not yet been written, no further judgement can be passed upon it.

Your Executive Committee has accepted the plan of Service Citizens for the publication of a history of Delaware to be written by Miss Katherine Pyle. Inasmuch as the book has not yet been completed, no further judgement can be passed upon it.

MANAGEMENT

The method of doing business as worked out during the past year is as follows: All books submitted to the Press are sent to the Manager's Office. These books are then read by the Manager and a report upon them prepared by him for the Executive Committee. If the Executive Committee considers the book worth while, the books are then read by persons best fitted to pass a judgement upon them. This method saves the Press the cost of having books read before it can be ascertained whether there is any likelihood of their being published. After the books have been read and approved, they are edited by the Manager. Following this, they are sent to Kells for manufacture. The process of manufacture having been completed, Kells ships them out according to instructions from the Manager. The Manager's Office keeps a record of the sale and distribution of these books, sending to Kells only the shipping directions. All money received by the Press from the sale of books is deposited by the Manager in a local bank and at periodical intervals transferred to Mr. Montaigne of the Service Citizens, who is acting as accountant for the Press.

ADVERTISING

Your Executive Committee has under advisement a plan of advertising, which will put into operation next fall when the book "An American Looks at His World" is placed upon the market. Inasmuch as the details of this plan have not yet been completed, I shall leave this matter for a later report.

POLICY

In closing, I wish to make a few remarks about the future policy of the Press. I believe that so far as possible the Press should avoid publishing books which enter into competition with other books in the same field. We have not the machinery for publishing books on as cheap a basis as have the large publishing houses. We do not have an organized sales force which is continually proclaiming our wares in the ears of the booksellers of the country. We have not sufficient capital to spend the thousands of dollars which are sometimes spent, to place books before the reading public so frequently that out of sheer desperation the public buys them.

For these reasons I feel that the Press should content itself with publishing books which because of their contributions to the sum of human knowledge, can be sold in limited editions at more than the average price. In this way the Press would have an assured sale for its books and would be taking less chances of loss of the capital invested than it would by trying to sell books of a popular nature which will either run into large editions or fall flat. In addition, by this kind of publishing the Press would avoid the ruinous forty–six per cent discount of Baker and Taylor; for the large majority of such books is ordered from the publisher without the intervention of any middle man.

Of course, I am aware that our capital would not be turned over slowly than have it tied up in books which could not be sold because of lack of advertising and too high a selling price for popular consumption.

Respectfully submitted,
Finley M. K. Foster, *Manager*

Unfortunately for the fledgling University Press, it was not financially sound enough or sufficiently organized to survive two monumental changes. Everett Johnson died suddenly in 1926 and without his leadership the Press of Kells foundered in spite of the efforts of many talented employees who did their best to save it. The Service Citizens charter expired in 1927 after having fulfilled all of their printing needs; their charter was not renewed which effectively removed the financial support of Pierre du Pont. The Press had never been a profitable enterprise (for example Delaware Notes was paid for by subscriptions from trustees and given away free of charge) and the faculty did not maintain an interest in its continuation. The end came in 1939.

In a letter to Mr. P. S. du Pont from Walter Hullihen the end of the University of Delaware Press was announced. "A meeting of the Board of Directors of the 'practically defunct' University of Delaware Press, of which you are a member, is called for Saturday, June 3, at 2 p.m., daylight, in the Lounge of Old College. The purpose of the meeting is to render the corporation 'wholly defunct' and to authorize the appropriation of the small balance of cash in the treasury of the Press to some useful University purpose. No books have been published by the Press during the past ten years and there are no funds sufficient to further publishing. It is therefore desirable that official action be taken to terminate the corporate existence of the Press and to dispose of the cash balance and books that still belong to it."[94]

In response to the letter Mr. du Pont wrote; "Thanks for your invitation to attend the funeral services of the University of Delaware Press. You do not add the usual words 'Please do not send flowers', but I take it for granted that none are expected."

"If it is necessary for me to be present, please notify me by telephone or otherwise. If the meeting is purely formal and a quorum will be present without me, I shall not attend." [95]

When John Perkins became President of the University of Delaware in 1950 he increased the funds allocated for publishing. For a short time cooperative arrangements were entered into with other university presses, including those of Rutgers, New York University, and Temple University. [96]

In 1975 the university entered into a contract with the Associated University Presses, one of several publishing firms controlled by Thomas Yoseloff, who agreed to publish, at his expense but with the University of Delaware Press imprint, scholarly books that are approved by a faculty board of editors, including books by authors who have no connection with Delaware. These books are printed as a service to scholarship and at no cost to the university except for the maintenance of an office and miscellaneous expenses..." [97]

New Schools for Delaware

Thank You Mr. du Pont

∞

In 1918 the Service Citizens funded a survey of the public school buildings of Delaware. The results fueled a bitter controversy over whether or not schools should be controlled by local commissioners or have to conform to State standards. Three professors from Teachers' College, Columbia University, gathered information and photographs of the majority of the schools in Delaware. The results were published in two volumes and each school received a score. A perfect score was 1000 points based on: 160 for Site, 200 for Building, 250 for Service Systems, 225 for Classrooms, and 165 for Special Rooms. (Special Rooms meant library space, rooms for manual training and home-making arts, a play and community room, and a room within the building for fuel.) [98]

Everett Johnson campaigned vigorously in favor of passing the School Code. The statistics from the professors' survey were presented in a 434–page book titled *The One Teacher School in Delaware* which was printed at the Press of Kells in 1925. The inscription read "Dedicated to Farm Boys and Girls of Delaware Patrons of Democracy". To appreciate the intensity of the opposition it is necessary to imagine the outrage felt by the average small town citizen upon being told the local school was not only unfit for children but immediate demolition of the building was recommended. Two typical school reviews follow.

Ogletown District No. 42 received 229 out of 1000 points with the following description;

> Ogletown is another of the very old, stone blockhouses.
> It is also located on one of the proverbial triangular sites
> in the fork of the roads. It possesses no single attribute
> which justifies its use for housing children. It is dark
> and depressing on the inside and unsightly from

the outside. The toilets are in a very insanitary
condition, vilely defaced and located within ten feet of
the class room windows, which are the only source of
ventilation. It is a crime against innocent children
to enforce compulsory attendance laws where such
accommodations are all that the community has to
offer.[99]

That was a school for white children. John Wesley No. 160
"colored" fared even worse with 160 points:

John Wesley school is nothing but a wretched,
dilapidated hovel. It is not fit for the housing of any
child. The clapboards are falling out, brick foundation
decaying away and the roof rotting in places. It is
unfortunately located near a cemetery and lacks
sufficient playground area as well as playground
apparatus. Children may with wisdom be kept at home
rather than housed in such a structure for the purpose of
"getting an education." [100]

The bitter debate over the School Code, was more than local
annoyance over three non-Delawarians condemning practically all of
the schools in Delaware. Small town politicians were reluctant to
relinquish their authority to control their local schools, no matter how
inadequate the schools might be. Some schools were actually burned
as a means of protest, which was probably a blessing in disguise!

Everett used his newspaper to dispel rumors and misconceptions
about the Code. As a means to educate the public and promote
support for the bill he ran a three—quarter page editorial in the *Post*,
June 25, 1919. It described the origins, the work of the commission,
and the provisions. He proceeded to describe the opponents and
supporters of the bill in the usual Everett Johnson fashion. Following
are some of the highlights of the editorial:

OPPOSITION TO ITS PASSAGE

Yes. By an honest opposition, fearing the wisdom of a change which seemed so radical. By an opposition, slow in decision, wanting more time to consider. By an opposition, by those adverse to change. By an opposition who wanted it for a party issue, as a political asset. By an opposition, who feared increased taxes saying, "Let well enough alone." By an opposition who wanted an extra session, in which to play politics. By a personal opposition to the Commission and the Administration. By an opposition who wanted to dictate the appointments. Yes, it was opposed honestly, opposed maliciously, opposed by fogyism, by ultra conservation, by political ambition, and by personal hatred. It was opposed by lack of understanding and opposed by false statement of facts.

SUPPORT OF CODE

Yes. It was supported honestly—and only honestly. The opposition whether honest, political or malicious never dared dispute that. It was supported by those who were thinking of their children, of the State, of Tomorrow. It was supported by citizens who were willing to sacrifice a personal opinion on some minor provision to the judgement of all. It was supported by men who were ashamed to be citizens of a state that ranked 33 in education in the 48 states of the Union. It was supported by men who were ashamed that Delaware ranked 34 in illiteracy. It was supported by men who were ashamed to be part of a state that spent less per child than forty other states. It was supported by men who laid aside party credit and town pride for their children. Democrats and Republicans were together in the work for the citizens of tomorrow. It was supported—and it is supported today by every mother in the State who is correctly informed of the provisions and opportunities given in this piece of legislation.

NO RIGHT TO INTERFERE

The statement that the State has no right to interfere with local affairs can best be refuted by reference to the Constitution. It says: "The General Assembly shall provide for the establishment and maintenance of a general and efficient system of free public schools."

The Schools are not local institutions but a part of a State system. The powers exercised locally are delegated by the General Assembly.

An impassioned plea was made to the readers of the *Post* in the July second, 1919 issue.

TO THE BOARD OF EDUCATION

The responsibility is yours. The honor and reputation of Newark will be judged by your actions. It's up to you—a stern serious problem from which you cannot escape.

In a word, The Code aims to improve our system of Education. That it will do this, no one has dared to dispute. No one need argue the need of improvement in Delaware. Our rank with other states is a blot on our history and a reflection on us here today.

The question up to you is one of Service to our Community, this State, and this Nation. The question is one of Service to your children and ours. More than that Service, not just for today but for tomorrow and all the morrows yet to come. The obligation to your selves, the responsibility to the Community you represent, the plain citizen's duty to your State, the service to your Country—all appeal to You.

For the safety of the State,
For America the Great,
And the freedom of all the World.
Adopt the Code.

Along with the new school code came a very unpopular increase in taxes. Everett chided his readers with a little insert in a column he called "Squibs". Springtime in Newark was a time for racing horses, a favorite pastime and a source of pride for the owner of a fleet steed. The little squib pulled no punches:

> "Funny isn't it, a man will drop a cool hundred to
> a spavin hoss and smile. He's a good sport. Then he'll
> kick on school tax. He's a poor citizen."

With Everett's editorial support, the School Code was finally passed in 1919 and revised in 1921. Of the schools built in the next eighteen years, one hundred and eight were built from funds provided solely by Pierre S. du Pont, including eighty-six schools for black children. [101]

Pierre's support ceased in 1927 and the *Post* carried the headline: "Pierre du Pont To Cease Building Schools—Chagrined at Attitude Toward His Efforts Will Probably Not Renew Need Of Service Citizens." In February, 1931 he sent a letter to the State Board of Education withdrawing his services for architectural support, supervision and accounting support for construction of school buildings. He was disappointed at the failure of the Legislature to appropriate sufficient funds for new buildings and he felt the citizens of Delaware had become too dependent upon him.

The collection of Pierre's personal letters at Hagly Museum contain many letters written by people intent on receiving a hand out. One in particular illustrates the attitude of dependency that was becoming all too common. Written by a schoolteacher from lower Delaware, who was enjoying the benefits of one of the new schools built by Pierre, she informed Mr. du Pont that the new school was without a flag and asked him to please promptly rectify the shameful situation by sending one. He responded by telling her to have a bake sale!

VOICES FROM THE PAST

∞

The College library that was formerly the *Newark Post* building, located on the South East corner of Main Street and South College Ave., was in poor condition and not suitable for its intended use. The idea of a new library, to also serve as a war memorial, was suggested back in 1918 by Delaware College President, Samuel C. Mitchell. Although Dr. Mitchell left the College in 1920, the seed was planted. Mitchell was replaced by Walter Hullihen who made the idea his favorite project but had to present the proposals three times to alumni before he was given the go-ahead in February 1922. A campaign committee was set up in September of that year, made up of Hullihen, H. Rodney Sharp, Henry Scott, H. W. Lyndall and Everett C. Johnson. The goal was to raise $300,000, strictly from private contributions.[102] The entire State took up the challenge and the full amount was raised from 26,690 contributors. The original provision called for a memorial in the center of the building consisting of a bronzed tablet bearing the names of those who died in the War and an accompanying hand–illumined, hand–engrossed book, with the names and life history of each person whose name appeared upon the tablet. The final result was a rotunda–like central room with four bronzed tablets placed in four triptychs. Near the four corners were the flags of the principal Allied Nations. In the center of the rotunda was a glass-topped case containing the so called "Book of the Dead". A detailed description of this volume, hand made at the Press of Kells, is in the Bibliography section of this book.

The dedication of Memorial Hall was held on May 23, 1925 with 1,200 people in attendance and lasted nearly two hours.[103] The most impressive feature of the ceremony was the presentation and acceptance of the *Memorial Book*. As Everett Johnson gave his speech, the Book rested on a side stand draped in the State Flag. At the close of his address, the flag was pulled away, and the audience got its first glimpse of the impressive volume. Governor Robinson, after his acceptance speech, called upon J. Alexander Crothers, Commander of the American Legion of Delaware, and turned the book over to him. It was then reverently carried up the steps into the rotunda and placed in its case as a bugler sounded "To the Color". The Memorial, including the Book remains there to this day. Everett described it in great detail in a two page article in the *Post*, May 27th, 1925 which covered the dedication ceremony.

The binding is of deep brown French calfskin. The paper is cream white Fabriano, made by hand in Palermo, Italy with deckled edges. The book weighs nearly twenty-five pounds, measures thirteen by nineteen inches, and is five inches thick. The front and back cover have imbedded lines dyed in black. On the four corners of the hand–tooled cover are gold diamond shaped studs representing The Diamond State. Imbedded in the middle of the front cover is a gold War Medal struck by order of the Governor and General Assembly of Delaware. The medal goes through the cover and the reverse can be seen on the inside. The front is the Seal of Delaware and the reverse reads; "In Honor of these Men Women from Delaware Who Lost Their Lives in World War this Medal is Struck by Permission of Act of the General Assembly 1925." (The same medal, in sterling silver, was given to Delaware veterans who served in the First World War.)

Only one book was produced and it is located on display at the University of Delaware Memorial Hall. When the heavy pages are turned, the name of each individual who gave his or her life in the War is revealed at the top of the page, lettered by hand. The hand lettering was done under the supervision of Stanley Arthurs, noted Delaware artist. It was Everett's intention to record the life history of each person, together with the insignia of his division, in color, at the very top. This work was never accomplished. In keeping with the original Book of Kells, which resides in Trinity College, Edinburgh, a ritual was followed wherein one page a day was turned.

The glass cover and stand now show signs of wear from students using it as a resting place for book bags or a writing stand. In later years Everett's wife Louise Johnson wrote in her memoirs, "In 1944, when I was working part–time in the Library, as I entered the building one rainy day, I was shocked to see it covered high with students' raincoats!"[104] It is doubtful that many students now realize the meaning behind Memorial Hall and without reading a small note

Memorial Book

Top: Front
Right: Detail of Medal

placed in the case with the Book they would have no idea what the book contains. Memorial Hall will be renovated in 1998 and hopefully the Memorial Book, and the rotunda will retain their place of honor in the building.

This speech was delivered by Everett C. Johnson at the dedication Exercises of the University of Delaware Memorial Library May 23, 1925.[105]

On such occasions as this, we of Delaware, are inclined to agree with Emerson that Institutions are but the lengthened shadows of the lives of men. Just as a man Caesar is born and we have a Roman Empire, so today by the lives and sacrifices of those who we honor, we have this Memorial to serve the generations yet to come. Fitting and appropriate too, for our State. Our traditions are tinged with Romance, our Past lighted with Ideals, our History recites Facts that make reading that inspires.In a crisis, Delaware never fails to respond. When Tradition whispers, History calls, when Humanity pleads and Christianity stands at bay, Delaware stands ever waiting at the Cross Roads of History following the footsteps of Destiny, ready to express in words and deed, in life or blood what we in our better selves have learned and felt.

"And how can man die better
Than facing fearful odds
For the ashes of his fathers
And the temples of his gods!"

And, too, Delaware does not forget.We love and recite the record of her past.From our heritage comes our Inspiration for the work of our day.History to us is a reverend and living philosophy.So in paying tribute to our Dead, we erect Memorials to serve our living. Marble monuments may appeal, towering shafts may awe, but to us a Memorial that garners the thought of the ages and guards the ideals of Men gives only true reverence to those having served, and inspires and leads on those who will and may. Indeed by such as this we translate their lives into our living and are prompted almost to say "There are no Dead."

A photo of Everett taken in a Philadelphia studio, cigar in hand.

Thus believing, mingled with our tears came the inspiration of this Memorial. Laying aside the brush of artist and chisel of sculptor, without thought of cold formality of official and legislative action, the heart and memory of this State conceived this Building as its feeble but best tribute to those sons and daughters who gave their lives at a Nation's and Liberty's call in the World War.

"O silent and secretly moving throng,
in you fifty thousand strong,
Coming at dusk when the wreaths have dropt,
And streets are empty, and music stopped.
Silently coming to hearts that wait,
Dumb in the door and dumb at the gate,
And hear your step and fly at your call
Every one of you won the War
But you, you Dead, most of all."

The Thought barely expressed when generous action followed, the story of which you have heard recited.

Aside from the collection and collecting of the World's thought and action, the rotunda of this Building has been reserved and has been designated as the Memorial Hall. In enduring bronze are inscribed the names of those "Rich Dead." In honored position rests the sacred desk. Embedded in its base is the bronze medal struck in Honor by Act of the General Assembly and your official signature. Flanking are your gifts of State and National colors, and in its case, Governor, you are requested to have placed this Book of the Dead.

It has been made by hand and has embedded, by your permission, replica of the official War Medal. Its cover is protected by studded diamonds typical of our State, and suggestive of the glory of service, it is sealed by the Gold Stars of sacrifice. At the headings of its pages are etched the names of those we honor. Inscribed below will be the life history of those sons and daughters as the facts are presented to us by relatives and official records.

Two hundred and seventy of these names make up the Chapter Headings, the dramatic and colorful Capital Initials underneath which our lives will be simple prose.

As one of the rank and file of our citizenship, designated to this responsibility, I present to you, Governor, this Book as our Memorial to those whose blood so richly tone its pages. I ask too, that in accepting, you honor our University and our State in dedicating this Building to the Memory of Sacrifice of yesterday and to the service of our day and tomorrow. Not long will be remembered our words but Time endures for those who gave.

In yonder years, as our children read the story of this day, may out of the flickering shadows come the whisper "These Dead shall not have died in vain."

Thus inspired, Delaware will again hold high the torch from Flander's Field. And as a Son of Delaware, and Champion of Liberty, or Daughter, a Mother of Peace, right well command.

Blow out, you Bugles over the Rich Dead.

After Everett presented the Book to Governor Robinson the Governor gave his acceptance address which was also written by Everett C. Johnson. [106]

With appreciation of the honor and reverent humility of the responsibility, I accept in the name of our citizenship this Book of The Dead wherein are enrolled the names of those, our Sons and Daughters, who gave their lives in the Great World War. In their sacrifice Liberty has advanced and Christianity endures. By their death we have enriched our heritage and "Nobleness walks in our ways again."

Sad is our recollection of our loss, there is, after all, an Inspiration for us to live and work in our day to finish the work for which they gave the last full measure.

True, as has been said, our traditions and History are Ideals translated into the Realities of Free Institutions. And well did these Sons and Daughters, to whom we pay meager but living tribute, do honor to their fathers.

So here, today, as we recite their story, may the voices from The Past sound clear to us. So, too, to you, our students here today, let me make appeal. As you read the story of the lives of our friends and kin and the records of the World's Thought and Deeds, try to catch a glimpse of the motive that prompted them and so live, that your deeds will honor their lives.

This Book, this building, is so in keeping with the thought and reverence expressed by our citizens that words would but feebly express our feelings.

> So, as Governor of Delaware, a State rich in
> tradition, proved in history, with reverence for the past
> and devotion of service to the future, I accept this Book
> and order that The American Legion conduct it to its
> honored desk where it will rest in the rotunda of this
> building, and too, by this action, I formally Dedicate
> this Building as the Memorial Library of Delaware at
> this, our State University. Beautiful in conception as a
> Memorial to the Dead, may it richly inspire and serve
> the living.

With Everett listed not only as the General Chairman but also as a member of the Executive Committee and General Committee[107] and with a print shop at his disposal, it is no wonder he would also do most of the printing needed. One of the first such printings was a leaflet titled Library and War Memorial Campaign University of Delaware 1922.[108] The leaflet was filled with information about the Memorial and what Delaware did for the War effort. Another printing was a small tri-fold leaflet titled *"Views, First Day's Work on The Memorial Library December 11, 1923."*[109] It contains views of students and faculty working side by side excavating the building foundation. Apparently they were not always digging in the correct spot but a good time was had by all. One of the photos shows the female students and is titled, "Women's College girls feed a hungry mob". A second photo showing the Color Guard happened to catch Everett just as he exhaled a puff of smoke from one of his favorite Cuban cigars!

Everett C. Johnson and Walter Hullihen signed a Certificate of Honor, nicely printed by Kells on 8 x 10 stock, for each contribution to the Memorial Fund[110]. The program for the dedication was also printed at Kells. All funds collected were earmarked for the building expenses and since there was no budget for printing, Everett donated the services of the Press of Kells, and supplied all printed materials connected with the fund raising gratis.

Eventually the University Library out–grew Memorial Hall and the new Library was built a short distance away in 1963. The Library was named in honor of Judge Hugh M. Morris, '98 and in 1998 boasted more than 2,200,000 volumes of books and serials.

LETTERS AND STORIES

THE PRIVATE SIDE OF EVERETT C. JOHNSON

∞

Everett C. Johnson was a man of letters. Journalist, editor, printer, newspaperman, were some of his titles. He put his ability to turn a phrase to good use, hammering relentlessly at the citizens of his alma mater, town, state and country, to take the lead, set the example and donate time, energy and money for the common good without complaining. All this he performed in the public eye. His editorials, essays and lectures were tailored to his audiences. He could compose sophisticated addresses for Governor John G. Townsend on demand and with equal facility write a column for the *Post* in down–home jargon replete with corn–pone humor. The intended audience dictated his style of writing and choice of words.

But Johnson also had a private side—a side reserved for close friends and family. The letters to his daughter Marjorie reveal a father struggling to put his feelings for his child into words. The words of Elbert Hubbard, whose literary style was greatly admired by Everett, provide a perfect insight into Johnson's letters written to Marjorie on her eleventh and eighteenth birthdays.

"We write for those who understand and the person to whom a letter is written gives the key that calls forth its quality. Great love-letters are written only to great women.[111] The following letters offer a rare glimpse into the private life of Everett C. Johnson:[112]

EVERETT C. JOHNSON, SECRETARY OF STATE

My dear Boots,

There isn't enough paper in Dover to tell you how much I think of you. Eleven years old, but I love you more than 11x your first birthday.

I want to say this, too. I think you are a wonderful girl and I expect great things out of you. You can do

"Little Boots" and "Big Boots", Marjorie and Everett shortly before his death.

almost anything you decide to do. So I want you to decide to study, to work, to be kind to mother and other people.

Folks who see you, like you. You are cheerful, a bunch of smiles and good nature. That's because of mother. So try to keep people liking you. Nothing would please mother more—and I would be happy as Ted with a bone.

I suppose you are as good when I'm away as when I am home, oh?

You treat me so good that it makes me feel like company— and I am not at all. I am just plain old Boots.

"Jes" about a million years ago, I dreamed about having a child just like you.

I thought it was a dream but it wasn't. For here

you are big and gay as life itself.

Everything I have, even my head if its any good to you, is yours. Its just the most fun to work for you— and you seem so much to appreciate it. So this is the end of my scrawl to you.

I can't say what I think but Boots ought to understand what other Boots mean.

Lovingly, Father

(Dover, August 4th, 10 PM., 1918, at Council of Defense Headquarters) Everett C, Johnson At The Newark Post Newark, Delaware. Tuesday 4:10 PM.

Dear old Boots.

Of course this could not be a letter except it insures the fact of getting a letter —then there "aint none". So it is like losing a fish after catching it. But Welcome to Aloha!. And you are I'm sure. Because you have a gay cheer that makes every one glad. That is not my opinion alone but unanimous.

And now Boots for a little compliment that I couldn't say to your face. Nor let it make you conceited nor again think there is no room for further advance. Here she goes.

I am a severe critic—the more I love, the more severe.

But your development and improvement in the last six months have been increasing delights to me. Doesn't that surprise you? You have a keen, quick, crit- ical, analytical, kind mind. And at times you surprise me with your sweep of imagination.

With these you have two rare qualities originality and sympathy.

I expect great things from you. They are yours with such little effort. Personality is scarce, and you have it in abundance. You have only a few facts to gather and our apprenticeship with the tools of expression—just enough to master technique and Great

Things are yours.

That's all and True.

So now play, catch the breath of the mountain air, catch the tails of its sunsets, the poetry of its moonlight: And after the thrill of the ride, the splash of the oar, the laughter of campfire—to (dance) amid the smell of fir and pine and sometimes, please, just sometimes dream of The Old Boots and awake again—a joy to all that live with your smile.

(Addressed "Aloha Club" at Comicut, (Corricut) ?. Pike, New Hampshire, June 30, 1925)

My Dear Girl—Marjorie

Great days these! Wonderful times! This day August 1st 1925 and Boots to pass in to Womanhood on the 4th Eighteen! My how I would like to see you that day! Do get on your horse and have someone take a good picture to have enlarged.

I should like to write you a letter today that you would long remember but the subject is too wonderful and day too seriously fraught with possibilities, that I sit here just overcome with all the yesterdays past and awed for the days to come. The deeper we feel, the less we say. So my birthday wish to you is this—On the night of the 4th when all is still and only Dreams and Silence are whispering out under Mountain stars, let your Ambitions slip out and listen to what they are saying. And they will be talking over your secret hopes, your life future with its work and play, its sun and shadows, its defeats and accomplishments, its will and determination to give and do for those around you, its honors, glories, home, children, its State and Country. All these things they will be saying. And what you in your best moments want most, is my wish to you this wonderful day. Would that I could give it to you! Would that I could go ahead always and clear the way! But then the thrill of mountain climbing is finding the trail and going up alone or with some one good and true pal, rather than following.

So, Boots, you go over. I'll stay here by this stream. You have youth. I have not reached the view I expected, so you find it for me. I'm tired and you are so young and then I would rather you have it anyway. My little ascent has been great—but you go on. It will be great to see you way up on the cliff of Life and Achievement —and wave to you.

Enough—away with "preachin". You have been a great good girl. And all my fussin' and "fussin" ways have been crude expressions of ambition and love. My "tongue-spanks" hurt me too (according to parental precedent).

So here is to you Boots, you 18 year old flat footed dream of mine!

Thank you for all the Joy given me—only give me more. And for you and yours (if successful) and all you want of the best to do—Luck and Good Cheer!

Here endeth the First Lesson found in the First Chapter of All Fathers to Fun Loving Children.

Well, your trip to the mountains sounds great. An event of a life time. Do you know that is considered a real achievement? I am so glad you passed the tests and were able to make it.

It seems to me that you are "Making Good" to an unusual degree. And you know how that makes me feel. I'm delighted too that you have decided on another weeks stay. Things are horribly dull here now. This period is the very worst.

The new man Smith is a working man. Of course I have not had time, nor he, to know of his peculiar fitness yet. But I am very much encouraged.

He moves in the "Cobb" house. They go to Foster's on Quality Hill.

Mother heard from "Winnie". Nothing dramatic

except she went to sleep, one day (?).

CONSTITUTIONS [113]

I am absolutely stumped. I have no idea how to finance, produce or dispose of them. Senator Bayard stopped in to congratulate Delaware and me on the honor conferred.

Tillie[114]dropped in for a chat and dinner. He is a good old scout. Full of enthusiasm for his work and Yale. He is the most serious fun getter I know. He even works up his sport to an advantage. This is a subtle suggestion. Your summer can be used next winter in getting A's and B's in English.

You surprise me in your reading. Am willing for you to lose another middy and wear my ties, it you keep that up. Well, if you have read this far,

Forgive the length and me. And for your birthday just Marjorie, we are together.

And with your flat feet and my flat head, we'll go quietly on. August 4th—you are a great day because of Boots. Yeah Boots ! Just Luck, Life and Love, Father

(Saturday Morning, August 1st 1925)

When Everett Johnson left Sussex County and headed North to enroll in Delaware College it was not his intent to tailor his education toward a political career. He majored in modern languages,[115] and his yearbook, The Aurora, recorded his ambition to serve in the military—an unlikely choice for a young man who had inherited his mother's frail constitution. His entry into the political arena was the logical result of Everett's many public appearances where he, with great facility, would tweak the conscience of his audience while challenging them to give their best for whatever cause needed support.

This penchant for public speaking first manifested itself during his college years as he participated in plays, competed in debates as a member of the Delta Phi Literary Society, and gave speeches advocating the addition of a Woman's College. In later years, according to his wife, Louise, he attended many political meetings; a trip with his father to hear Theodore Roosevelt speak at Havre de Grace, Maryland made a lasting impression.[116] As a result of these appearances Everett was drafted as a Republican candidate for the Legislature in 1910.

His ability to captivate his listeners with a mixture of dry wit and wisdom made him popular in the business world in such gatherings as The Grange, Newark's Aetna Fire Department, and especially the Wilmington Rotary Club of which he was an active member. Fellow Rotarian and newspaperman William F. Metten, (editor and later owner of Wilmington's "Every Evening") was a Democrat and in spite of Everett being a staunch Republican the two became close friends, working together for the betterment of Delaware's newspapers.

Business and politics often go hand in hand and in spite of himself, Everett became increasingly more influential in Republican politics. An unsigned clipping from the 'Every Evening' paper poked fun at Johnson's verbal proficiency with heartfelt good humor. It most probably came from the pen of Walt Mason who wrote "Rippling rhymes." [117]

> Some publishers can make remarks with paper, type and ink, and there their brief resources end for telling what they think; but Johnson is a versatile and oratoric bird, who vocalizes thrillingly the deadly printed word, who tells it Lazarus come-forth and makes it live and throb, who spellbinds all the critics and electrifies the mob.
>
> He used to be an editor, plain simple, just and mere, who took a yard or two of slugs to make his meaning clear, but when he made his first address the public rose and yelled, and ever since to speak and speak he's frequently compelled, for while he runs the Newark Post with weekly waves of ink, we're always glad to have him rise and tell us what we think. He's been the Secretary of the State wherein he thrives. He helps the University in lightening our lives. He boosts for it and Newark as the stars by which to steer. He

banquets with Rotarians and often has their ear. He is
in many vital ways a citizen of class, whose merits
would be difficult to equal or surpass.

A favorite family story, recounted by Everett's daughter Marjorie,
shows another side of her father. While perfectly able to rise and
deliver a speech he had prepared ahead of time, the man of words
would draw a blank at dinner parties when it was suddenly his turn
to produce an impromptu poem as part of the after-dinner
entertainment. On one memorable occasion, when the hostess
suddenly pointed to Johnson (who was lost in his thoughts of
Roosevelt) for the next bit of rhyme, he blurted out to the
astonishment of all, "T is for Teddy, D is for Damn. J is for Johnson,
That's who I am!" Predictably, he was excluded from such parlor
games in the future, much to his relief.

Any discussion of Johnson's political ideals must take into
account his extensive research into the life and leadership of Abraham
Lincoln. He admired Lincoln above all men and his personal library
included fifty-two books on the speeches, writings and biographies of
the "Great Emancipator." Everett's gift of oratory was first brought to
public attention as the result of a speech delivered before the joint
session of the Delaware Legislature on the occasion of Lincoln's
birthday in 1911. He held members of the two Houses spellbound for
an hour and was invited back every year for a repeat performance.[118]
On February 12, 1927, one year after his death, his traditional
Lincoln's birthday speech was sorely missed. [119]

There is something missing in Delaware's official
observance of Abraham Lincoln's birthday these
days...the realization of why that something is
missing caused many a Delaware heart to ache this
February 12th.
...Lincoln's birthday celebration did not seem
complete, in legislative years, unless Everett Johnson,
himself a former member of the House, addressed the
legislators on the subject of Lincoln's life. His Lincoln's
Birthday Address came to be known in all parts of the
State, Delawarians flocked to Dover to hear him deliver

it and the old State House would not accommodate the
crowds that assembled there on such occasions."

The address was so popular it was finally printed at Kells. The
earliest edition was quite plain, with a drab olive green cover.
Succeeding editions were of a larger format, on heavy handmade
paper, tied with white silk thread. The cover, designed with great
reserve, simply says 'Abraham Lincoln' in gold letters with an
exceptionally detailed embossed profile of the President in the lower
right-hand corner.

One paragraph in his speech reveals a side of Johnson's character,
which was not conducive to making a profit in the business world.
Never a clever businessman, this passage reveals his disdain for what
he considered the anti-intellectual, commercial side of life.

All over this country today, men just as we,
steeped in the practical things of life, are laying aside
their duties of the hour and acknowledging that hero
worship still lives, by paying tribute to a man. And

Everett's famous Lincoln speech printed into a booklet at Kells.

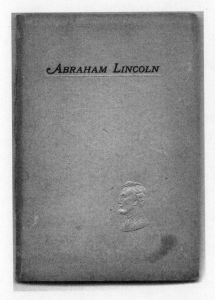

though we tramp the path which towering genius dis-
dains; though we may never acquire distinction where,
by the stroke of a pen, we can emancipate slavery, we
have yet a duty to perform in seeing to it that the greed
and avarice of today enslaves no freeman. To us comes
the duty to teach those slaves how best to enjoy freedom with its responsibilities; and too it is for us to see
that no freeman bow heads in slavery to the commercial
lash of the times.

The booklet was subsequently used by the Lincoln Society of
Wilmington, which had its origins in 1929 in a meeting at the
Wilmington Country Club with a small group of male admirers
of Abraham Lincoln. The official history of the Lincoln Club of
Delaware (by Albert O. H. Grier and Harold Brayman) lists Everett
C. Johnson as one of the 1929 Charter Members present at the first
dinner meeting.

CHARTER MEMBERS

Those present at the first dinner-meeting who
thereby became "charter members," were John
Bancroft, Joseph Bancroft, City Librarian Arthur L.
Bailey, Everett C. Johnson, Professor James A. Barkley,
Newlin Booth, Henry T. Bush, James I. Boyce,
Reverend Dr. C. L. Candee, J. Allen Colby, Rt.
Reverend Philip Cook (bishop of the Protestant
Episcopal Diocese of Delaware), Jasper E. Crane, Dr.
Burton P. Fowler, Charles H. Cant, Congressman
Robert G. Houston, Edgar H. Hoopes, Jr., former
Congressman William H. Heald, Dr. Walter Hullihen
(president of the University of Delaware, Newark,
Delaware), John B. Jessup, Joseph C. Lawson, Robert P.
Lane, J. Warren Marshall, William C. Mahaffy, Henry
C. Mahaffy, Hon. Hugh M. Morris (Judge of the
United States District Court of Delaware) , William F.
Metten, Edmund Mitchell, Jr., William R. Mans, John
H. Mullin, John P. Nields, Lewis Rumford, David J,

Reinhardt, Henry F. Scott, William F. Sellers, Willard
A. Speakman, Dr. William C. Speakman, Harry T.
Springer, Frank G. Tailman, Willard F. Van Riper, G.
Morris Whiteside II, Irving Warner, Alfred D. Warner,
Jr., Reade Wildrick, Joseph S. Wilson, Frank E.
Schoonover and Albert O. H. Grier. (Taken from
Lincoln Club of De. A History)[120]

Everett did accomplish a great many tasks but this was not one
of them since he died in 1926, three years before the event took place.
The first issue of the *Newark Post* began with quotations from
Abraham Lincoln and several following editions featured highlights
of his life and presidency. One quotation became slightly altered in
the re–telling—unfortunately it was the bit of Lincoln wisdom most
often repeated by Everett, a favorite phrase which had its origins in a
conversation between Lincoln and his close friend, Joshua Frye Speed.
The president had just resolved to pardon all the men who had been
imprisoned for resisting the draft in Western Pennsylvania after
listening to an impassioned plea from the mother and wife of one of
the prisoners. Speed, knowing the President had recently been
suffering from ill health, made the observation, "Lincoln, with my
knowledge of your nervous sensibility, it's a wonder that such scenes
as this don't kill you." Lincoln's reply was, "Speed, die when I may
I want it said of me by those who knew me best, that I always
plucked a thistle and planted a flower when I thought a flower
would grow."[121]

Everett's version, which was part of his famous Lincoln's
Birthday speech, was slightly different, "I want to so live that when I
die those who knew me best will say, "He planted a rose and plucked
a thorn wherever he thought a rose would grow." It was later
rearranged by an unknown typographer to read, "I want to so live
that when I die those who knew me best will say, 'He plucked a thorn
and planted a rose wherever he thought a rose would grow." The
Lincoln Club of Delaware, which assumed it was correct, used this
version.[122] Everett and a group of friends had discussed founding the
club prior to his sudden death in 1926 and for this reason he is listed
as a charter member even though the organization date is recorded as

being 1929.

Whether thistles and flowers or roses and thorns, Johnson lived his life guided by the underlying philosophy. He died in his sleep of heart failure; the book found next to him was his newest purchase, Lincoln's life as told by Carl Sandburg, titled *The Prairie Years*.

Everett Johnson was known for his ability to be optimistic in the face of great odds. On one occasion life seemed to weigh heavily on the overworked editor and he wrote the following story which has a timeless message and was later printed in booklet form by Kells

THE LOG IN THE DAM

My little girl received a picture puzzle the other day, from a friend who had been visiting her. Last night after the household was asleep, I was sitting at my desk trying to work. In reviewing the old year, things didn't seem to come out right—everything dead wrong. They had been wrong all day. Little worries of details had formed a conspiracy, seemingly against me. Honest opinions had been challenged, motives questioned, —In their solid alignment even the evening lamp and favorite book failed to dispel the fears, resulting from a too hard day.

Impossible—What's the Use – Misunderstood— that Trinity of Defeat, stood before me and demanded my surrender. In the language of the street—or better, the country road—I had the blues. Seeing the picture puzzle before me where "Boots" had left it, I began, almost unconsciously, to put the fantastic pieces together. I experienced no difficulty in matching the cards. Then came a card, rather jig–saw in shape, apparently of little importance, yet it puzzled me to find its place. Not until that card was used could I find place for the others. My curiosity was aroused. I wanted to see the complete picture. Forgetting thoughts of self of a few moments before, I set to work in earnest. Finding the position for my little insignificant, fantastically cut card, the picture was soon complete. There on the desk before me was a beautiful scene of peaceful nature, a wooded stream. In the distance was the old mill, with its poetic wheel. Painted, I guessed, by one who had played there in boyhood, it had the technique showing the touch of an artist. Yet these touches were so blended that in admiration of the picture, one lost sight of the minute details that made it great.

I looked at it long. I could almost hear the splash of the moss covered paddles, the whirring moan of the great stones. Watching the sun sinking here in the west back of the old mill hole, I forgot the worries of the day and boyishly prided myself on my success with this simple little picture puzzle.

But the jig—saw card—so insignificant in itself, yet necessary to the picture! Why, that's myself! Perhaps I have a place, after all. The New Year means a new day, another opportunity. I'll try again.

I tore up the picture reluctantly and found the card representing my mental state of the hour previous. It was an old log in the dam. I smiled to myself—I am part of the world's old dam and here I was resenting the accusation.

Yet the dam was necessary. The old log was necessary to the picture, to the mill and to the grist of the neighborhood.

So I'll take, again, my part tomorrow,—a log in the dam.

The Old Man, In the Newark Post, At the Shop of
Kells. Newark, Delaware

On a lighter note, in his college yearbook, classmates made note of Everett's affinity for auburn tresses. A brown paper bag, in a bureau drawer at his daughter Marjorie's house, contains locks of her hair after it fell victim to her first haircut some 70 years ago. The event was so traumatic she was still feeling pangs of remorse telling the tale.

"My hair was always curly, but not the sort of curly I felt was attractive. My mother and I decided it was becoming too unruly and so, one afternoon I joined the more progressive girls of the time by getting it "bobbed." Well, when my father came home and saw what I had done he was so devastated all conversation ceased and he refused to look at me all through dinner and the rest of the evening. It wasn't until the next day that he began to recover from the hurt."

The curly brown locks were placed in a bag, still adorned with pink and blue hair ribbons, but no amount of sighing would ever put them back.

A story related by Elizabeth Taylor, who at the age of seventeen was the last person hired by Everett, shows an attempt to prevent such calamities in the future:

"We were standing at a table putting bindings on with hot glue. Mr. Johnson came in and I didn't know him very well because I had just started there. I had long hair at the time and he came over to me and put his arm around me—scared me half to death! He hugged me and he said, "Don't ever get your hair cut." So that was Mr. Johnson. That's the kind of man he was."

THE "OLD MAN OF KELLS"

THE "OLD MAN OF THE ATLANTIC"

∞

O ne of the last causes championed by Everett C. Johnson was the preservation of the old lighthouse at Cape Henlopen. It also proved to be a lost cause. He was fiercely proud of his state, and the lighthouse ranked among the oldest of all the historical structures in Delaware. His father, Captain Isaac had introduced him to the sea, and the beacon of light had often guided them on their way past the shifting shoals off Cape Henlopen.

His personal bookplate illustrated his love for things nautical; they depicted a sailboat, heeling into a stiff breeze, with the inscription taken from a poem, *The Book*, by Emily Dickinson; "There is no frigate like a book to take us lands away."

When Everett and Louise built their final home on the piece of ground adjoining Kells, in addition to the mantle with its light-house, the hallway of the house has a ship's desk built into the wall, a further indication of his ties to the sea.

One of Everett's favorite possessions, a model of the ship *Crescent Moon*, was given a prominent place on the mantle of the stone fireplace in the Whim at Kells. Given to him in 1924 by a close friend, Ella Wilson, he wrote of it in a thank you letter; "Thank Miss Ella for my ship. It stands on the table heading in toward Henlopen Light, and if I were to put my dreams aboard, the Delaware Legislature would never be able to appropriate sufficient money to open up Indian River inlet where she sank."

In the March 4, 1925 issue of the *Newark Post*, Everett wrote:

> "Old Henlopen" is not just a bit of sentiment of a
> few who feel History and Tradition but it is known in
> every port the world over. No building in our border is
> so crowded with Facts, History, and Tradition as this
> Tower. Age marks its starting by a patent of 200 acres
> in 1762, building began in 1765 and lighted in 1767.
> Ninety-three feet high, (height varies according to

Everett's personal bookplate.

different sources and stages of erosion) she has stood sentry in Peace and War, in Storm and Calm, 1767 to 1925. Before Concord, before Rodney, before Cooch's Bridge, before 1776, before 1787. Before 1798— twenty-one years before old City Hall of Wilmington was built. Old Henlopen had served so nobly and well.

Have we a right to let it go without some of our effort and some of our effort's return known as contribution of money. (Punctuation and capitalization are Everett's)

That the plight of the lighthouse went unnoticed until it was actually teetering on the very edge of the sand dune is not surprising. All too often historic buildings are lost due to simple inertia and apathy on the part of citizens who do too little too late. In the case of the lighthouse, the commission trying to save it simply ran out of time. The ever-shifting sands proved to be the nemesis of the tower. The original site of the lighthouse was one quarter of a mile inland, protected by a growth of pine trees with a stream of fresh water running past on its way to the ocean, which at that time seemed very far away. [123]

The westward drifting of the sands eventually submerged the greater part of the woods, leaving bare only the tops of the tallest trees. The remaining pines were cut down leaving the tower at the mercy of the elements. As if the effects of wind and shifting sand dunes weren't enough, the ocean was constantly nibbling away at the shoreline. The final factor in the sequence of events leading to the fall of the light was the erection of the Delaware Breakwater in 1840. It fulfilled its mission of creating a refuge for ships but in so doing proved fatal to the lighthouse. The currents were now directed shoreward, increasing the effects of the waves in their destruction of the shoreline.

Everett would repeatedly belabor the point that the government was responsible for the creation of the breakwater and therefore the government should take the necessary steps to reverse the situation and prevent the lighthouse from tumbling into the sea.

In his editorial of March 4, 1925, he quoted the engineer's report presented to Governor Robinson:

> If the government has placed a structure, which however successful it may have been in the past of the purpose for which it was designed, has deflected the current onto a beach and caused its destruction — then unquestionably, the community and the state so damaged, has a certain right of redress at the hands of the government.

On August 6, 1924, the *Post* featured a photo depicting one of two paintings of the lighthouse by noted Delaware artist Stanley M. Arthurs, who would later be commissioned to paint Everett's memorial portrait. One of these paintings was given to Senator Bayard, probably in the hopes that it would spur him to greater action. At this point the sea was a mere eight feet from the base of the cliff.

On September 30, 1924 (the date the light in the tower was extinguished as a safety precaution), a committee representing the State Service Clubs prepared a report to the lighthouse commission.

An oil painting, done in 1924 by Stanly Arthurs and donated to Senator Bayard in an effort to help save the Cape Henlopen light.

Senator Bayard was reported as being "extremely interested and supportive" of any efforts to save the light. Everett appealed to his fellow Delawarians to take action.

OCTOBER 1, 1924 *Newark Post*

OLD HENLOPEN LIGHT

Old Cape Henlopen Light goes out tonight. To anyone with reverence for the Past, this is sad. Nor is the sadness mere sentiment. Tradition whispers, History calls, gratitude bows before us-and more than all, Service speaks in a language only understood by those of the Sea. Service is a big word today and the story of Henlopen and its keepers is dramatic as are all stories of Lights at Sea. Harbor beams flashing out over dark waters truly serve!

But enough. Our story found and known of Henlopen, later-not tonight.

Sad as is the Event of the darkening Tower, older than our Government and Flag, to be replaced by a tripod lantern of short–lived mechanical structure, so typical of today's rush, it is sadder still, that to ourselves—citizens of Delaware—this has occurred. Those in charge of Lighthouse Service at Washington have for years appealed to Congress for the saving and maintenance of this historic, beautifully constructed Tower-and without avail. They today, see and feel its worth and interest more than we have expressed. This Federal Board, without State Associations such as ours, has given time and voice for its preservation where in Delaware, Silence has reigned.

Henlopen Light goes out— and the fault is ours.

The Tower can be saved—mayhap even the Light restored if nautically safe and serviceable—Shall we do it?

The future of Henlopen Light depends upon the citizens of Delaware. And in the decision, our character and reverence will be portrayed. What has this Day done to us that we forget so often the Men and Services of Yesterday? Shall we keep this Monument as a Memory showing reverence to the Past and giving inspiration to the Future?

No, this is not mere sentiment, either men. Nor do not laugh to furnish excuse for indolence and neglect. It is, by actual engineering statistics, practical, which so much appeals to those who oppose.

Our action in this either portrays or betrays our manhood.

Old Henlopen Light can be saved.

Everett C. Johnson was named permanent chairman of an organization to be known as the Henlopen Lighthouse Preservation Committee. The members received authority from the Secretary of Commerce to "enter upon and occupy the Cape Henlopen Lighthouse

Reservation for a period of five years from January 1, 1925, and to perform such construction work thereon as necessary to protect and preserve the light tower and the site thereof from destructive action of the elements."

Noting that back in 1883, when the bark Minnie Hunter was sunk north of the light, the shoreline had begun to build, the board thought they had a low cost solution to the problem. (Previous estimates for two bulkheads had been quoted at $29,600 and $40,000.)[124] Everett described his plan in the guise of a tale told by the old light itself. It was titled, "The Spirit Of The Light Speaks To Delaware" and it appeared in the *Newark Post*, September 16, 1925. It reads in part:

> Through my friend, to whom I have told my story, I learn that there are at Norfolk, some two hundred wooden hulls, some of which have winged to a safe harbor by my light. These have been dismantled of all that is of value, and are to be burned.
>
> What better end could some of them meet than to

The Cape Henlopen Lighthouse after the light was extinguished.

save that which in its time has saved them and their predecessors? As they are doomed to destruction it would not be much more than towage to secure some of them, twelve or fourteen, and bring them to rest at my feet. Five should be laid from East to West, two North to South, three from West to East and the others directly at my feet. Those would break the sweep of the tides, dispel the force of the Easterly gales, and help to build the shoreline of the Cape... ...Tomorrow may be too late, next month may be too late, next year WILL BE. By that time both the hulls that would save me, and I, will be gone and an ache will be in your heart, when you gaze at the spot where once I stood, guarding by day and by night, through storm and calm, in winter gales and summer beauty the Cape of Delaware.

On March 3, 1926, the *Post* informed its readers: "Gales Sweep More Earth From Henlopen's Base; End Is Near Says Report." The sandbank at the foot of the light was now perpendicular to the side of the lighthouse.

Sadly, neither the eloquent pleas nor the imaginative plans would be enough to save "The Old Man of the Atlantic." At 12:45 AM, April 13, 1926, one wave too many carved away the last bit of sand supporting the tower. [125]

A Sonnet Addressed To The Henlopen Light

No more will your now sightless eye glare red
Upon the everlasting restless wave;
Tis tragic pun of Fate, or man, your grave
Should many others form just such a bed!
Your long and lonely life of serving all,
In calm or storm unfailing, must enthrall
The man who thinks, with great and awful dread
When he looks on his own dark selfish way--
A poor comparison. And you're to go,
"Unhonored and unsung," out from the Aye

Of things into an everlasting No.
But thus too often is good work repaid:
The one who tries to shed a light, betrayed.

Contributed to The Post[126]

Perhaps the unorthodox plan printed in the *Post* September 2, 1925 would have provided a better ending:

> ...But can you not see more clearly the old Henlopen standing proudly and safely for the ages yet undreamed of on the campus of the State University—a glistening gem in a gorgeous emerald setting? Can you not hear much more distinctly the ringing shouts of carefree college youths, the melodious laughter of bouyant college girls, mingling with the mellow sound of chimes floating down the old Henlopen, as it announces the approach of twilight to tomorrow's generation at the University of Delaware?
>
> To everyone—do you realize, are you actually aware that one of Delaware's greatest historical treasures is in a terribly perilous position? Is the Henlopen Light to be saved? Are the people of "the first state" going to fail? Are the governmental authorities of the State going to allow the Henlopen, that "good and faithful servant" of former times, to topple to a disgraceful end into the ocean?
>
> It is not going to be a case of the light that failed," but in a few days it may be a case of "the people who failed." What's the answer?

Best Seller

"There is Nothing Like a Good Constitution"

∞

The quote was hand written in one of the books found by the authors. It was signed Henry J. Bailey. That publication would prove to be the mainstay of Kells and was a small, unpretentious book. Unable to find a copy of The Declaration of Independence and The Constitution of the United States in one convenient volume, Everett decided to print his own. This passion for helping citizens become familiar with their government manifested itself as early as 1911 when, as a member of the House of Representatives, he introduced a bill authorizing the Secretary of State to have printed copies of the Constitution of the State of Delaware.

Johnson printed The Constitution of the United States and The Declaration of Independence in the *Post* in 1924 and was surprised at some of the responses he received. Some of his readers admitted it was the first time they had read the documents since their school days.[127]

The first printing, in 1924, was a small edition given to friends. It contained an error on page 61 in Amendment V which read: nor shall private property be taken for private use; It should have read…for public use. The authors have not found the error in any editions other than the first one.[128]

The first commercial edition consisted of an order from the Joseph Bancroft Company of Wilmington for 2,500 copies to be bound in their own book cloth, which were distributed to "every man, woman and child in their employ."

Harry Harkins of the Hotel du Pont had a special edition printed and placed a copy in every room of the hotel. The Waldorf Astoria followed suit and Congressmen and Senators read copies in a Washington hotel.[129] Several editions followed. In 1924 and 1925 every high school and university graduate received a copy of the book with their diploma. The inside front cover contained a lengthy bookplate, which read:

"The rights with which the Declaration of Independence proclaimed all men to be endowed by their Creator and the duties and responsibilities of preserving the Government instituted through the Constitution to secure those rights give rise to and bound the principles of American citizenship.

Around the conception and defense of these principles is written the development of our Nation; upon their maintenance the enjoyment of the rights of life, liberty, property, happiness and safety depends. To keep ever before us the opportunities and obligations embodied in these fundamental truths this volume has been printed for the graduates of the University and the High Schools of the state of Delaware for the year 1924."

The book also contained a leaflet giving a quotation from Lincoln.

Local banks, The Continental Fiber Company, The Lions Club of Wilmington and The Rotary Club all ordered special printings. It was printed in at least thirty different bindings, receiving "compliments and comments and kind words from friends, strangers all over the country, and an occasional word from up in Canada." The leather bound De Luxe edition of the book was accepted by the prestigious Grolier Club of New York and placed on their shelves.[130]

Everett had great hopes for the book in 1926, the year of the Sesqui-Centennial celebration to be held in Philadelphia. It was to be an official souvenir and the special edition was to be bound in buff and blue, the Colonial colors of the state of Delaware. It contained a frontispiece, a facsimile of the Declaration of Independence, and a five-page insert in facsimile of the Constitution from a photograph made just previous to the document being placed in the Library of Congress. A special copyrighted design of the Liberty Bell was embossed on the cover. Everett was proud of the fact that the edition was printed at his shop which was located on a road leading from the Old Academy, where three of the signers of the Declaration of Independence were educated, to Cooch's Bridge, where the flag was first unfurled in the battle of the Revolution.

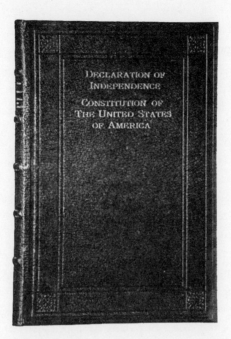

The De Luxe leather bound edition of the Declaration of Independence and Constitution of the United States of America; the little book that paid the bills.

Despite the great popularity of the book, poor attendance at the Sesqui-Centennial resulted in few sales. Johnson had counted on the souvenir edition to erase most of Kells' debts; instead, after his untimely death, on February twentieth, 1926, those remaining at Kells found themselves in the awkward position of having to ask Curtis Paper Company to allow them to return the unused paper he had purchased.

A great many copies remained unsold. As of June 1928, Kells had on hand 2600 copies of the Sesqui edition of the Declaration of Independence & Constitution. Total cost for the lot, $1,690. (65 cents each, sold at Sesqui for $1.50).

The promotion and sale of this little book at times caused Johnson great consternation. In a letter dated February nineteenth, 1926, the last day of his life, he wrote to his good friend John Townsend and described one of the typical problems preventing further successful marketing of the book. The letter is copied here in its entirety, as an illustration of Johnson's subservient yet chiding manner, so often characteristic of his editorials. [131]

February 19, 1926
Honorable John G. Townsend
320 Cass Street,
Tampa, Florida

My dear Governor:

This is just to thank you for all your kindness to me in my round down your way. Things in Delaware are just as hot as they are in Florida though the sun is not shining. I landed home in a blinding snowstorm and found the weather conditions in perfect keeping with political condition. The wet and dry issue; the Secretary of State; the indisposition of the Governor; the Sesqui-Centennial and the ambitions of Henry P. Scott are all running as usual.

A very interesting thing happened yesterday. I had arranged that Delaware be given the honor of present-ing the Boy Scouts copies of the Constitution on the Fourth of July, expecting to follow that with a meeting with the National Executive Committee in New York, with the idea of starting a national campaign led by our State. The Delaware committee, of which Mr. Scott is a dominating force and member of the National Committee, adopted the idea with more than the usual enthusiasm, claiming that here was an opportunity for Delaware to be First again. The resolution was passed and laid out on the minutes when up spoke the young genius, Frank du Pont, saying "why pay 80 cents, we did that once for our hotels, but are now printing them ourselves for a quarter. I would be glad to furnish the 750,000 for the United States for that amount." Under the spell of such oratory Mr. Scott decided that it would be well to take the matter under advisement.

There is such a thing as ethics but it is found mostly in books. I had been lead to believe from my reading that the day of hoss thieves was over, even in the far west, but as the days go on I find I'm living myself in that very atmosphere. If I were now intimate with the Governor I should ask for my first appointment—that is of special Constable, which would give me permission to carry a gun. Incidentally, I may make a boomerang myself, because on the fly–leaf of this particular book I'm the only one who can place the official souvenir imprint, but I guess I am licked in this particular instance. Thus the penalty of my refusing to form a sales corporation financed by Wilmington citizens.

I certainly was impressed with the work that Paul is doing. With a little supervision on your part and the responsibility that he has in directing such a big thing, I have every confidence that he is going to make a big man of himself. I cannot conceive of such a personality as his failing. Julian is more conservative than his father, and Jack is too familiar with the wiles and tricks of men to be fooled.

It was certainly good of you to rush around all day Sunday in order to show me a bit of the flippant world that I wanted so much to see. The possibilities in Florida are wonderful, and I will believe any story; but how in the world a few of you big Delawareans who go down there and see what can be done in a piece of marsh land as is found at Venetia and will permit the land around Rehoboth or Fenwick's to lie idle is beyond me. With the road facilities that we have, in touch with a third of the population of the United States, and the desire of at least a million people to have a home by the sea without the jangle of a merry–go–round or poker game, there is a fortune and a field for real service right here in Delaware. I wish when you get through down there that you and your equipment would come back and start a sub-division down in Sussex County. I'll advertise for a corner lot. Of course you have not read this far, and probably only the beginning, so here is the end.

Thank you as usual.

Yours very truly,
J/M Everett Johnson

Booksellers often wrote to Johnson trying to make The Constitution as printed by Kells a purely commercial proposition but they never succeeded. The book was later used to further personal causes, something Everett never intended and would not have sanctioned. A perfect example of this is the purchase of several hundred copies, left over from the Sesqi-Centennial, that were rebound in blue Du Pont Fabrikoid. These were bought by Pierre S. du Pont to be distributed amongst the members and supporters of The Association Against The Prohibition Amendment, of which he was the executive chairman. Cards were inserted in each copy stating they were given with the compliments of the Association. [132]

The final insult occurred when an edition, printed by Kells, appeared in 1934, also in blue Fabrikoid, which bore no Kells imprint or copyright. The only variation from the previous editions was the inclusion of the twentieth and twenty–first amendments to the constitution.

SQUIBS

"It's 'gentz the Constitution" was his final argument.
"Have you read the Constitution?"
"No of course I haven't. Do you think the State would allow them to be hawked around? Only the judges and lawyers can have a copy of the Constitution."

TOMMORROW NIGHT WILL BE MY PARTY

∞

By 1926 Johnson's health had deteriorated and he was fighting a daily battle with exhaustion. He declined invitations, avoided parties and limited the number of guests at home. Even the effort to carry on conversations taxed his small reserve of energy necessitating occasional weekends at a quiet retreat, shielded from social obligations and jangling telephones.

Louise relates a story in her memoirs that illustrates how easily her ailing husband could be defeated by unforeseen events. "He had once lived in Philadelphia when he was young and had enjoyed the Mummers' Parade. One New Year's Day he decided he would go to see it again. He would watch the parade and then he would stay all night at the hotel. Later that night I heard him return home. There was a midnight train that stopped at the Pennsylvania Railway Station at Newark. His story was, that as he went into the hotel to watch, he saw former Governor Miller, who had had the same impulse. Governor Miller talked and talked. Everett's only escape was to take the train home."[133]

His many illnesses, beginning with pneumonia in 1903 and culminating with influenza during the epidemic of 1918, had seriously damaged his heart. A less strenuous lifestyle might have prolonged his years but that was never an option for him. In an interview with author Richard Carter, Louise, at the age of 94, remembered Everett's struggles to expand the Press of Kells. "But he just didn't have the strength. He smoked (cigars) all the time and he was just getting weaker as the years went on. I could see it. If he had an illness it was terrific, and he had plenty of illnesses. And this work, it was just too much for him, the headwork and the body work. And when he'd come home at night he was just crawling. He just couldn't get in the house fast enough. So it was just a case of overwork."[134]

February 19, 1926 was the date of the Junior Prom of the University of Delaware held at the Hotel duPont in Wilmington.

Johnson (far left) at groundbreaking ceremonies for Memorial Hall, the camera caught him just as he exhaled a puff of cigar smoke.

Marjorie, who was president of her sophomore class, was invited to attend the dance by Cornelius Tilghman and her parents were asked to participate in the receiving line. Everett declined the invitation, choosing instead to remain home and rest in preparation for the next evening when, as president of the Alumni Association, he would be a keynote speaker at the Annual Midwinter Banquet. As Louise and Marjorie prepared to leave he assured them "I'll get along fine. Tomorrow night will be my party."

He had recently returned from a trip to Florida where he attended the convention of the Del-Mar-Va Press Association as a delegate.[135]Colonel Theodore Townsend, at a meeting of the Press Association held after Everett's death, told of "an extemporaneous speech Mr. Johnson made at a dinner in Florida, where he chose as his topic "Dreamers." Col. Townsend said it was the most moving word picture he had ever listened to and that at the end of the speech when Mr. Johnson, exhausted by his efforts, left the dining room, an assemblage of 600 people paid him the tribute of silently standing till he had passed from the room."[136]

Suffering from fatigue, he took an early train home in order to avoid lengthy conversations with his friends. Despite observations by those close to him in those last days that his health seemed to be "better then usual," he may not have been completely recovered from the demanding trip.

Johnson's favorite method of regaining strength was to retire with a good book. This particular evening he chose a recently published history of Abraham Lincoln, the latest addition to his collection of fifty–two volumes on the subject of his favorite president. Titled *The Prairie Years* by Carl Sandburg, it was a book he would never finish.

Marjorie stayed with friends in Wilmington after the prom and Louise returned home around 2a.m. She noticed a light shining under Everett's door and assuming he was still reading she did not disturb him. The next morning, realizing he was not downstairs, she went to his room where she discovered he had died in his sleep. The family physician, Dr. J.R. Downes, was summoned and he determined Everett had suffered a fatal heart attack. The book on Lincoln was by his side along with a green piece of notepaper bearing the Kells logo on which he had written in pencil, "There is no frigate like a book to take us lands away."

Louise telephoned Marjorie and to spare her from anguish during the long ride back to Newark, simply told her to come home. As Marjorie remembers, "It wasn't until the car pulled into the driveway where several family friends were waiting to lend their support, that I noticed the front door was draped in black crepe and realized my father was gone."

Everett Johnson was buried on February 23, and his obituaries appeared in all of the major Delaware newspapers. A clipping from the Wilmington *Morning News*, described the funeral in great detail and after the passing of over seventy years the reader still experiences the feeling of sadness felt in Newark on that day.

The University suspended all classes after noon and most of the students attended the service joining faculty, former members of the legislature, prominent business men and three former governors of Delaware: They were, Simon S. Pennewill, who was Governor when Everett served in the Legislature and appointed him a member of the Board of Trustees of the University of Delaware in 1911; Charles R. Miller, Senator in 1911 when Everett was a member of the House, and John G. Townsend Jr., his life–long friend under whom he served as Secretary of State.

The funeral was held at his home on Park Place and by the time the service began, approximately 1,000 people had crowded into the area between the house and Kells. At two o'clock, as the grandfather clock ceased tolling, Reverend Richard W. Trapnell, rector of St. Andrews P. E. Church in Wilmington began the prayers assisted by Reverend Frank Herson, pastor of the Newark M. E. Church. At Louise's request, the quartet of the Wilmington Rotary Club, sang one of Everett's favorite songs, "Crossing the Bar" by Tennyson.[137]

Six employees of Kells carried "The Old Man" to the hearse, which led a procession of 100 cars to where, "A little mound of fresh turned turf, conspicuous against the white snow in the picturesque little Welsh Tract cemetery near White Clay Creek, marks the last resting place of Everett C. Johnson... The grave was completely surrounded with floral wreaths which included floral tributes from employees of Kells, the Aetna Hose Hook and Ladder Company (of which he was a member), the student bodies of Delaware College and the Women's College, as well as from many individual relatives and friends."

The newspapers tributes more than made up for the absence of eulogies at the funeral and one of the most eloquent came from his close friend and fellow journalist William Metten:

> I have never known a man who literally gave of himself more frequently, more generously, more whole–heartedly, to the many causes which enlisted his support than Everett Johnson, and my friends, it will be many a day before we find in this state a man who can compare with him in that respect.
>
> Never of robust health, but uncomplaining, of an ambition and determination that are rarely approached and certainly never excelled, a person that made friends everywhere, a kind and generous nature, he never declined a call for service. I have known him time and again to speak at some function when he should have been home and in bed.
>
> In those dark days when our state and our

government were calling for men and for money, as
Secretary of State under Governor Townsend, I venture
to say that no man in Delaware, I care not whom you
name, did more valiant work or rendered more
patriotic service than Everett Johnson. And when the
end came, only a few days ago, you saw not only his
friends and neighbors stand with bowed heads to honor
his memory, but the people of the entire state expressed
a sorrow that has never been equaled, certainly not
in my recollection. His was a life of service, and if we
read aright, there must be a splendid reward awaiting
such a man. [138]

Everett's grave is marked by a modest, rough–hewn granite
tombstone, which has only the dates of his birth and death, along
with those of his wife, Louise, who survived him by forty–six years.
There are no clues that a man of letters lies buried there—not even
his favorite quotation from Hamlet, one that he used many times in
the Post to bid farewell to those friends who had passed on before
him—"And the rest is silence."

Five clippings were found in his pockets after his death: a
mystical poem titled *Phantasy*, an article praising the *Post* on its' fifteenth anniversary, a short poem called *Playing the Game*,
dedicated to the unsuccessful candidates for the election of November
4th, and two pieces of paper that give us pause. The first is a poem;

> *Alert and still in my grave arrayed,*
> *Like a sentinel I'll be lying,*
> *Until I hear the loud cannonade,*
> *The neigh of the chargers replying.*
> *Then over my grave will my Emperor ride,*
> *The swords will be flashing and falling!*
> *And hearing a voice, I'll arise from the dead:*
> *My Emperor, my Emperor is calling.*

The second merely says, in Old English font, …And the rest
is silence. [139]

"30"

THE END OF KELLS

∞

After the sudden death of Everett Johnson in 1926, his wife Louise was left with the operation of the *Newark Post* and the Press of Kells. Efforts were made to sell the plant as a going concern and after negotiations with several parties it became apparent that the sale in the regular trade channels could only be effected at a price far below the real value.

John Townsend felt that it would be in the best interest of Mrs. Johnson to attempt to develop a permanent profitable business along the lines laid down by Mr. Johnson and at the same time the opportunity would be afforded to carry out Mr. Johnson's principles and ideals. A number of factors made this extremely difficult. The most obvious was the loss of the inspiration, dedication, and popularity of the "Old Man". Mr. Bowden in his estimate of jobs done by Kells believed that one–half of the work was drawn in by the popularity of Everett alone.[140] Before his death, Louise was relegated to gathering social and other news and finding fillers for the paper. This in no way prepared her to run the business by herself. Louise stated "It seemed that I was helpless as far as Kells was concerned. Everett had always left business behind him when he came home." [141]

The other problems were financial. A new and expensive addition was nearly completed on the Kells building leaving a mortgage on the building of $5,000 and a Real Estate mortgage of $13,512.[142] The expected income from the sales of the Declaration of Independence book at the Philadelphia Sesqui—Centennial was to help offset the mortgages but because of poor sales this had not materialized. Everett had purchased $1,000 worth of new type for the De Luxe Edition which was in fact not needed. The circulation of the *Post* prior to Everett's death was over 2,000 and quickly dropped to less than half of that after his death. To complicate matters Everett had failed to keep proper operational and accounting books.

Two of Everett's close friends, John G. Townsend and P. S. du Pont, offered their assistance in keeping the name and business of

182

Everett C. Johnson alive. Charlotte C. Mahaffy, an employee at Kells and a close friend of Louise, was asked to manage the operation. Miss. Mahaffy turned to Everett's friends for help and Dr. Odell referred her to Frank A. McHugh who was financial secretary to P. S. du Pont. What McHugh needed in order to give his advice was a review of the "Capital position and Profit and Loss Account". In a letter to Miss. Mahaffy dated March 22, 1926, he bluntly stated that since no standard or conventional ledger had been kept he was unable to be of assistance. He was only able to recommend that a person qualified through experience with publishing and printing do an appraisal or survey of the business. [143]

The American Type Founders Company did an inventory of plant equipment, exclusive of paper stock, ink, furniture and fixtures. The inventory resulted in the following appraisal:

Composing Room Equipment	—	$17,000
Press Room	—	23,500
Bindery Equipment	—	6,000
Miscellaneous Equipment	—	2,500
		$49,000

The value of the building and land was appraised at $50.000 giving a total value of land, building and equipment to $99,000.[144]

Even with this information they still lacked direction. The information was shared with du Pont and Townsend, and du Pont responded in a letter to Mahaffy saying "...This is disappointing, but I must confess inability to suggest a plan, although I should welcome the saving of the institution to Delaware." Mr. du Pont again drew on his vast resources and called upon Charles H. Bowden, Manager of the Du Pont Printing Division. Mr. Charles H. Bowden, prior to the death of Mr. Johnson, had been consulted by him rather frequently in connection with the running of the Press of Kells and especially in connection with the purchase of equipment and securing certain type of experienced operators. This contact developed a friendship between Mr. Johnson and Mr. Bowden and Mr. Bowden, upon Mr. Johnson's death, was more than willing to interest himself in endeavor and ascertain what was the best thing to do.

The burden of running both the *Post* and the Press of Kells soon became too much for Louise. In the later part of 1927 the Press of Kells, Inc. was organized with John G. Townsend, Jr., William G. Mahaffy, and Charles H. Bowden as directors. Kells Inc. purchased the equipment from Mrs. Johnson and paid her $1,500 per year rent. They were to run the business and eventually purchase the building, and in this way Mrs. Johnson would receive a much higher price than could be obtained in any other way. This arrangement would enable the Johnson Estate to liquidate various obligations and provide Mrs. Johnson with some immediate income.[145] Because the building was designed to house a printing plant it was not easily converted for any other use.

Mr. Bowden pointed out if the printing plant was liquidated at that time not only would there be a large loss on the sale of the building, there would also be a still larger loss if the equipment was sold as second–hand. Both of these losses were to be guarded against if possible. The following article in the *Post* tells of the split:

Aug. 3, 1927

Kells Incorporated by Group of
Everett Johnson's Friends

At the State House, Dover, there was filed yesterday a charter for the Press of Kells, Incorporated. At a stockholders meeting, held at noon today in Wilmington, officers of the new corporation were elected.

The stock – holders of The Press of Kells are a group of close personal friends of the late Everett C. Johnson, who have taken over The Shop of Kells in order that the ideals of Mr. Johnson's that characterized and guided Kells might be kept active and fruitful, and that dreams, that were in process of realization at the time of Mr. Johnson's death, might reach maturity.

The officers elected were: Former Governor John G. Townsend, president; William G. Mahaffy, vice – president; Charlotte C. Mahaffy, secretary and treasurer.

The incorporators named on the charter were

William G, Mahaffy, Charlotte C. Mahaffy, and Rodman S. Mahaffy.

Mr. J. Spencer Brock was elected general manager of Kells by the stock – holders, and is now in full charge of the plant. Mr. Brock was formerly manager of the Flester – Owen Press, of Philadelphia, and later Philadelphia manager for the International Paper Company.

Rodman S. Mahaffy was appointed resident agent.

The Newark Post was not included in the incorporation and will have no connection with the new organization, except that The Press of Kells will print *The Post* for Mrs. Everett C. Johnson, publisher.

The following stockholders (limited to friends of Everett Johnson) purchased stock at $100. Per share: [146]

John G. Townsend	$12,000
Pierre S. du Pont	10,000
William G. Mahaffy	12,000
Charlotte G. Mahaffy	5,000
Rodmon S. Mahaffy	1,000
Balt. Trust Co.	6,000
Lammot duPont	10,000
Frank duPont	5,000
William B. Foster	2,000
Charles H. Bowden	2,000
C. H. Weston	1,000
Spencer Brock	1,000
W. F. Metten	500

Mr. Bowden felt from the beginning that if the *Post* could absorb the *Newark Ledger* (owned at that time by Mr. Alfred I. du Pont) the combined business, advertising and subscription lists would be sufficient to make a paying proposition.

It was hoped that the Press of Kells could either purchase the *Ledger* at a reasonable figure or that friends of the University of

Delaware would want to purchase it so that the property might go to the University. In either event the objectionable features of the "Ledger"would be eliminated. The proposition was discussed among the University and had been given active consideration, however, it later fell through.

Everett had always been the sole Editor and Publisher of the *Post*. Directly after his death the heading of the Editorial page listed Estate of Everett C. Johnson – Publisher, Mrs. Everett C. Johnson – Editor, and Charles B. Jacobs, Jr. – Associate Editor.

Mrs. Johnson retired as Editor of the *Post* August 1st, 1928; this position was filled by Charles Jacobs. She then sold the *Newark Post* to Kells Incorporated but continued to own the building and property.

The following notice was printed in the *Post* August 1, 1928.

> Beginning with this issue, The Newark Post will be owned and published by The Post Publishing Company, and edited by Charles B. Jacobs, Jr.
>
> The Post Publishing Company believes that The Newark Post, founded in 1910 by Everett C. Johnson, is an important and valuable institution in the town of Newark, and is an effective medium for promoting the ideas, ideals and ambitions of the founder of the paper.
>
> The Post Publishing Company hopes that it may be able to increase the value of the Post both to the State and to the town of Newark. Arrangements have been perfected by The Post Publishing Company with the Press of Kells, Incorporated, whereby the publication and distribution of The Newark Post will go forward from The Shop of Kells, by and through its new editor.
>
> Mrs. Everett C. Johnson, the retiring editor, bespeaks for the new management and the new editor the same courtesy and support which has always been accorded the paper by the people of the community and the press of the State.

The Board of Directors felt that with the securing of a competent manager and salesmen, and with the proper type of operating organization, the volume of business could be brought up to a point where it would be possible to make a reasonable profit.

The efforts during 1928 and the early part of 1929 were devoted to getting an organization together on the basis of The Press of Kells being a quality press and not an ordinary country print shop. The goal was to try and secure the same high class of work that had been available in 1925—26, namely: The du Pont letters, the Service Citizens studies, the University of Delaware publications, and special printing for the DuPont Company Dyestuffs.

Mr. Bowden on the expectation of being able to get this higher class of work had recommended Mr. J. Spencer Brock for Manager, because of certain characteristics he had, his high ideals, and because of his extensive experience with a high class of printing. The Board of Directors agreed with Mr. Bowden on his selection.

There was no way of knowing at that time that this type of work was not available and that The Press of Kells for an indefinite number of years would have to depend largely upon the ordinary type of

The third location of The Newark Post building, which still stands on Thompson Lane in Newark.

competitive printing. The collapse of the stock market in 1929 and 1930 added to the financial burdens of the struggling business.

A conflict between the Mahaffys and Mr. Brock over how the shop was to be run lead to Mr. Brock resigning as Manager in April, 1929 and Mr. B. F. Carley, who previously had been used as a salesman, became the Manager. Mr. Mahaffy, at a board meetings, stated that if he had his way he would fire the Manager, the salesmen and the foremen and proceed to run the shop as a country printing shop, apparently being willing to abandon the idea of maintaining Kells on the basis of its being a quality shop.[147]

Based on an analysis of the 1935 audit, there were insufficient assets to offset the indebtedness, and in addition to the stockholders losing the $68,500 that had been put into the Company, there was nothing whatever left from The Press of Kells for Mrs. Johnson — not even enough to pay her the rent due for the use of the property during the last five or six years.

The Press of Kells was sold to Woodyard Publication of Delaware, Inc. in 1936 and the tangible assets of the Press of Kells were sold at a trustee's sale in June 1940 to Woodyard Publications, Inc. of Spencer, West Virginia owned by Edward D. and Henry C. Woodyard. The Woodyard brothers held a deed of trust from the Delaware Corporation, which was sold for $5,000. The equipment was shipped to Wytheville, Va. and was installed in another plant of the Woodyard Corporation. Woodyard Publication of Delaware, Inc. also owned The Dover Index and Laurel State Register.[148] The last book the authors could find printed by the Press of Kells was *Delaware Tercentenary Almanack & Historical Repository 1938*.

The Delaware State Corporation charter was repealed in 1939 for non–payment of taxes for the preceding two years. With the removal of the equipment the only thing that remained after 1940 to keep the memory of Kells alive was the building and what it had produced.

The *Post* was sold and moved to Thompson Lane in 1935. Louise and Marjorie lived for a time in the building which was turned into Kells Apartments and which remained the property of Mrs. Johnson until 1945. Mr. and Mrs. Henry Mote added six more apartments and sold the building to the YWCA in 1961.

The *Newark Post* continued on Thompson lane with Charles H. Rutledge as Editor. In 1937 Richard T. Ware became editor of the

Post while it remained in the hands of the Woodyard Brothers, and in October 1940, Ware continued as editor with co–owners Dr. Wallace M. Johnson and Robert Armstrong who was an undertaker. Ware was able to acquire all the stock in the corporation some time later. He was able to keep the Post "independent"which is printed on the masthead, but leaned towards the Republican Party. Unlike Johnson, Ware did not print an editorial feeling that taking sides was not worth the enemies it would gain. Freely admitting he did not have a "journalistic calling"he only wished to serve the community with a readable paper. To better service the community he appointed Frank N. Megargee as editor while acting as owner and publisher. (Post 8–29–48)[149]

SCRAPBOOK

CLIPPINGS FROM THE POST

∞

April 27, 1910

A man died and went to Heaven. St. Peter showed him around. Everything was pleasing—everybody was happy except a band of people who were in chains. The stranger asked the reason for this. St. Peter replied: We are compelled to do that—they are from Newark, and if we were to turn them loose they would go back home.

∞

September 13, 1916

HE SHRIVELED UP

A man was afraid of a thunderstorm and crawled into a hollow log. The thunder rolled, the rain poured down in torrents, and the log swelled up until the poor fellow was wedged in so fast that he could not move. All his past sins began to pass before him and he suddenly remembered that he had not paid his newspaper subscription. It made him feel so small that he was able to crawl out of the log through a knot hole.

∞

June 1, 1910

> "I am not bound to win. But I am bound to be true; I
> am not bound to succeed but I am bound to live up to
> what light I have."

Abraham Lincoln

"A man that never makes mistakes never attempts anything."

Theodore Roosevelt

The above quotations state the position of the publisher of this paper. It is perhaps a matter of little concern what this paper says, but of whatever concern it may be it will follow out that policy. It will fail or succeed on those lines. We have been asked to state our policy – our politics our creed. This will be done when we think it wise. Rest assured, we are not ashamed of either.

This paper is going to stand for what we think is right. Our methods of fighting what we believe to be wrong, are to us, the best suited to this work. When we think differently we shall change, but no one, by threat or coercion, can change our views nor can that method of warfare have any effect on us.

With what can they reproach me as a writer? I have always taken the part of the weak against the strong. I have always lived beneath the tattered tents of the conquered and slept by their hard bivouac. It is true, I have cancelled a number of too pompous adjectives which certain names have appropriated to themselves; and now and then I have also pricked the bubble of some bloated self-conceit. But the persons whom I have treated so were on the side of the enemy, and I had the right to explode their airs. I did not violate the law of war against them; and if they complain about me, it is just as if an old soldier of the empire should complain because he was wounded at Austerlitz. Call it personalities – what of it? Everyone has his own way of making war, the others shoot into the masses at half the height of a man; but I select my man and take a good aim. And if a plumed crest happens to pass by my door, I always give him the preference.

∞

February 2, 1910

This column will be consistent, as was Cromwell, who said; "Read your bible but keep your powder dry." or Grant, when he said: "I intend to fight it out on this line if it takes all summer," then said—

"Let us have peace."

∞

December 2, 1914

COUNTRY NEWS EDITOR

One who holds the peace of the Community in his hand by suppressing most of the news.

To Run a Newspaper

To run a newspaper all a fellow has to do is to be able to write poems, discuss the tariff and money questions, umpire a baseball game, report a wedding, saw wood, describe a fire so that the readers will shed their wraps, make $1 do the work of $10, shine at a dance, measure calico, abuse the liquor habit, test whiskey, subscribe to charity, go without meals, attack free silver, wear diamonds, invent advertisements, sneer at snobbery, overlook scandal, appraise babies, delight potato raisers, minister to the afflicted, heal the disgruntled, fight to a finish, set type, mold public opinion, sweep out the office, speak at prayer meeting, and stand in with everybody and everything.

– Contributed.

∞

July 28, 1920

YES, EDITORS SOMETIMES MAKE MISTAKES

They're More Conspicuous Than Those Of Others

The editor of a newspaper is not infallible and makes mistakes the same as any other human being, but no one knows this better than does the editor himself. The nature of an editor's work makes his mistakes more conspicuous.

We have noticed a number of squibs in our exchanges regarding mistakes. These items lead us to believe that other duffers besides editors are subject to this malady. The editor's mistakes stand out more conspicuously than most other professional men's because every issue of his paper is an open letter to the public.

A fellow may happen along and inform his neighbor that there is a new set of twins at Hick's place and if later it develops that the twins were a boy no one pays any attention to the originator of the false rumor. But should it appear in the paper as originally reported, the father will in all probability be down and exchange bullet courtesies with the editor.

Again when the village belle chances to get tied up to some worthless cuss, whose only qualifications are that he can chew tobacco and relate suggestive stories, the whole town may with impunity review the past history of the two and it cuts very little ice. But if the editor happens to spell the groom's name with an "o" instead of an 'a' and overlook to record the fact that the bride is a member in good standing of the Ladies' Aid Society they both would be insulted and mercilessly flay the editor and his Gimlet.

What is strange about the mistakes of a newspaper man is the fact that no matter how many errors he makes in lying about another man's qualities he never lays himself liable to be punctured with a thirty-two, or lynched. Indeed it is a funny old world.

Everybody makes mistakes. The only ones who never make them are slumbering in the cemeteries- and it is not unlikely that some of them are there because the doctors also make mistakes.

A man often makes a mistake by marrying when he should have taken a post graduate course in how to support himself. A fine woman often is in error when she wantonly throws herself away on some fool who can sing coon songs like Caruso but couldn't make a noise like a loaf of bread to save his life.

A boy makes a mistake when he thinks he knows more than the entire staff of teachers, including the principal of the schools. The world is plumb full of mistakes and mistake makers.

If the newspaper man should take the pains to record them all he'd make the mistake of his life and die on the bed of the press with his shirt sleeves rolled up and his boots on.

∞

November 15, 1922

NEWSPAPER BUSINESS IS DIFFERENT

"A newspaper is quite a bit different from any other line of business. When once established in a good, live, thriving community it goes on forever while other lines of business may change management occasionally, but the same old paper is issued and read day after day and year after year. There is no use getting peeved at the editor. If he starves out, there is always some one to take his place. You may kill off all the editors you please, but when you come to kill off a well-established newspaper you may just as well give up, for some day it is going to publish your obituary."

∞

February 1, 1922

Let me direct the newspapers and I care not who teaches in your schools, who preaches in your pulpit or who legislates in your Halls of Assembly.

∞

August 29, 1923

EXTRA! EXTRA! EXTRA!

"May I print a kiss on your lips?" I said,
  And she nodded her sweet permission.
So we went to press, and I rather guess
  We printed a full edition.

"One edition is hardly enough,"
　　She said with a charming pout.
So again on the press the form was placed
　　And we got some "extras" out.

Doing business without advertising is like winking at a girl in the dark. You know what you're doing but nobody else does.

The Newark Post
Welsh Lane
Newark Delaware

∞

February 1, 1922

The world do move. It was amusingly wonderful the way the old Anti-Suffrage editors proposed women for membership into the Press Association. Then it snowed.

∞

December 16, 1914

Dear Old Kris,
I hope you can bring me a tricycle, a sweater, a skating cap any color you choose, a pair of driving gloves, suit of harness and blanket for Chum. I like tan harness. I named my pony Chum. He is growing fine. I wish you could bring Anabel Jarmon a pony.
Thank you,
With love from
Marjorie Johnson.

∞

January 14, 1920

An Ad—for Advertisers

THE POST is different — -everybody admits that. Even our enemies.

Again, we edit our Ads with the same care as we edit our news. No Gold Bricks, no luring sensations, no Get-Rich-Quick Proposals. We have no scandals in our columns, either news or advertising.

No G. A. R. Hero is saved by Camouflage Booze, no Society Belle of Skedunk saved by "Pink" Grace adorns our pages. We exploit no patent pills — tut–tut, liver, asthma and dope cried for have not our O. K. Such ills are for physicians and for nature.

We back our Ads. They are worthy and have our guarantee. We are proud of them and their association. We know them.

Honest Good advertised by Honest Men are welcomed to The Post. And they do say, those who have tried, that Advertising in The Post pays. So when contemplating your Spring Campaign, place your Ad where you are at least satisfied with your associates. Ads, as well as men, are sometimes known by the company they keep.

THE POST AD MAN.

∞

March 28, 1923

IT WASN'T THE POST

A recently arrived business man in Newark had occasion to see THE NEWARK POST. He inquired the location. "Turn down South College Avenue and THE POST is the first funny looking building you come to," were the explicit instructions given by the Main Street Loafer and General Information Bureau. Our new citizen started out one evening and following closely information given, stopped at the "first funny looking building he saw."

And it wasn't THE NEWARK POST but a disgraceful architectural, advertising-bedecked frame structure within town limits.

∞

June 1, 1910

I don't agree with all he says but durned if I don't like his paper.

∞

September 6, 1916

THE NEWARK POST

The Paper that is read by everybody worth while and others.

Everybody reads it whether they like it or not. Whether in business or in the social whirl; in public life, or plain every day citizen; in college or out; in Limousine or Ford or just a walking curiosity, you need THE POST.

Some take it seriously, some take it as a joke—some just a nuisance.

Any way it is a necessity.

When it criticises the other fellow you'll laugh, when you are knocked, you get mad. But if you ever subscribe, you will never miss an issue. It makes you think —and there is where we succeed.

Somebody said it was like power, you couldn't control it. A college man says we are crude, unacademic; a citizen we are trying to be a high brow.

—All of which makes it interesting.

∞

October 10, 1923

"SIX MONTHS WILL WIND IT UP"

That was the comment of the local knocker and loafer back in 1910 when the Newark Post was started.

"Have you seen the Tower of Failure?"

That was the Inquiry when Kells was being erected down on Welsh Lane. "Newark's Monument to Folly", it was called.

That was seven years ago when we moved down here.

Yet "Six months" has rolled by–and the years too and Kells still lives and The Post has never missed an Issue since December 26th, 1910. Last week, our sales, inquiries and orders reached the highest yet —and we are dreaming still. The Kells Tower holds samples of Printing unsurpassed in Delaware.

Thus doth the Knocker, boost.

∞

December 23, 1913

SQUIBS

Our style and purity of diction is often the subject of sarcastic smiles among present day students. Crude in expression, blunt in punctuation as our writing is, our readers will appreciate the niceties of our mother tongue as given by one of the coming literary lights. The conversation was something like this:

> "Yes, this is my last year at old High. I try out Delaware next year – that is if I slide through. Have worked off all my Math except Trig and that's a cinch. 'Merican Lit is simply a trot, believe me! They say Sy's English Lit is fierce and that he is long on themeing. Sorry to leave old High, but ti's so long to Tipperary – and it's shy on pep. So long, old pal, got to bone on my Lit. She's a bird for tomorrow. How about Latin? Remember the song, "My pony boy.' Good night shirt!"

∞

February 2, 1910

Listen to your own instincts; they will tell you the truth. Have courage enough to believe them and to obey them. Never let such a microbe as the love of popularity get into your moral life. You can get along without the praise or even the approval of other people. But you cannot get along without the approval of your conscience. I would not give a fig for a person who is always taking his color from his surroundings, always deriving his moral judgments, not from his sense of right. But from his idea of what other people will think.

∞

May 11, 1910

GET BUSY

The study of History is either present or future, never past. The Philosophy of History should always look toward the future-progressive not regressive. It is impossible to look backward and judge aright. The correct vision is ahead. Pessimists are created by the study of History-constant looking backwards.

There would be no such thing as pessimist if Forward was the cry. A man who studies History progressively and does not see the world is growing better, either is a fool or is not capable of good reasoning.

I am tired of the Past. I have just returned from the funeral and instead of contemplating, finding out how much better he was than I am, of how he made mistakes, lived in a more auspicious and opportune time, that he was stronger than I — his good points all this is rot. (I do not ask you to pardon the use of the word — it is in the dictionary and its meaning is very clear.)

This is the result of looking backward. Look ahead of you. The time is not out of joint. Stop cussin' spite. You or someone else was born to set it right.

So get at it. Step in his place. Stop rubbering. Don't crane your neck. The end is straight ahead. Look at it and go for it and when your Present becomes Past, the Future seeing your success, will take your place with a better will.

By doing so Perhaps you will stop this retrogressive idea and the next generation will be the better for your having lived.

The happiness of the Future depends on the Present. The Past is dead. We are grieved, but let us take the death as a Philosopher.

Fill his place.

You are three hours late now, and the Fast Express will soon enter the block.

The rail you want to watch is ahead. If it snaps in your going over it, the Freight will, if engineered aright, attend to that.

Look ahead.

∞

December 2, 1914

A PRINTER

The only man who knows more than he pretends.

∞

How The Knocker and Booster were Created

Some one has said that "when the Creator had made all good things, there still remained some work to do; so he made beasts and reptiles and poisonous insects, and when he had finished, there were some scraps left, so he put all things together, covered it with suspicion, wrapped it with jealousy, marked it with a yellow streak, and called it a Knocker."

"This product was so fearsome to contemplate that he had to make something to counteract it, so he took a sunbeam, put it in the heart if a child and the brain of a man, wrapped these in civic pride, covered it with brotherly love, gave it a mask of velvet and a grip of steel, and called it a Booster; made him a lover of field and flowers and manly sports, a believer in equality and justice. And ever since these two were, mortal man has had the privilege of choosing his own associates."

∞

May 18, 1910

Views Of A Kicker

Some weeks ago your paper had a letter from one of our citizens suggesting that we boom the town as a summer resort.

This is a good idea, but it would require a good ad writer to display our advantages and beauties so as to cover up the unsightly things in this town.

What would he say about pig–pens?

What would he say about carrying the offals from butchering in the back yards?

What would he say about over–flowing cesspools?

What would he say about our stagnant gutters and paper being thrown on the street?

Newark can be made a popular summer resort, but not until the Board of Health, the Town Council and the citizens themselves get busy.

If Newark can forge ahead as it does under the criticisms, personal bickerings and petty jealousies, ye Gods, Mr. Editor, what would it do if everybody got in the band wagon?

I am not an old resident here, but I have lived here some years, and never have I seen a town with more chance than this.

One of the strange things is this — When I came here I inquired about the manufacturers and very few citizens know anything about them. They had no more idea of what the paper and fiber mills were doing than I did, who had received only outside information.

You have gotten in a rut and nothing less than a calamity will ever bring you together. You couldn't start a pig race and have the whole support of the community.

Get together.

A KICKER

(note- a kicker is different from a knocker-a kicker is trying to change things.)

∞

April 27, 1910

The Council effected a strong organization, and a good administration is looked for. But after running out of heavy–weights in the scientific world they completed the Board of Health by appointing a long-haired farmer by the name of (Everett) Johnson, from Pencader not even a citizen of the town. He sprang from the malarial districts of Cypress Swamp; and has spent a great deal of his life under a doctor's care. We expect to report the condition of his property to the Board of Health, and if this does not answer-the state Board.

A warning to him now is, that for the health of the town, we have removed that "taurus" (scientific name for what is known in Sussex as Bull) from the side of Strahorn's barn. It is causing nervous prostration and cold feet to our citizens.

Another thing we suggest that he have the water plug removed from the middle of the pavement in front of the primary school building. It may not be unsanitary, but it will cripple someone. Awkwardly gaited, he tripped over it the other evening, and if we were to publish what we overheard him say, he would never be placed on the Board of Health.

∞

Was it Lincoln who told about the steamboat which had to stop for lack of steam every time its whistle blew? A lot of people we know are blowing the whistle too hard to make much headway. Bank some and keep going.

∞

February 16, 1910

"To avoid unkind criticism - say nothing, be nothing, do nothing."

∞

May 24, 1922

OUR REPLY TO OUR ENEMIES

Some one has said "To win a friend is an accomplishment; but to win an enemy is an achievement." Enemies are great influences in our lives. They challenge us to do better and bigger things. To sum up the work of a man, we must take in consideration those who maliciously oppose him. A man worth while makes enemies and has peculiar pride in him. Beware of him who has only friends. The old Persians sensed their value when they prayed, "Give me this day an Enemy."

How to handle an enemy is something difficult. At times they are annoying. For our reply, our Ideal of History is both an Inspiration and constant source of comfort. His words fit so many occasions and are always so delightfully full of common sense.

So again we use the language of Lincoln – and this is our reply:

"If I were to read, much less answer, all the attacks made on me, this shop might as well be close for all other business. I do the very best I know how – the very best I can; and I mean to keep on doing so until the end. If the end brings me out all right, what is said against me won't amount to anything; if the end bring me out wrong, ten angels swearing I was right would make no difference."

∞

July 16, 1913

There are different grades of cowards as well as different classes of heroes. The most contemptible coward is a newspaper man who refrains from writing his honest opinion with the fear of loss of business or popularity.

∞

October 15, 1924

"When we build, let us think we build forever. Let it not be for present delight nor present use alone. Let it be such work as our descendants will thank us for, and let us work as our descendants will thank us for, and let us think, as we lay our stone, that a time will come when those stones will be held sacred because our hands have touched them, and that men will say as they look upon the labor and wrought substance of them 'See! This our Fathers did for us.' "

—— John Ruskin

April 13, 1921

ORIGIN OF THE PRINTERS CHAPEL

The name CHAPEL was the name applied to every printing office at so early a date that its origin is in doubt as to whether it was derived from the fact that William Caxton set up his first press within the unused St. Anne's Chapel in Westminster Abbey, or from a bit of pleasantry on the part of some ungodly soul gifted with a sense of humor.

An ancient poem in praise of the craft has it:

> "Each printer, hence, howe'er inblest his walls,
> E'en to this day his house a Chapel calls,"

The father of the Chapel was the oldest printer in the shop. It was his duty, in case of a disagreement or quarrel between two craftsmen to "Call the Chapel" to the imposing stone and to try the case. His decision was absolute, and the loser had to pay a fine, "For the good of the Chapel" what today in city sweat shops is called a bucket of suds."

Regarding the Devil, we read in an ancient volume:

> "We're the furthest from good when the church
> we are near.
> So in each Printer's Chapel do Devils appear."

The custom even today in small shops of using a headstone in the composing room, probably originated from the Chapel idea — church yard was the burying ground.

∞

May 4, 1910

Take a little grouch, some honest criticism, some blue blood, some good blood and bad blood, some old scores to settle, serve it first wet and then dry, in first one bank then another. Get four good men out. Serve a little scanday (scandal?) on the side and then let loose the dogs of war and you will have a school election.

∞

October 12, 1921

PUSSY DEAD AND SOLDIERS MOURN

A big cat, hero of the war, in the French lines at Amiens, has just died. Dispatches from Paris carry this news and the war record of "Diamond," as a tribute to the mascot of French soldiers.

The cat appeared one day, probably from a household in the rear of the lines, and refused to leave the soldiers. He was immediately named and adopted. Every day he went on a tour of inspection and indulged in a little scouting expedition of his own, crossing no – man's land, picking his way through the entanglements to the very edge of the German front trenches.

The French soldiers in order to protect the cat, tied a package of cigarettes around his neck and a card with the words: I bring you cigarettes; do not kill me." Since the war, Diamond, being a veteran has had the best of care and his death is mourned by many of the Poilus for whom he was a lucky mascot.

∞

December 31, 1913

TARIFF

No Republican can discuss tariff without some Democrat going up in the air, contradicting his argument. There is one thing, however, the Tariff has not lowered, – the slit in the skirt is higher now than ever known since the time of Nero's fire.

∞

September 25, 1923

NO WONDER

The ship captain and the chief engineer had a dispute as to which was the most important man aboard the ship and agreed to change places.

Soon the captain came up covered with oil and grease. "Chief!" he called, "you have to come down here. I can't make her go."

Of course you can't," replied the chief; "she's ashore."

∞

December 31, 1913

Referring to a public man's aversion to being spick and span a country paper announced:

> "Maguire will wash himself before he assumes the office
> of town councilor."

This made Maguire furious, and he demanded an apology, which appeared thus:

> "Maguire requests us to deny that he will wash himself
> before he assumes the office of town councilor."

Oddly enough, this only enraged Maguire the more.

∞

July 9, 1913

When you hear a man boasting of his judicial temperament, watch him when he approaches the ballot box–he'll stuff it if you don't.

∞

September 1, 1920

Everett, aged six, had been left with a neighbor while mamma and papa attended an amateur theatrical.

When they were alone together, the neighbor remarked, "Your mother certainly looked nice. She was certainly dressed up."

"Yes'm" Everett responded, "She had on everything new she got for Christmas 'cepting her percolator!"

November 11, 1914

SOME SHOP NEWS

An interesting comment on business! A week or so ago a young lady came into the office and inquired for the prices on programs. She was a stranger — a prospective customer. We went to considerable trouble to estimate on her specifications. Our price happened to be just $17. She, by this time had shown her ignorance of the cost of printing. Her program of eight pages and cover passed away in her gasp. We suggested the eight pages without cover for $15. Still too much. Fearing to insult her, we risked, however, the suggestion of an ordinary folder 8 1/2 x 11 for $10.

She thanked us and said she would consider.

Down the street she went. Now the story comes back thus:

> "I just left yon job office and received my worst blow.
> The price first named was $17. When I said this was too
> high he said $15, and in a few minutes was offering to
> do the work for $10."

As a tip to the circulated story—she never explained the difference of the stock and make-up of the job for the different prices. The prices remain the same and a 4-page folder costs less than an 8-page and cover.

A bell rings when she returns.

∞

March 6, 1918

BE SURE—THEN GO AHEAD

A man once ordered his tailor to make him a suit of clothes. When the cloth was cut and basted the tailor called his customer on the phone and asked him to come in and try on the suit.

"Oh, I've changed my mind about that suit," replied the other. "I've decided to make this one I have on last me for another season. Anyhow, I don't much care about the pattern you showed me the other day – it isn't snappy enough. Much obliged, but you may just cancel that order and call it off."

Now, do you suppose that the tailor meekly abided by this instruction, pocketed his loss and said cheerfully: "That's all right, Mr. Dresser, no trouble at all. You must be the judge, of course. If you don't like it, we're sorry. But when you are again in the market we hope that you will give us another chance."

Assuredly not. Yet this is exactly what many a buyer of printing expects of his printer under like circumstances, and unfortunately there have been printers weak enough and foolish enough to accept such treatment not only with meakness and humility, but with an abject surrender that would seem to concede that such a course of conduct was altogether proper.

Somehow the printing business has never succeeded in gaining from the public the same recognition that is accorded to other lines of manufacturing and merchandising. Many a business man looks with frank amazement at the printer who would dispute his right to cancel an order, provided the impressions of the type are not actually inked upon the paper. That a big part of the cost of an ordinary printing job comes before the presses begin their work, is often ignored.

Mr. Businessman learn this fact. It will save money for yourself.

∞

August 22, 1923

WHY THE WINDOWS WERE WASHED

"Why do you wash the windows? It isn't your work. You wouldn't get anyone in a city shop to do that. They would quit first."

The above was the comment made to one of the girls at Kells. Why she did it is interesting. No one asked her but everyone appreciated it. Her position is one of the most important in the plant. Her work in many instances is the final touch that distinguishes the craftsmanship. Her word in many cases is final. Her position is one of unusual responsibility. On this particular day, there was a little lull in her work and she seized the opportunity. "Fine, she said, let's wash the windows." It never occurred to her that it was a menial task or that her dignity was lowered or that it in any wise reflected on her position.

Then why did she do it. She might have taken a seat in a corner and waited until her work was ready. Why? It was the spirit of Kells. It was love for the beauty and dignity of labor. She couldn't explain it herself. "Just because I wanted to" was her interpretation. A simple story but fraught with meaning. She is a part of Kells. Its success is her subsconscious (sic) desire; its work is her work. Of such is the Shop of Kells. A little different, a little odd but this spirit is making friends and doing work worth while. Interest in her job and Kells is why she washed the Windows.

∞

October 18, 1916

BOY WANTED

A boy wanted with Pep, Punch and Perseverance to learn the Printing Trade. It is an opportunity for a boy not afraid of work; who dares stick to his job. He must have wit and a desire to become a Craftsman worthy of the name. For a year, he is worth about errand-boy wages. After that if he has learned the lingo, not afraid of ink and elbow exextion, (sic) he has made good and starts to get some returns in his work and pay envelope.

Boys without this desire and Printer's Grit need not apply at KELLS.

∞

September 27, 1916

WANTED – JUST ONE GIRL

Our Bindery Department is growing. We have the stock on hand to do some real binding. A book is in process that will be bound in a dainty purple sheepskin. It will be sewed. There will be a hand illumined initial. To know how to do this, is a profession. It is Art craft that demands study, thought, and skill. College girls all over the country are taking up this work. It needs the dainty touch of the girl who has the eye for color and symmetry and neatness. An opportunity will be offered to some Newark girl to learn. When the work begins, an artist experienced in the craft will be in charge. A helper, an understudy, will be needed. Here is a chance. In the meantime, we can find work in the department. She can become acquainted with the surroundings, learn the technical lingo of the Shop. Also she will be learning the rudiments of binding.

The hours are short, — 48 of them a week.

KELLS.

Apply in writing.

∞

June 7, 1916

COST OF PRINTING AT KELLS

First let us say that the customer must get what he wants, when he wants it, and a little better than he expected.

What will this service cost is a legitimate question. It is, after all, a business proposition. The usual businessman is willing to pay a reasonable price, giving a reasonable profit.

Printing is a class of work in which there are several points for consideration. In the simplest job, several operations are necessary.

1st. Stock. The choice of paper oft times makes or mars the appearance of the finished job.

2nd. Type. Very essential. Size, style, spacing. Old English would be absurd in a Steel Product catalogue. Bookman would not be in keeping for a Price List.

3rd. Press Work and Ink. The job is made ready. Too dark, ink running heavy, impression too strong. One, two, three, or more trials before the final O. K. Then care throughout the run.

4th. Dry thoroughly, then folding, either machine or by hand which must be done with utmost care. Trimmed, wrapped ready for delivery on date promised. These and many other operations enter into the simplest job.

The cost for this at Kells is reduced to the minimum. Every operation is accounted for, charged to the job on a 5–minute basis. Cost are figured on floor space, machine operation space, labor investments, office and all overhead Light air arrangements, Cut Cost Cabinets, labor saving devices, cut out lost motion. A Job makes a complete circuit from office back to office direct, without going back and forth. Our furniture cabinet with 3460 pieces at your hand has the advantage over the old timer of 120 pieces, half locked up probably in other jobs. Our Cut Cost Cabinets, so called, just installed, save time, – everything necessary from the composition end of the job right at the man's finger tips.

New machines make the press make — ready not only better, done in one – forth of the time; folding, accurate, better than possible by hand, as fast as the feeder can touch the guide. Take the cutting stock, alone, our power cutter by touching a button saves time and labor.

You can readily see that modern equipment, with all that goes with maximum production with least effort causes prices to be lower, rather than higher. Labor and not machinery makes up the cost of a job. Any machine, any arrangement, that will lessen labor, make the work pleasanter, is saving on the cost of the job and, incidentally, adds very materially to the grade of work. High grade machinery facilitates the efficient handling of the job, relieves the physical strain and gives the workman more energy for thought. And to think, is a big factor in a print shop.

So these are some of the vital factors that enter into our cost system, enabling us to give quality, service at a moderate cost. Much less than those of the old poorly lighted, ill – equipped sweat shop. We add to the cost a fair profit, which we spend for a living and the study of the Art of Printing.

∞

February 23, 1916

"Art is not a thing – it's a Way," said that Master Printer, William Morris. At Kelmscott, Morris with his craftsmen, worked and experimented. They loved type. They studied colors. They learned paper. They put their soul in it – and sometimes forgot the clock. They worked the regulation hours for honest pay – then slipped back after supper to play, trying out another tint, designing another border. Surrounded with all the known appliances to carry out the mechanics, in a shop simple in construction, designed for comfort, with an outlook that appealed, these printers with William Morris, snatched printing from a purely commercial accommodation, and again revived the Art of the printed page. Today to own a Morris book is to have an Art treasure. His designs of borders and type are now on exhibition at the British Museum. He was an Artist because of the "Way" he worked.

Printing at our Shop has always been considered Art and not a Job. Because of the Way we go at it. Given the appliances, the chance, the boys and girls in the Shop have put their heart in it. Every new piece of printing has an idea back of it. The kid who makes a suggestion gets the credit. He is complimented on his work,—if not up to standard—his best, he gets good–natured thunder for falling down. Often times he is his own sternest critic.

No, we have not turned out any masterpieces—not yet. But the kids have done things with a smack of originality in them. Things different. They are becoming less afraid all the time. They are daring to put more of themselves. A bit crude sometimes, (not always, mind you). they love to see their best in printed type and colors. They are artists in the making.

Despite carping critics, they are not imitators-they are students, catching an idea, a method when and where they can. We are reading and studying the masters more every day. No, we are not imitators, not because of any grandstand moral scruples, but it isn't any fun. Our crude selves, with our heart in it—that's fun.

This new Shop was designed with a foot rule, a No. 2 Faber and what wit the owner possesses. There's method in his madness. The main Shop is lighted on all four sides, the office on three sides. Other rooms have their lighting features. Open air, sunshine, space dominate the place. In construction, rugged stone, straight lines, tile walls—all have their reason. Simplicity dominates. No "fille de lieus," no false walls nothing bizarre, it is a simple building erected for work, a place where a man, a boy or girl can do his best. We disagree with one of our big business men, who said, "Why I thought any kind of building would do for printing plant." No, not for our kind. While this is commercial in that it must pay its way and the grocers, it does not ring with this sweatshop talk.

Industry today with all its cost producing details would disagree with this man. Our light, air, surroundings are material assets—they are methods that help the workman. He produces more. They help Make him an artist.

So this is the reason we say this is a place where Printing is considered an Art and not a Job. It's the way we do it. Locally, our new building is questioned, smiled at, but every customer is a friend who wishes us well. Gradually but surely the work of these country boys is winning recognition. The mystery of the place, is that one man, who can't do these things, takes keen fun in furnishing the opportunity. He wants neither praise nor credit—it's fun.

We do Printing in a Way that makes it Art—for a consideration.

∞

April 29, 1925

Today there is Kells and we are dreaming still. There have been good days full of cheer and hard, hard days, dull, cold sordid. There have been days when we smiled but there was but little cheer in it for we saw the laughs of the crowd. There have been nights when we looked tomorrow's Pay Roll in the face and flinched. It takes nerve to face a Pay Roll in a country newspaper plant. We have faced Defeat, so close that we could touch its dull dreariness. Then would come Determination and a good day. We have sacrificed much of material gain in order to hold true to our original standard.

And today there is Kells. It has produced some printing worth while. Pardon a boast, but our color work has the unsought praise of The Lambs and Our Constitution has been accepted by The Grolier——and we are proud. Our Plant is our pride— and Down at Kells come old friends and new, increasingly as days go by. Some do us honor and now call us "Quality Folks" but the Best is Wawayanda—Just Beyond and Kells dreams to produce its Greatest Work in 1925—and Realization of its actual beginning is in the Spring's hovering mists.

Yes, it's a Dream—lets hope.

∞

July 18, 1917

A LITTLE TALK ABOUT PRINTING

Cheap investments never pay. Of nothing is this more strikingly true than of printing. Every man of affairs knows the cheap little folder that comes in the morning mail. Whether it advertises farm machinery, cow feed, or a pumping system—the one impression it gives is cheapness. Cheap paper, cheap printing, cheap ideas, from cover to cover. Isn't it logical to conclude the wares for sale are also cheap? And so the pamphlet travels on—straight through, from mail-box to scrap basket.

But then, too, there comes the attractive little folder, modest or pretentious, to suit the value of the commodity or the firm's pocket book. Everything about it is well done. It is well thought out from cover to cover; typography, arrangement, and press work are of the best. "My firm is on the job," it shouts at everyone. Somehow the little folder seems too good to throw away. We drop it into a drawer for reference, and unconsciously classify all that it represents with efficient service and thorough–going business.

∞

WHEN KELLS WAS A DREAM

QUALITY FOLKS

The old Southern darkies recognized those who were above them by the name—quality folks. To us quality folks are those who do better work, who render better service than the ordinary run of folks. Heinz qualifies for that with his 57 varieties; the Studebaker Wagon Company, the Oliver Plow Company, John Wanamaker—all these and others in their class are quality folks. But one doesn't have to be of national importance to be reckoned in this class. One can be "quality folks" in a small community. All you have to do is to do a certain kind of work a little better than the best. That is the open sesame to that society.

Jones out in Wisconsin, is making better sausage than any one else, while Mary Elizabeth makes those who like good candy bend the knee to Syracuse. Out there in Pittsfield, Mass., is the Caxton society. These lovers of good printing are publishing a series of brochures which are fitted with the best literature. Thomas Mosher of Portland, makes the best books in the country. One can caress a Mosher book, and always be sure that within the covers one can find something high grade. The Roycrofters came into existence because Elbert Hubbard stumbled into William Morris and caught the germ. Out in Los Angeles, James Grifis has set up the Golden Press among the orange trees and roses. He sends out his beautiful little magazine "Everyman" to try to bring folks to see that the Golden Rule is really greater than the majority think, and that a laugh is worth ten frowns in every market.

An ideal we have is that some day there will be a little shop in Newark that will do good things in printing. It is a dream—not of a country job office, but of a little art shop. A dream perhaps—but that the Newark Post some day will be considered and loved as a little weekly paper at Newark, Delaware, that is good, that is doing good, that is different, and that we may be classed among the

QUALITY FOLKS—because we are doing good work, a little better than the other fellow can.

KELLS

∞

May 4, 1910

TO THE MAN WHO SETTLED THE POST

Sparklets has passed into the glowing embers of the Past; Citizen has gone to other hunting grounds and Neutral will never see the light of day. Tauras, belching forth fumes of tobacco smoke, is hitched to the Post. The long haired farmer will soon sit in councils of the scientific world on the Board of Health. The debris of the wreck of the Gentleman's Limited, which occurred last Saturday, has been cleared away. The citizens tremble as the sparks fly from the live wire of Council. The Board of Trade is dead and W. H. Taylor stands weeping at the bier. The storm that burst in the New Century Club has passed. The Wets are almost landed high and Dry. The Matinee Idol has left the Avenue. The professors who were so unceremoniusly buried, have arisen. Amid all this the POST has stood firm, and stands today unscarred. You have not lost your head. Don't do so now, and you will find as the storms gather that Newark will cling to the POST that has been settled in our midst.

God Speed and success, and when "I can't buy it in Newark, I'll get it in Wilmington."

WHITE CLAY

∞

March 07, 1928

ATTACKED BY ROOSTER

Miss Nora A. Lindell had a harrowing experience last Friday morning, when she was attacked by a large and pugnacious rooster, knocked across a ditch and, severely belabored by the enraged bird's bill and spurs.

Miss Lindell was on Cleveland Avenue, on her way to work, when she received an unexpected and hard blow in the back, which knocked her off her feet and over a small ditch. As she fell she saw her assailant was an enormous rooster. The bird after knocking her down, flew at her legs and concentrated his attack on them. Miss Lindell finally managed to beat the bird off and make her escape.

The attack was entirely unprovoked as Miss Lindell had never seen the fowl before. It is thought that the feathers on Miss Lindell's hat may have caused the rooster to become envious.

END NOTES

∞

1. Everett C. Johnson Collection, University of Delaware, Special Collections.

2. Wilson Lloyd Bevan, History Of Delaware Past And Present Volume IV pages 314-316 "Everett C. Johnson".

Joan Easley, The University of Delaware News March 1980 "A Case Study in Small Town Journalism".

Robert J. Taggart, Everett C. Johnson (1879-1926): Political Visionary and Eternal Optimist Delaware History Volume XXV Number 4 page 215-236.

Thomas Beckman, Arts & Crafts Printing in Delaware: Everett C. Johnson and his Press of Kells Collections Volume V 1990 pages 22-37.

3. Curtis Paper Accession, Longwood Papers, Hagley Museum and Library.

4. P. S. du Pont Papers, Longwood Papers, Hagley Museum and Library.

5. Hudson Cemetery Records, Delaware Historical Society.

6. Williams Papers, University of Delaware, Special Collections.
7. Tuppy unknown author c. 1870.

8. Newark Post 25 September 1918.

9. Everett C. Johnson Collection, University of Delaware, Special

Collections.

10. George D. Strayer The General Report On School Buildings And Grounds Of Delaware Bulletin of the Service Citizens of Delaware Vol. 1 Number 3.

11. Robert H. Robinson Visiting Sussex Even if You Live Here 1976.

12. Ibid.

13. Ibid.

14. Richard B. Carter Clearing New Ground - The Life of John G. Townsend, Jr.

15. Henry C. Conrad History of the State of Delaware volume II page 606.

16. Newark Post 18 April 1923 "Reverend Herson Returns".

17. Old Country Churches of Sussex County.

18. Francis A. Cooch Alumni News "College Life 1889-1893" Volume V May 1934, number 16 page 11.

19. Newark Post 3 March 1926 reprint from Every Evening.

20. Louise S. Johnson A Narration of Many Memories Several Detours and A Few Thoughts page 39.

21. Newark Post 14 February 1917.

22. Oral History Tapes, interview with Louise Johnson 1975, University of Delaware, Special Collections.

23. Everett C. Johnson Collection, Photo copies of Engelhardt Baltimore City, Maryland, The Book of its Board of Trade University of Delaware, Special Collections.

24. Ibid.

25. Everett C. Johnson Collection, Unidentified newspaper clipping, University of Delaware, Special Collections.

26. Op. Cit. Narrations Page 42.

27. Ibid Page 44.

28. Ibid.

29. Op. Cit. Clearing New Ground p. 309.

30. Newark Post 17 July 1912 page 4.

31. Op. Cit. Narrations page 51.

32. House Journal, State of Delaware 1911.

33. Alfred D. Warner "History of the Women's College" Delaware Note Twentieth Series 1947 p. 16.

34. John A. Munroe The University of Delaware A History p. 162.

35. Elisha Conover The University News 1938 p. 4 "Delaware Then and Now".

36. University News 1938 pg. 5.

37. Winifred J. Robinson History of the Women's College of the University of Delaware 1914-1938.

38. John Wiley & Son A History of Graphic Design "The Arts and Crafts Movement" p. 179, 180, 189.

39. Ibid p.36.

40. Louise Johnson interview,   University of Delaware, Special

Collections.

41. The Note Book Of Elbert Hubbard The Roycrofters 1927, p.29.

42. Letter undated to Warner from Vallandigham, Warner Scrapbook, University of Delaware, Archives.

43. Letter to Charles H. Bowden to J. Spencer Brock May 7, 1928, Hagley Museum & Library.

44. Ibid.

45. Newark Post 14 November 1923.

46. Evans Papers, Letter to Hugh Rodney Sharp from Everett C. Johnson June 1915.

47. The Delaware Bulletin, October, 1924 p.3 University of Delaware, Archives.

48. Newark Post 28 April 1915.

49. Evans Papers, Letter to Evans from Johnson June 3, 1915 and Letter from Evans to Mitchell June 23, 1915.

50. Narrations p.53.

51. Taped interview with Louise Carter 1977, Richard Carter.

52. Marie Via Head, Heart and Hand.

53. Narration p. 54.

54. Newark Post 6 January 1916.

55. Newark Post 23 February 1916.

56. Narrations p. 47.

57. Newark Post 22 August 1917.

58. DuVal Cleaves History of C&L Printing Company, Harry H. Cleaves, Owner 1948.

59. Narrations p.55, 56.

60. Newark Post 7 September 1921.

61. Ibid 31 March 1926.

62. History Of Delaware Past And Present, Volume III p. 55.

63. Quality Folks, Newark Post 13 April 1910.

64. Hagley, Early Business of De. Curtis Ledger Books.

65. Constance J. Cooper The Curtis Paper Co. Cedar Tree Press, Wilm. De. 1991 p. 41.

66. Articles on Fabrikoid, March 1929 Du Pont Magazine p. 16, Vol. XXIII No. 3, September 1919 p. 6.

67. American Type Founders Catalog.

68. Newark Post 28 April 1915 "Newark Post".

69. Newark Post 23 October 1912.

70. Newark Post 39 April 1913.

71. Narrations p. 58.

72. Edward N. Vallandigham Fifty Years of De. College, 1870-1920 (Newark [1920]), p. 98, 99 Kells.

73. Narrations p. 74.

74. Narrations p. 71.

75. Ibid p. 72-74.

76. Ibid p. 69.

77. Everett C. Johnson Collection University of Delaware, Special Collections.

78. Carter p. 156.

79. Ellen Rendle P.S. We Love You The Cedar Tree Press, Inc. 1993.

80. Everett C. Johnson Collection University of Delaware, Special Collections.

81. Narrations p. 81.

82. What Is The Service Citizens of Delaware 29 July 1919.

83. Ellen Rendle P.S. We Love You The Cedar Tree Press, Inc. 1993 p. 3.

84. An Appreciation To Pierre S. Du Pont From The Foreign-Born Mothers Of Delaware. Hagley, PS Papers.

85. Hullihan Papers, "The University of Delaware Press" p.745.

86. P. S. du Pont Papers, Longwood Papers file 10/A, Hagley Museum and Library.

87. Hullihan Papers University of Delaware Special Collections p. 745.

88. University of Delaware Alumni News, 1922. "The University of Delaware Press" p.23-25.

89. Elbert Hubbard, Little Journeys to the House of Eminent Orators

- Vol. XII March 1903 No. 3.

90. Letter from Pres. Hullihen to Henry Thompson 3 July 1923, Hullihen Papers, UofD Archives.

91. Letter To the Stockholders and Board of Directors of the University of Delaware Press, Hagley.

92. The University of Delaware Press, Report of the Manager, 11 July 1923, Hagley.

93. University of Delaware Alumni News, September 1922.

94. PS papers, Hagley.

95. Ibid. #643.

96. Munroe 440.

97. Munroe 440.

98. Bulletin of the Service Citizens of Delaware, Volume I Number 3, p.26.

99. Ibid. p. 72.

100. Ibid. p. 175.

101. Ellen Rendle P.S. We Love You The Cedar Tree Press, Inc. 1993 p. 4.

102. Munroe p.256.

103. Newark Post 27 May 1925.

104. Narrations p. 88.

105. Everett C. Johnson Collections, University of Delaware, Special

Collections.

106. Ibid.

107. Personal Collection of Marjorie.

108. Ibid.

109. Hullihen Papers, University of Delaware, Archives.

110. Ibid

111. Elbert Hubbard, Little Journeys to the House of Eminent Orators - Vol. XII March 1903 No. 3.

112. Private Collection of Marjorie.

113. Press of Kells, Declaration of Independence / Constitution of the United States of America.

114. Cornelius A. Tilghman.

115. Everett C.Johnson's Transcript Delaware College University of Delaware, Archives.

116. Narrations p. 50.

117. Johnson Collection, newspaper Clipping, Special Collection.

118. Every Evening, Wilmington De. February 20, 1926 p.1.

119. Johnson Collection, newspaper clipping Special Collection.

120. Albert O. H. Grier and Harold Brayman Lincoln Club of Delaware, A History.

121. William H. Herndon and Jesse W. Weik, Life of Lincoln p.425 (World Publishing Company, 1949).

122. Program Lincoln's Birthday Nineteen Hundred Thirty-four, Wilm. De.

123. John W. Beach Cape Henlopen Lighthouse and Delaware Breakwater 1979 Dover Graphic Association Dover, Delaware p. 27.

124. Charles W. Staniford Report for Proposed Protection for Care Henlopen Lighthouse, Printed in Newark Post 4 March 1925 p.10.

125. Op. Cit. Cape Henlopen Lighthouse and Delaware Breakwater p.71.

126. Newark Post 18 November 1925 p.4.

127. Newark Post 22 July 1925 p.4.

128. P. S. du Pont Papers, Longwood Papers file 10/A, Hagley Museum and Library.

129. Newark Post 22 July 1925 p.4.

130. Ibid.

131. Everett C. Johnson Collection, University of Delaware, Special Collections.

132. P. S. du Pont Papers, Letter to Bierre from W. H. Stayton 14 August 1928, Longwood Papers, Hagley Museum and Library.

133. Narrations p. 87.

134. Richard Carter taped interview of Louise Johnson 1977.

135. Newark Post 29 September 1926.

136. Everett C. Johnson Collection, unidentified newspaper clipping "Hundreds Mourn as E. C. Johnson is Laid to Rest".

137. Ibid.

138. Metten's Eulogy.

139. Everett C. Johnson Collection, Special Collections, University of Delaware.

140. P. S. du Pont Papers, Letter to G. H. Bowden from W. B. Foster, Longwood Papers 10/A, Hagley Museum and Library.

141. Narrations p.89.

142. Ibid.

143. P. S. du Pont Papers, Letter to Charlotte Mahaffey from Frank McHugh, Longwood Papers 10/A, Hagley Museum and Library.

144. P. S. du Pont Papers, Letter to G. H. Bowden from W. B. Foster, Longwood Papers 10/A, Hagley Museum and Library.

145. W. B. Foster "Outline of Policy" Press of Kells, Longwood Papers 10/A, Hagley Museum and Library.

146. "Press of Kells Inc." Longwood Papers 10/A, Hagley Museum and Library; letter to P. S. du Pont from Helen M. Wanser 20 July 1929.

147. W. B. Foster "The Press of Kells" 22 October 1935 p.7, Longwood Papers 10/A, Hagley Museum and Library.

148. Newark Post 27 June 1940.

149. Newark Post 29 August 48.

BIBLIOGRAPHY

ITEMS PRINTED BY THE NEWARK POST AND
THE PRESS OF KELLS

∞

Each book, pamphlet, motto card, and magazine is listed in order of the year it was printed followed by an alphabetical listing of the title. Measurements given include width followed by height and total number of pages. In some cases this is followed by the type of paper used determined by watermarks. Following is a description of the binding and any notable parts in the text. A more complete description and points of particular interest about the publication can be found in the Appendix. Any quotations come from Kells' own descriptions or comments. It should be noted that any item listed that does not contain the *Newark Post* or Kells imprint has been confirmed by other sources. Unless otherwise noted the authors have examined each item. The items tied with silk or cord are uniquely tied using three holes, this makes the binding more secure than the two hole method. The most prominent feature found in the majority of the Kells printing is the use of Bookman Oldstyle.

Published by

The Craftsmen of Kells

Newark Delaware

1 9 2 1

∞

1912

∞

1. SPECIMENS OF ENGLISH PROSE COMPOSITION. SELECTED BY WILBUR OWEN SYPHERD, PH.D. AND GEORGE ELLIOTT DUTTON, A.M. OF THE DEPARTMENT OF ENGLISH, DELAWARE COLLEGE.

4 7/8" X 7 1/4" 151 pages.

Brown cloth binding with title printed in gold on spine. Blank pages are left at the end of each chapter for students' notes.

IMPRINTS: Printed at the Shop of Newark Post, Newark, Del.

NOTE: Possibly the first book printed by what later became the Press of Kells and the first of several printed for Sypherd.

∞

2. CALENDARS

The Newark Post printed special calendars with "sepia tint on deckle edge card". Exclusive rights to the subject matter printed on the calendar were optional for the buyer.

∞

3. DELAWARE COLLEGE CATALOG

The authors have not located this catalog and only found mention of it in a letter to the Sunday Star from President Harter. The letter was advising the Sunday Star that the Newark Post would be printing the catalog.

∞

1913

∞

4. ALUMNI ASSOCIATION DELAWARE COLLEGE ANNUAL REUNION

5" X 7 1/4" 8 pages tied with blue silk.

Bound in heavy ivory stock with blue lettering underlined in gold.

IMPRINT: "Newark Post Press" printed in blue on the second to last page.

NOTE: The reunion was held at the Hotel du Pont in February 1913. Everett C. Johnson gave a toast to the Delaware College and the State of Delaware. The text printed in blue with gold headings and borders.

∞

5. **AFFILIATED COLLEGE, AN ACT PROVIDING FOR SECURING THE SITE, ERECTING, EQUIPPING AND FURNISHING BUILDINGS FOR A WOMEN'S COLLEGE AFFILIATED WITH DELAWARE COLLEGE, AT NEWARK, DELAWARE, AND TO PROVIDE THE METHOD OF PAYING FOR THE SAME.**

4 1/4" X 9 3/4" 8 pages with DOUBLE ANTIQUE paper.

Ivory color pamphlet is a reprint of a bill signed by Governor Miller on March 31, 1913.

IMPRINT: NEWARK POST PRESS printed on bottom of the back cover.

∞

6. **DELAWARE COLLEGE REVIEW**

By staff and students.

7" X 10" 28 pages.

Stiff paper cover printed in blue with the seal of the college in the center. The color of the cover changes between issues. To help defray the cost of the publication advertisements were obtained from local business. The October 1913 issue of The Review announced: Everett C. Johnson has been awarded the contract for printing the "Delaware College Review" at the plant of the Newark Post, where distinctive "printin" is done.

SUBJECT: Literary articles on current affairs.

IMPRINT: Shop of The Newark Post. A Plant, where Printing is considered an Art, and not a Job. We Print for the Elect.

See Appendix.

∞

1914

∞

7. THE DELAWARE FARMER

7" X 9 7/8" numbers of pages per issue varied, numbered consecutively.

Ivory color paper cover with title printed in black and underlined in red. Each issue contains half tone pictures.

IMPRINTS: On the back cover "Shop of The Newark Post Newark Delaware" printed on a sign with an ink ball.

First issued January 1914; printed by Kells for at least four years.

See Appendix.

∞

8. PANAMA CANAL

Folder courtesy of The Farmer's Trust of Newark

"First of a series of leaflets on the building of the Panama Canal, printed in three colors."

The authors have been unable to locate any of the folders and all information obtained came from the Newark Post that further wrote, "The historical and pictorial value of the folders assures them a permanent place in the files of all those interested in the great movements of the world."

∞

9. LOUISE HOMER CONCERT PROGRAM

2/18/1914

The authors have been unable to locate a copy of the program and the only mention found has been in the Newark Post.

∞

10. DELAWARE COLLEGE IN THE SERVICE OF THE NATION

AS INTERPRETED IN THE ADDRESSES DELIVERED ON THE OCCASION OF THE INSTALATION (SIC) OF SAMUEL CHILES MITCHELL AS

PRESIDENT OF DELAWARE COLLEGE, AND OF THE BUILDINGS OF THE WOMEN'S COLLEGE OF DELAWARE, AND THE INSTALLATION OF WINIFRED J. ROBINSON AS DEAN, ON OCTOBER TENTH, NINETEEN FOURTEEN.

6 1/4" X 9 3/4" 64 unnumbered pages with ENFIELD (Curtis paper) tied with silk.

The paper cover has the title printed in black and a blind stamped College seal.

SUBJECT: The title explains the main theme of the combined speeches.The booklets were presented to the College for alumni, trustees, and distinguished visitors.

See Appendix.

∞

11. VIEWS OF DELAWARE COLLEGE
By Delaware College

6 1/4" X 9 1/4" 28 pages unnumbered.

Brown paper binding with dark brown print. A series of 27 half tone pictures of campus buildings cover each page. The only text other than the title page is a caption under each photo giving the name of the building. A three-page centerfold shows a panoramic view of what is now Old College and Recitation Hall with finely dressed students and guests on the open lawn. The caption reads "Commencement Day at Delaware College".

IMPRINT: The sign–like imprint and ink ball is on the lower right corner of the back cover with Shop of The Newark Post Newark, Delaware.

∞

12. STATE ELECTION BALLOTS
Newark Post October 21, 1914; "Work has begun on Saturday on the printing of the half million ballots for the coming election which requires about 24 tons of paper. 30,000 will be sent as sample ballots to voters throughout the State. The ballots will be about 18 inches in length with Republican, Democratic, Progressive, Prohibition and

Socialist nominees grouped in separate columns." The authors have not been able to locate the ballots.

∞

13. THE NEWARK TRUST AND SAFE COMPANY

"This book was designed, printed, set to color and embossed by those working here. Special mention should be made of embossing and press work, executed by our Harry Cleaves."
The authors have not located this printing for Newark Trust and obtained the information from the Newark Post March 25, 1914.

∞

14. "A little magazine from a neighboring town which promises to become a monthly affair four colors, cover embossed" The authors have found no further information and the only report of the unnamed magazine was found in the Newark Post March 25, 1914

∞

1915
∞

15. ACTS OF THE GENERAL ASSEMBLY RELATING TO THE TOWN OF NEWARK AND ORDINANCES RELATING TO ITS GOVERNMENT / PUBLISHED BY THE ORDER OF COUNCIL.

By Newark, Delaware, Published by order of Council 1915
6 1/4" X 9 1/4" 132 pages with marginal notes and index.
Light brown, cloth covered board binding with red label and gold print on spine.

∞

16. ORDINANCES RELATING TO THE GOVERNMENT OF THE TOWN OF NEWARK DELAWARE.

By Newark, Delaware Council
6 1/4" X 9 1/4" 54 pages.

The ordinance half of the book #15 is bound in gray stiff paper cover on the front and white on the back. The title is printed in black with a red underline under the word ORDINANCES, and "Published by order of Council 1915" printed in black on the lower right hand corner of the cover. 200 copies printed.

∞

17. ENGLISH COMPOSITION FOR COLLEGE FRESHMEN
By Wilbur Owen Sypherd and George Elliott Dutton.
7 3/4" X 10 1/4" Part I, 180 pages Part II, 154 pages.
Part I and II are bound in dark blue, cloth covered board, with gold lettering on the spine.
IMPRINT: To the left of the preface is printed "The Post Press Newark, Del."
NOTE: Part II is made up of loose leaves so the 50 examples could be changed.

∞

18. ALUMNI NEWS
Volume I, #1, was printed from January 1915 up to 1935. The name changed to University News and the publication was intended to be printed Quarterly. The format changed from 5 1/2" X 8 1/2" with 4 pages, to a small newspaper design of 21" X 15 1/2" in Volume IV, # 1, June 1918. The first issue to carry the Shop at Kells imprint was December 1916, Volume III # 1.

∞

19. PRINT OF COMPANY E OF NEWARK--ORGANIZED MILITIA OF DELAWARE AT CAMP MILLER
A copy of the print was reproduced in the Post and was described as suitable for framing.

∞

1916

❧

20. THE PRESS OF KELLS
5 1/2" wide X 4" high with four leaves inside a card stock tied in brown silk.

The cover has the gold script, embossed Kells and blind embossed triangle. Inside is a color print of the Kells shop with the first two sections of the building completed and a quote from Hamlet. "You're welcome, master, welcome all. Welcome good friend."

See Appendix.

❧

21. DELAWARE SONG ALMA MATER
7" X 11"

"The music is printed on WEDDING ANTIQUE BRISTOL stock made at Curtis Paper Mill Newark De. The Song, set in Packard, printed in black. On the margin is a sunset scene of the Dorm, paneled, blind embossed. A torch of wisdom in gold sets off the idea, so that it makes an attractive card for framing."

❧

22. THE SHAKSPERE FESTIVAL
8" X 12 1/4" 28 page OLD STRATFORD paper.

Ivory color cover bound with cord with the embossed title and head of Shakspere. The text was complete with orange side notes. The printing was limited to 1,000 numbered copies. (The " e and a" in Shakespeare had been left out of the modern day spelling.)

"Layout and composition by Shultz, makeup and embossing by Cleaves, and press work by Balling."

See Appendix.

❧

23. THE SHAKSPERE FESTIVAL ANNOUNCEMENT
3 7/8" X 5 5/8"

The heavy ivory paper has a double fold making 6 pages of

announcements and information. Title and fleurons printed in red.

∞

24. SHAKSPERE (Motto Card)
4 3/4 " X 8 5/5"
The card stock has the embossed head of Shakspere with one of his quotes printed in green. A red poinsettia made it suitable as a Christmas card. It is not known how many different quotes were used. The authors have been able to locate two varieties.

∞

25. THE TALE OF TWELFTH NIGHT or WHAT YOU WILL
By Charles and Mary Lamb
6" X 7 3/4" 33 pages OLD STRATFORD watermark.
Ivory stock cover bound with white cord with an embossed head of Shakspere. A hand tinted initial letter begins the text and each page has a green double line at the top.
"So here ends the story of the Play Twelfth Night as it was written by Charles and Mary Lamb. Printed and done into this booklet by the Craftsmen of Kells at Newark, Delaware, in the year 1916, being the 300th Anniversary of the death of William Shakspere."
IMPRINT: At the end of the book is the Kells triangle printed in green.

∞

26. DANCE PROGRAM FOR THE JUNIOR PROM
"Was placed on exhibit in a printing art display in Philadelphia."
The authors have not seen the program.

∞

27. CREED AND DEED: Wherein is given the story of The Visit of the Good Bishop in Les Miserables to the Conversationalist and a Portrait of the Bishop as found in the words of the Master, Victor Hugo

By Hugo, Victor, 1802-1885
4 1/2" X 6 3/4" 65 pages OLD STRATFORD deckle edge paper.
The purple sheepskin cover with purple endpaper has the title deeply
imbedded in gold. Purple is also used for page numbers, line fillers,
chapter headings, and initial letters. A few of the books were hand
illuminated and came in a special box for Christmas. Body set in
Bookman.

IMPRINT:

> Compiled and Printed into this Book by the Craftsmen
> at Kells, at Newark, Delaware
>> This book is Number____of an edition of one
> hundred and one copies printed at Kells in the town of
> Newark, Delaware, in the year nineteen hundred and
> sixteen.

COLOPHONS:

> And so here endeth our little book of the story of
> the visit of the Priest to the Conventionalist. Reading
> again the story, we have gained, let us hope, a greater
> sympathy with TRUTH. The Craftsmen here in
> keeping with custom old whisper-God Speed.

See Appendix.

∞

28. ABRAHAM LINCOLN; AN APPRECIATION BY EVERETT C. JOHNSON DELIVERED BEFORE THE GENERAL ASSEMBLY OF DELAWARE, ON THE TWELFTH DAY OF FEBRUARY, NINETEEN HUNDRED ELEVEN.

By Johnson, Everett C.
5 1/2" X 8" 6 pages tied in silk, ALEXANDRA paper.
The stiff, ivory-colored paper cover has Abraham Lincoln's bust
embossed on the cover. The uniquely tied pages are made up of six
leaves French folded. The booklet is a fitting tribute to the speech.
First given in 1911, the booklet was not printed until after 1916.
IMPRINT: The Kells device on the booklet is unique in that it features a rounded off triangle without the 1916 printed in the lower H.
COLOPHON:

> At the request of kind friends, this appreciation of that

Master Man, Abraham Lincoln, is printed into this
booklet.

By the Craftsmen at the Shop of Kells which is on
Welsh Lane, Newark, Delaware.

NOTE: Everett Johnson was well known and sought after for his
speeches on Lincoln.

∞

29. A CULTURAL-PRACTICAL COLLEGE EDUCATION FOR WOMEN
By Women's College of Delaware
5 7/8" X 3 1/2" 8 pages tied in silk.
The paper cover is printed in black with bold underline and Women's
College seal in gold. It contains five half tone photos and course
descriptions.
IMPRINT: Early oval Kells imprint on the back cover.

∞

30. MOTTO CARDS
Divinity By Hugo, Victor
Les Miserables By Hugo, Victor
My Symphony By Channing
8 3/4" X 13"
Title printed in red with motto printed with Old Style Bookman and
Kells triangle embossed.

∞

1917
∞

31. THANKSGIVING PROCLAMATION 1917
4 3/4" X 9 3/4" 12 pages, only 4 with printed text, DOUBLE
ANTIQUE paper.
Heavy white stock binding tied with white silk cord. The Old
English type, printed in gold, with embossed state seal. Governor
John G. Townsend and Secretary of State E. C. Johnson signed the

Proclamation.

∞

32. COMMENCEMENT DELAWARE COLLEGE JUNE TENTH TO JUNE THIRTEENTH NINE HUNDRED AND SEVENTEEN.
3 1/4" X 6"
Tri-fold pamphlet ends with a half-tone picture of Old College being remodeled in 1917.

∞

33. FOURTH ANNUAL REUNION OF THE NEWARK HIGH SCHOOL ALUMNI ASSOCIATION, HANNA'S CAFÉ WILMINGTON, JUNE NINE, NINETEEN SEVENTEEN.
3 1/2" X 4 1/2" 12 pages.
Stiff ivory paper cover tied with cord.
The cover displays an American flag in red and blue with quote from Oliver Wendell Homes printed in blue.

∞

34. THE BLUE HEN
8 1/2" X 11" 207 pages Cameo Plate paper.
Blue "Fabrikoid" binding has a leather spine with title and date printed in gold.
IMPRINT: The last printed page has a Kells advertisement and on the back of the book is a small Kells Newark, Delaware. The last line of the Foreword; "…and The Craftsmen at Kells for their interest as well as technical skill."
The yearbook contains many fine photos, some in color, of the University campus during a time of transition.
SUBJECT: Delaware college (men's) yearbook.

∞

1918
∞

35. CHRONICLE

7 1/2" X 11 1/4" 146 pages.

Blue "Fabrikoid" binding with the title and date printed in gold.

IMPRINT: On the last printed page; And so this is where The Chronicle was printed, Kells Where Master Craftsmen study and work at the Art of Printing, Welsh Lane-Newark, Delaware.

SUBJECT: The yearbook was for the first graduating class of the Women's College and appears to be dedicated to expressing the hardships the women suffered during their four years of college.

∞

36. THE GOSPEL ACCORDING TO SAINT JOHN AS FOUND IN THE KING JAMES VERSION

6" X 73/4" 127 pages DOUBLE ANTIQUE paper. Body copy set in 12 point heavy face Cheltenham type.

Bound in gray board, tipped with sheepskin. "St. John" stamped in gold on the cover and initial blocks for hand coloring. Paragraphed and not versed. "Initial letters and ornaments were made specially for this publication."

IMPRINT:

> Printed at the Shop called Kells, Which is on Welsh
> Lane in the Town of Newark, State of Delaware, United
> States of America. 1918

COLOPHONS:

> And so here endeth the Gospel according to Saint John.
> Done into this book in Cheltenham type by the
> Craftsmen at Kells in the year Nineteen Eighteen.

See Appendix.

∞

37. WIN-THE-WAR CONFERENCE HELD UNDER THE AUSPICES OF THE STATE COUNCIL OF DEFENSE FOR DELAWARE AT WILMINGTON, WEDNESDAY, JULY 10, 1918.

5 1/2" X 9 7/8" 36 unnumbered pages.

The white paper cover has the title printed in black with a quote printed in red along with the raised state seal. The back cover has a blue embossed hen and three chicks. Throughout the booklet are quotes printed in red. Introduction by Everett C. Johnson, Director General. The authors located a Kells receipt made out to J. G. Townsend, Jr. for the printing of 1,000 programs for the Win-the-War Conference at a total cost of $225.85 which amounts to less than twenty-three cents each.

∞

38. WIN THE WAR
By State Council of Defense
9" X 12" 12 pages cover stock with DOUBLE ANTIQUE paper.
The large pamphlet printed in black type with orange headings, initial letters and fleurons also made use of callouts. The first issue was dated September 1918, published under the auspices of State Council of Defense by courtesy of a patriotic citizen. This hard to find pamphlet is filled with stories on how Delaware citizens may help the war effort, along with suggestions for daily living during war time. It is a real treasure of information on Delaware during the war.

∞

39. PROGRAM AS ARRANGED by PRESIDENT MITCHELL & MEMBERS of FACULTY of DELAWARE COLLEGE for the ENTERTAINMENT of the DELMARVIA PRESS ASSOCIATION
4" x 7 1/2" 8 pages tied in blue silk on DOUBLE ANTIQUE paper.
Bound in heavy ivory color stock with a fancy "Delaware" printed in blue, and a gold University of Delaware seal on the cover.
IMPRINT: A blind embossed Kells triangle on the back cover with "Courtesy of Newark Post" printed in gold.

∞

40. ANNUAL BANQUET OF THE ALUMNI OF DELAWARE COLLEGE
4 1/2" X 7 3/4" 8 pages.

Heavy ivory stock cover tied with blue silk. Delaware raised in gold with hen and 3 chicks raised in blue. City Club Wilmington, Delaware, January twenty-sixth nineteen eighteen.
IMPRINT: Kells triangle on last page.

∞

1919
∞

41. DELAWARE STATE HIGHWAYS; THE STORY OF ROADS IN DELAWARE FROM THE DAYS OF THE "BEASTS OF *BURTHEN"--TO THE ROAD TO TO-MORROW". PREPARED AND PUBLISHED BY THE CLEARINGHOUSE OF THE DELAWARE STATE PROGRAM.

BY DELAWARE STATE HIGHWAY DEPT.

6 5/8" X 10 1/4" 53 pages.
The tan, stiff paper bound booklet, with eight photos and state maps, shows before and after photos of the main roads in Delaware. The cover has a deeply impressed shield enclosing the state crest.
IMPRINT: Kells device on the inside back page.
NOTE: Many of the photos and much of the information was also printed in the Newark Post.
* "Burthen" is an archaic form of the word burden.

∞

42. MOODS, A MODERN RUBAIYAT, ALSO TO THE MEN OF SORROWS AND OTHER POEMS.

By Bell, Jerome B.
6 1/4" X 8 1/2" 62 pages with deckle edge.
The binding is green paper over board and has a wide tan spine with gold lettering.
IMPRINT: On the cover page is Kells, Newark, Delaware 1919. A vignette is printed at the end of each chapter.
NOTE: The book contains a mounted portrait of the author.

43. DELAWARE MAGAZINE
Published monthly by Delaware Magazine Publishing Co., at
Newark, Delaware.
Kells took over the printing of this magazine September, 1919
Volume I number 5. Louis J. Allemann, Business Manager and W.
Arthur Wise, Managing Editor.

∞

44. AMERICANIZATION IN DELAWARE, A STATE POLICY INITIATED BY THE DELAWARE STATE COUNCIL OF DEFENSE.
By Lape, Esther Everett
5 1/8" X 9 1/8" 48 pages.
Body copy set in Bookman Oldstyle.
Ivory color binding with black and orange print, and an embossed seal
of the state.
IMPRINT: The material shows no imprint but has all the usual signs
of Kells work, Bookman Oldstyle type with distinctive swash ligatures
of words "The" and "of" and orange ink.
NOTE: It was not uncommon for printed articles done for the state by
Kells to lack an imprint while Everett was serving as Secretary of
State.

∞

45. THE BLUE AND GOLD
11 1/2" X 8" 144 pages.
The blue "Fabrikoid" binding has the title and date printed in gold.
IMPRINT: The last page has a picture of Kells along with, Kells
Where Master Craftsmen study and work at the Art of Printing Welsh
Lane-Newark, Delaware. The Foreword has, "…Also, we wish to
express appreciation for the artistic workmanship of Kells Master
Craftsmen."
SUBJECT: Women's College yearbook.

∞

1920

∞

46. BLUE AND GOLD
8 3/4" X 11 1/8" 208 pages.
Blue "Fabrikoid" binding with title, date and Women's College seal stamped in gold.
IMPRINT: Kells, Where Master Craftsmen study and work at the Art of Printing, Welsh Lane-Newark, Delaware.
SUBJECT: Women's College yearbook.

∞

47. FIFTY YEARS OF DELAWARE COLLEGE 1870-1920
By Vallandigham, Edward Noble 1854-1930
5 7/8" X 9 1/4" 153 pages.
The hardback copy is bound in the college colors, blue and gold, with a vignette showing a sunset scene of Old College on the cover. The light brown paperback has blue lettering with a single page map of current and proposed buildings on the University Campus.
SUBJECT: History of Delaware College.
IMPRINT: The title page has Kells, Newark, Delaware. The Kells is in the oval format.
NOTE: The book was printed in 1920 to celebrate the Fiftieth Anniversary of the College Re-opening. Vallandigham graduated from Delaware College in 1873. Everett Johnson absorbed the cost of printing the book.

∞

48. WHAT DELAWARE MAKES AND SPENDS: THE STORY OF STATE REVENUE AND EXPENDITURE / PREPARED AND PUBLISHED BY THE CLEARINGHOUSE OF THE DELAWARE STATE PROGRAM. / HOW FAR IS DELAWARE'S FINANCIAL SOLVENCY A MATTER OF CHANCE.
By Delaware State Program Clearing House, 1920
6 1/2" X 10 1/2" 55 pages.
Light blue-green paper binding with title printed in blue and the state seal. The body and text is printed in Bookman Oldstyle.

IMPRINT: On the back cover The Kells imprint with triangle device.

∞

49. GOOD ATTENDANCE AWARD
4" X 6"
Ivory cardstock printed on both sides. The front has a hand-tinted scene from Delaware and the reverse a short history of the scene. Printed on the front is a short inspirational message from Governor Townsend concerning good school attendance. Bellow this is the inscription "Awarded to_____ for Good Attendance for the month of October, nineteen hundred and twenty."
As the date changes so do the scenes.

∞

1921
∞

50. THE INAUGURAL ADDRESS OF GOVERNOR DENNEY, DELIVERED AT DOVER ON JANUARY THE EIGHTEENTH, NINETEEN TWENTY-ONE.
By Denney, William D.
7 1/8" X 11" 15 pages.
White paper cover with black print, tied with white silk.
IMPRINT: The booklet contains no Kells device or imprint but is clearly printed by Kells. The cover and title page make good use of the distinctive Kells typeface with swash ligatures of words "The" and "of".
NOTE: Governor Denney replaced Governor Townsend as Governor of Delaware and had wanted Everett Johnson to stay on as Secretary of State. Everett declined the appointment.

∞

51. CONVENTION OF THE AMERICAN ROADBUILDERS ASSOCIATION
8" X 12" 50 pages.
The convention was held in Chicago and the book was printed with

half tone and three-color work.

The authors have not located the book and it is believed that Thomas Colman du Pont attended the convention in Chicago.

∞

52. KELLS-THE STORY OF THE VISIT OF A VAGABOND PRINTER TO THE SHOP WHERE MASTER CRAFTSMEN STUDY AND WORK AT THE ART OF PRINTING.

By Vagabond printer, [John Schultz]

4 1/2" X 7 3/4" 17 pages.

The type used was Bookman Oldstyle along with italic and swash from ATF.

Brown paper binding tied with brown silk cord. Distant picture of the Kells Shop, with hand illuminated orange sunset sky, tipped in opposite the title page.

IMPRINT: The cover is embossed with KELLS and the triangle. The inside title page has KELLS and the triangle printed in orange, as is the initial letter. To the left of the title page is a mounted illustration of the Press of Kells.The date is not printed in the book but the contents and reference in the Newark Post indicate it was printed in 1921.

See Appendix.

∞

53. THE LOG IN THE DAM

By Johnson, Everett C.

3 1/4" X 6" single leaf folded once.

Ivory paper with the title in gold.

SUBJECT: Inspirational thoughts by Everett C. Johnson, Everett's daughter submitted it to *Reader's Digest* and it was printed in 1995.

∞

54. THE ENGLISH BIBLE: BEING A BOOK OF SELECTIONS FROM THE KING JAMES VERSION

Edited, with introduction and explanatory notes, by Wilbur Owen
Sypherd, Professor of English at the University of Delaware
7" X 8 5/8" 550 pages light linen rag.
Dark blue fabric binding with gold lettering on the spine.
IMPRINT: Both the triangle and Kells printed on the spine.
NOTE: Second Edition, printed by The Press of Kells for the
University of Delaware Press, in December 28, 1923 is slightly larger
than the first addition.
See Appendix.

∞

55. THE BLUE HEN'S CHICKS IN CARICATURE
Sketches and Captions / by Gee Tee Maxwell, prepared and published
in collaboration with the Delaware State News, Dover Delaware.
8 1/4" X 12" 89 pages.
Dark blue "Fabrikoid" binding with the title stamped in light blue on
the front. An oval DUPONT FABRIKOID trademark is stamped in
gold on the spine. Volume I printed on the title page.
IMPRINT: "Printed at the Shop called Kells, which is on Welsh Lane
at Newark, Delaware 1921". The back cover shows the two Kells
devices.
See Appendix.

∞

56. BLUE KETTLE, THE
By Women's College staff and students
5 1/2" X 8 1/4" 40 pages tied in silk.
Volume I, number I, was bound in white paper with blue print. The
cover shows a kettle over a fire and was printed December 1921.
Volume I number II and III changed to a yellow cover with black print
and the kettle was changed to a teapot over a fire. They were printed
in April and June 1922.
IMPRINT: Printed at Kells, Newark, Delaware with no printed
device.
NOTE: The publication only lasted until the fall of 1923 at which
time the staff joined the Review staff.

∞

1922

∞

57. POEMS TO IANTHE

By Landor, Walter Savage, arranged, with an introduction and notes, by Finley M. K. Foster.
7 1/4" X 12 1/2" 16 pages.
Brown "Fabrikoid" binding with the title stamped in gold and a wide tan spine. The de luxe edition is limited to 125 numbered copies and has ivory paper over board binding.
IMPRINT: On the title page "Published by The Craftsmen of Kells Newark, Delaware". MDCCCCXXII.
See Appendix.

∞

58. DREAMS AND OBSERVATIONS BEING VERSES OF FANCY AND FACT

By Benson, Alden Richardson 1860-1927
4 3/4" X 7" 142 pages with deckle edge and top edge gilt. BAY PATH BOOK/MADE IN U.S.A. paper.
Brown "Fabrikoid" binding with dark brown spine and gold title printed on the front and spine.
IMPRINT: Kells triangle on the spine and "Printed at the Shop called Kells Newark, Delaware" printed on the title page.
NOTE: The author is a former Secretary of State from Delaware and has his picture tipped in after the title page.
See Appendix.

∞

59. A JANUARY SUMMER

By Sharp, Dallas Lore, 1870-1929
5 1/2" X 7 3/4" 37 pages.
The binding was done in two different styles. The dark blue cloth-covered binding is stamped in gold with a paper label depicting a drawing by R. Bruce Horsfall. Most of the pages have etchings by

Horsfall. The book was also done in a heavy cardstock cover in light tan with paper label.

IMPRINT: Printed at the Shop called Kells Newark, Delaware.

NOTE: The book was published for the Service Citizens of Delaware and carries the previous copyrights; Copyright 1919, Duffield & Company, Copyright 1922, Dallas Lore Sharp.

See Appendix.

∞

60. THIRTY HOME LESSONS FOR FOREIGN-BORN WOMEN IN DELAWARE
By Hart, Helen

8 1/4" X 10 3/4" 62 pages.

Brown paper cover with the title in dark brown type. The book is a series of simple lessons in English with a generous amount of free space on each page.

IMPRINT: The lower right corner of the back cover has the oval Kells.

NOTE: Helen Hart was the Secretary for the Americanization Committee of the State Defense Council.

∞

61. UNIVERSITY OF DELAWARE AND STATE WAR MEMORIAL CAMPAIGN COUPON BOOK
3" X 5"

The pink coupon booklet for contributions to the campaign. "...the sum of____dollars per month for twenty months payable in 10 bimonthy payments beginning October 1, 1922". The students were given a little green card "Above all, what is asked for is - Every Alumnus in the game at the kick-off and hitting the line with all his strength One hundred per cent Alumni! AND IT'S A TOUCHDOWN SURE. Sum of____dollars per month for twenty months."

∞

62. LIBRARY AND WAR MEMORIAL CAMPAIGN, UNIVER-

SITY OF DELAWARE 1922
4 1/4" x 9 1/2"
The multifold pamphlet is printed in black on white with some highlights in red.

∞

63. A LIBRARY AND WAR MEMORIAL FOR THE STATE OF DELAWARE
7 1/4" X 10 1/2" 16 pages Bay Path Book paper.
The ivory paper cover is tied with white cord through three holes. Program of the campaign dinner given at the Hotel DuPont on October the twentieth, nineteen hundred and twenty-two, Everett C. Johnson General Chairman. The second page has a tipped in view of Old College. The last page is illustrated with a hen and three chicks and inscribed "This Program has been given through the Courtesy of a friend". [Everett C. Johnson]
The back cover has the Kells triangle embossed.

∞

64. THE BLUE AND GOLD
11 1/4" X 8 3/4" 165 pages.
Blue "Fabrikoid" binding with title in gold.
The yearbook does not have many campus photos but it does have a two-page fold out of all the students of the Women's College students.
IMPRINT: Kells Where Master Craftsmen study and work at the Art of Printing Welsh Lane-Newark, Delaware.
SUBJECT: Women's College yearbook.

∞

65. DELAWARE, ANNUAL OUTING OF THE SONS OF DELAWARE OF PHILADELPHIA UNIVERSITY OF DELAWARE MAY THIRTEENTH, NINETEEN HUNDRED AND TWENTY-TWO.
5 3/8" X 9 1/2" 8 pages MADE IN USA ALEXANDRA paper.
White cardstock cover tied with white cord. On the cover Delaware

and the letter A are printed in gold with the rest of the title printed in blue, as is the text. Kells printed the annual program with the same format for several years.
IMPRINT: Courtesy of KELLS

∞

1923
∞

66. NATIONAL EDUCATION IN THE UNITED STATES OF AMERICA, BY DU PONT DE NEMOURS, TRANSLATED FROM THE SECOND FRENCH EDITION OF 1812 AND WITH AN INTRODUCTION BY B. G. DU PONT.

By Du Pont de Nemours, Pierre Samuel, 1739-1817.
5 3/4" X 8 3/4" 161 pages with University of Delaware Press watermark, gilt top edge.
Dark blue "Fabrikoid" binding with gold stamped title and blind stamped border. The light brown dust jacket with dark brown lettering advertised the publication of *An American Looks at His World* and *Negro School Attendance in Delaware*.
IMPRINT: University of Delaware Press, Newark Delaware 1923. Printed from Type, February 1923. Printed by The Craftsmen at Kells Newark Delaware.
This was the first book printed by The Press of Kells for the University of Delaware Press.
See Appendix.

∞

67. LIFE OF ELEUTHERE IRENEE DUPONT, FROM CONTEMPORARY CORRESPONDENCE 1778-1834.

Translated from the French and with an Introduction by B. G. du Pont.
5 3/4" X 8 3/4" with 11 volumes totaling 3613 pages plus a 159 page index, University of Delaware Press watermark.
The binding of each volume is done in light blue paper over board with a white paper spine and a blind stamped crest on the cover. A color print of Bois des Fosses by Stanley Arthurs is tipped in. The end

papers of volume 1-4 have a partial map of France showing the location of the estate of Du Pont de Nemours.

IMPRINT: University of Delaware Press Newark, Delaware 1923.

Copyright 1923 by Pierre S. du Pont.

Printed in The United States of America by the Craftsmen of Kells at Newark, Delaware. Only two hundred and fifty copies were printed for private distribution.

∞

68. NEGRO SCHOOL ATTENDANCE IN DELAWARE

By Cooper, Richard Watson and Cooper, Hermann

8" X 11" 389 pages, Curtis Velvet Finish paper, 1200 copies printed. Dark blue "Fabrikoid" binding with gold lettering on the front and spine and the U of D Press diamond. It contains 141 tables and 82 maps along with diagrams and graphs.

"Printed by The Craftsmen at Kells, Newark, Delaware" is inscribed on the copyright page.

See Appendix.

∞

69. AMERICA'S SAFEGUARD OF LIBERTY

By Morris, Hugh M. U.S. District Judge for the District of Delaware. 5 3/4" X 11 1/4" 20 pages.

Ivory stock paper tied with cord, title printed in black.

IMPRINT: Kells triangle, Courtesy of Kells Newark, Delaware.

SUBJECT: An address delivered by the Honorable Hugh Morris before the students of the University of Delaware at Wolf Hall on May 15, 1923. The entire speech was also printed in the Post May 16, 1923.

∞

70. SUPPORTING AND DEFENDING THE CONSTITUTION

By Henry Campbell Black, LL.D.

16 pages.

Heavy stock cover.

An address delivered before the Delaware State Bar Association in

Wilmington, May 8,1923.
Printed by Kells for the University of Delaware Press. The publication was paid for by Judge Hugh Morris and a group of lawyers in Wilmington.

⌘

71. AN AMERICAN LOOKS AT HIS WORLD: VARIATIONS ON A POINT OF VIEW / BY GLENN FRANK.

By Frank, Glenn 1887-1940.
5 1/2" X 8 1/2" 364 pages.
Blue "Fabrikoid" binding has the title printed in gold on the cover and spine, with a preface by Joseph Odell. 2,500 copies printed.
IMPRINT: U of D Press The Craftsman at Kells
See Appendix.

⌘

72. PRINT OF BOIS DES FOSSES

By Arthurs, Stanley
"Four color print of an Oil Painting printed from copper plates with brush stroke effect."

The "brush stroke effect" was accomplished by a slight embossing of selected parts of the print. The print was tipped in the first volumes of Life of Eleuthere Irenee duPont, from Contemporary Correspondence 1778-1834.
See Appendix.

⌘

1924

⌘

73. THE DELAWARE BULLETIN

Published four times during the College Year by the Alumni Association of Delaware College of the University of Delaware.
7 3/8" X 10 3/8" 15 pages.
The paper cover has the title printed in red with a triple line border in blue. Theodore R. Dantz, Press of Kells employee, is listed as being

on the Editing Committee. Volume I. Number I. September 1924.

∞

74. KAPPA ALPHA DANCE PROGRAM
"A white and gold program held together by silk cords of red and yellow."

∞

75. LECTURES ON HISTORY AND GOVERNMENT: SERIES ONE, 1923-1924, DELIVERED AT THE UNIVERSITY OF DELAWARE, UNDER THE AUSPICES OF THE DEPARTMENT OF HISTORY AND POLITICAL SCIENCE
University of Delaware with an introduction by G. H. Ryden. Lectures by H. M. Morris, Willard Saulsbury, R. H. Richards, Henry Ridgely, and J. P. Nields.
6 1/8" X 9 1/8" 155 pages.
Reddish brown "Fabrikoid" binding with the title printed in black.
IMPRINT: The Press of Kells printed the book for the University of Delaware Press. Kells triangle is on the bottom right of the title page.
See Appendix.

∞

76. DECLARATION OF INDEPENDENCE AND CONSTITUTION OF THE UNITED STATES OF AMERICA
First printing 4 3/4" X 7 1/8" 83 pages
Second printing and all following printings 6 1/4" X 9 1/4" 83 pages.
The first printing of the Kells copy is the smallest and the rarest. It was printed by Kells to be given to Johnson's friends. The cover is light brown "Fabrikoid" with a dark brown spine and the title printed in gold. Most of the subsequent printings are set in the same type and layout. The bindings vary not only with new additions but also within the same editions.
See Appendix.

∞

77. LINCOLN ON THE CONSTITUTION
4 1/8" X 7"

The folded single sheet has an embossed head of Abraham Lincoln on the cover and a quote by Lincoln printed inside. A copy was placed in every copy of the Declaration of Independence and Constitution printed by Kells.

∞

1925

∞

78. AMERICA AS INTERPRETED IN THE DECLARATION OF INDEPENDENCE, TOGETHER WITH THE PRIVILEGES AND RESPONSIBILITIES OF CITIZENSHIP, AS SET FORTH IN CONSTITUTION OF THE UNITED STATES.
5 1/2" X 8"

Heavy white stock cover tied with cord with an embossed Delaware seal. The initial letter "A" is printed in red with the remainder of the title in black. The first page has a US flag embossed in color. The text is printed in black with side notes in red.

Presented by the Service Citizens of Delaware To_____ Upon declaration of his intention to become a citizen of the United States.

The only copy the authors have been able to locate is in the Historical Society of Delaware.

∞

79. THE ONE-TEACHER SCHOOL IN DELAWARE, A STUDY IN ATTENDANCE.
By Cooper, Richard Watson and Cooper, Hermann
8" X 10 3/4" 434 pages, Curtis Velvet Finish paper.
Bureau of Education Service Citizen of Delaware
Dark blue, cloth cover binding with gold lettering and a blind stamped border. Several graphs and charts along with six photos of Delaware schools dominate the book.
IMPRINT: University of Delaware Press Newark Delaware 1925.

Printed from type, August, 1925. Printed by The Craftsmen at Kells
Newark, Delaware
NOTE: Dedicated to "Farm Boys and Girls of Delaware. Patrons of
Democracy. "

∞

80. PROGRAM of EXERCISES of the DEDICATION of the MEMORIAL LIBRARY at THE UNIVERSITY OF DELAWARE at NEWARK the TWENTY-THIRD DAY of MAY, NINETEEN HUNDRED TWENTY-FIVE
6 3/4" X 10 1/2" single fold.
Heavy ivory stock with deckle edge top and bottom. "The" and "of"
done in Kells style.

∞

81. THE SENIOR CLASS of NEWARK HIGH SCHOOL PRESENTS " COME OUT of the KITCHEN.
5 3/4" X 8 1/2" 10 pages.
The program contains several local business advertisements with a
small section to cover the Cast of Characters.

∞

82. MEMORIAL BOOK
13" X 19"
The binding is of French calfskin in deep brown. The paper is white
Fabriano, made by hand in Palermo, Italy with deckled edges. The
book weighs nearly twenty-five pounds and is five inches thick. The
front and back cover have imbedded lines dyed in black with a gold
diamond stud at each corner. In the middle of the front cover is a gold
War Medal struck by order of the Governor and General Assembly of
Delaware.
See Appendix.

∞

83. PARENT TEACHER ASSOCIATION POSTER

Two distinctive art posters on illiteracy were distributed by the P. T. A. districts in Delaware. The posters were from original paintings done by J. Eads Collins, a prominent Wilmington artist. The Post printed the following description: "The first poster mailed represents a moonlight scene in Sussex, with the famous pines and sand of that territory a prominent factor in the painting. A young man stands in bewilderment before a sign he cannot read. The sign says 'Opportunity School--seven to nine p. m.' The second poster has for its main motive the figure of a woman, draped in the blue and gold of Delaware, lifting her eyes, she catches a vision of the Stars and Strips emerging from a passing cloud. She is arrested by the thought 'The first star in the flag is mine.' The printing of the posters involved four-color process printing and was completed the other day by the Craftsmen at Kells. They are believed to be the largest ever printed in the State."

∞

1926

∞

84. DELAWARE.

By State of Delaware. Published by the Bureau of Markets of the State Board of Agriculture State of Delaware. Copyright 1926.
6" X 8 7/8" 77 pages.
Stiff paper binding with a photo of the Cape Henlopen Lighthouse. 13,000 copies printed.
History, description, travel, and economic conditions.
IMPRINT: On the back of the last page: "Printed by the Craftsmen at Kells Newark, Delaware" with triangle.
See Appendix.
See the same title printed in 1932 for a second edition.

∞

85. DELAWARE ALUMNI NEWS

Published by the Executive Committee of the Alumni Association at Newark, Delaware.
6 3/4" X 11" four page paper.

"A tidy newspaper for 1200 Graduates; no pictures; no editorials; just news". The Editor was T. R. Dantz, manager of the Press of Kells. It was mailed free to alumni and seems to be a fore-runner of the current University of Delaware Messenger.

∞
1928
∞

86. PAMBO
Published by the Press Club, Women's College.
6 1/2" X 9 3/4" pages range from 40 to 50.
The paper cover carried a range of designs from a simple Pambo inside a double box to artful silk screening. The printing was done on paper containing varied watermarks including Strathmore Courier, Linweave Text and Suede Finish.
See Appendix.

∞

87. BLUE AND GOLD 1928-1929
9 1/4" X 12 1/4" 190 PAGES.
Blue "Fabrikoid" binding with embossed door stamped in gold.
IMPRINT: Kells.
Subject: Women's College yearbook.

∞

88. DELAWARE NOTES
Fifth Series, 1928
6" X 9" 94 pages on University of Delaware Press paper.
Light tan paper over board binding with a paper label printed in dark brown.
Sixth Series, 1930
6" X 9" 152 pages on University of Delaware Press paper.
Brown paper over board binding with a paper label printed in dark brown.

See Appendix.

∞

89. COLONIAL FINANCES IN DELAWARE
By Rodney, Richard Seymour 1882-1963 Associate Judge, Supreme
Court of Delaware.
6 1/4" X 9 1/4" 68 pages deckle edge with UTOPIAN paper.
The first edition was bound in blue paper over board, with tan spine,
and a tan paste–on label printed in blue. The last page is inscribed;
Five hundred copies of this edition were printed for Wilmington Trust
Company in December, 1928 of which this copy is Number____.
Another 1500 copies of the books were later printed for Wilmington
Trust.
The second edition is the same size and differs from the first by hav-
ing a stiff paper cover with reversed colors. It has the same number of
pages and water marks with The Press of Kells, Inc.
printed at the bottom of the last page. It was also printed in 1928 but
is not a Wilmington Trust limited edition. A nice feature of both is
the facsimiles of documents and paper money.
IMPRINT: On the bottom of the last page The Press of Kells, Inc.
Newark, Delaware.

∞

90. OFFICIAL FLAG OF DELAWARE
Printed in color on heavy enameled paper. The official Delaware State
flag established in 1914.

∞

1929
∞

91. THE UNKNOWN SOLDIER
By Dawson, Coningsby 1883-1959
6 1/2" X 9 1/2" 48 pages with deckle edge and UTOPIAN (Curtis)
paper.

The binding of the autographed edition is black paper over board with gold silk-screened lines and stars. The last page is inscribed: "One hundred and ninety-nine autographed editions have been printed of which this is number......

The unsigned edition is bound in blue with gold spots and a gold paste on label with a brown spine.

It is not known how may unsigned, unnumbered copies were printed.

IMPRINT: Newark - Delaware The Press of Kells Inc. 1929

∞

92. PROGRAM OF THE FIFTEENTH ANNIVERSARY OF THE OPENING OF THE WOMEN'S COLLEGE OF THE UNIVERSITY OF DELAWARE ON OCTOBER TENTH, NINETEEN HUNDRED AND TWENTY-NINE.

3 1/2" X 5 3/4"

Bi-fold card stock with a single front-page deckle edge has a half tone illustration of the women's College on the front and contains the activity schedule.

∞

93. TOWER HILL SCHOOL 1929-1930

By Tower Hill School.

7" X 11" 183 pages.

The binding is yapped, reinforced brown paper cover, printed with green and gold, showing the state of Delaware and State seal.

IMPRINT: On the lower right corner of the back cover The Press of Kells, Inc. Newark.

NOTE: Many of the Board of Trustees of the school were close friends and associates of Everett.

∞

1930

∞

94. LIVES OF VICTOR AND JOSEPHINE DU PONT

By Du Pont, B. G.

6" X 8 7/8" 273 pages DUCHESS paper.

The full Morocco binding and turn-ins have marbled end-pages and top edge gilt. The spine has the title stamped in gold with gold boxes between the raised spine bars and triple gold boxes on the front and back cover. Printing was limited to only three hundred copies intended for private distribution, not individually numbered.

IMPRINT: Printed in The United States of America by the Press of Kells, Inc. at Newark, Delaware 1930.

∞

95. OFFICIAL PROGRAM OF THE TWELFTH ANNUAL MEETING OF DELAWARE STATE EDUCATION ASSOCIATION.

4" x 8 3/4" 47 pages.

Blue paper cover has the title and hen with three chicks printed in gold.

IMPRINT: Triangle and THE PRESS OF KELLS, Inc. Newark, Delaware printed on back cover.

∞

1931

∞

96. MISCELLANEOUS SHORT ADDRESSES

By Conwell, Charles S.

4 3/4" X 7" 140 pages WARREN'S OLD STYLE paper.

Light blue "Fabrikoid" binding with gold lettering on the cover and spine. Copyright 1931 by Conwell. Opposite the title page is a tipped in half tone of the author.

IMPRINT: Published by the Press of Kells Inc. Kells is also printed in gold on the spine.

See Appendix.

∞

97. DRY LAW, FACTS NOT FICTION 1890 - COMPARATIVE FACTS - 1931, SENSATIONAL DRY RAID FACTS, DELAWARE FACT FINDER FACTS.

By Wilson, Harold David (Three Gun)
4 5/8" X 7 1/2" 224 pages.
The second edition, printed by Kells, bound in blue cloth over board with title printed in gold. The dust jacket done in tan paper with title printed in blue. A first edition has not been found. The book contains photos and cartoons. At a dinner in honor of Wilson, Kells printed the menu in the shape of a gun.
IMPRINT: The Press of Kells, Inc. Newark, Delaware

∞

1932

∞

98. DELAWARE

By State of Delaware
6" X 9" 77 pages.
Published by the Bureau of Markets of the State Board of Agriculture, State of Delaware.
Stiff paper binding with a color photo of peaches on a tree.
The book contains many of the same photos as the 1926 publication along with the same brief history.
IMPRINT: Printed by the Craftsmen at Kells 1932.

∞

99. DU PONT DE NEMOURS, 1739-1817

By Du Pont, B. G. (Bessie Gardner)
6" X 8 3/4" Volume I 179 pages Volume II 235 pages.
Full Morocco binding with turn-ins, (this one will fool you; it is really "Fabrikoid") marbled end-pages and top edge gilt complete with an open sided fitted case. Copyright 1933 by Pierre S. du Pont
IMPRINT: On the page facing the preface, Printed in The United States of America By the Craftsmen of Kells (The Press of Kells, Incorporated) At Newark, Delaware with Kells device.

∞
1934
∞

100. BRANDYWINE BULLETIN
Editor Otteni, Ernest
Business Manager Mahaffy, Rodmond S.
Published every Tuesday by The Press of Kells, Inc. the twelve-page newspaper had a weekly circulation of 8,000 copies in the Brandywine area.
Printed by Kells from January 15, 1934 to December 10, 1935.
See Appendix

∞
1935
∞

101. THE AMERICAN LEGION AND AMERICAN LEGION AUXILIARY OF KENNETT SQUARE, PENNSYLVANIA PRESENTS HISTORIC DELAWARE / PRODUCED BY JOHN T. HALL; DIALOGUE AND CONTINUITY WRITTEN BY JOHN T. HALL; OUTLINE BY CHRISTIAN C. SANDERSON; INCIDENTAL MUSIC BY CHRISTIAN C. SANDERSON AND HIS POCOPSON VALLEY BOYS; MUSIC BY GEORGE MADDEN AND HIS ORCHESTRA.
9" X 12" 60 pages.
DESCRIPTION: The cover has a multi-color print of Lafayette at the Battle of Brandywine by Frank Schoonover.
SUBJECTS: Longwood Open Air Theater June 20th through 22nd, 1935 programs.
IMPRINT: On the bottom of the back page is printed The Press of Kells, Inc., Newark, Delaware.

∞

102. PROGRAM OF THE COMMENCEMENT EXERCISES OF THE UNIVERSITY OF DELAWARE.

6" x 9" 8 Pages with KINGSLEY paper.
High quality rag paper with black print.

∞

103. D'ANDELOT AND BELIN FAMILIES
By Laird, Mary A. B. Du Pont (Mary Alletta Belin Du Pont), 1878-1938
8" X 11 1/4" 60 pages.
Dark blue cloth over board cover binding with gold lettering. Many of the pages are fold—out extensions for the family tree. A second edition was made up of 100 copies with some additions.
IMPRINT: The left side page prior to the index has in small print, The Press of Kells, Inc. 1935.

∞

104. A COLLECTION OF RECIPES
By du Pont, Irene S.
5 3/4" X 7 1/8" 191 pages P. M. FABRIANO DUCA D'ESTE paper. Green "Fabrikoid" binding.
The book contains 66 recipes on 91 pages and has 100 blank pages in the back for the writing of personal recipes. The recipes were collected from Irene du Pont's mother and friends and cleverly illustrated with drawings of frogs.

∞

1936
∞

105. LITTLE KNOWN HISTORY OF NEWARK, DELAWARE AND ITS ENVIRONS
By Cooch, Francis Allyn with introduction by George H. Ryden.
6 1/4" X 9 1/2" 297 pages.
Medium blue, cloth over board binding with gold letters. It contains 25 photos with an extensive index that could read as a Who's Who in Newark. The white dustjacket has a likeness of Levi G. Cooch.

IMPRINT: PRESS OF KELLS printed on the spine and the title page.

∞

106.   ABRACADABRA...; OR ... ONE DEMOCRAT TO ANOTHER
By Rand, Clayton
5 1/2" X 7 3/4" 101 pages.
Light blue board binding with dark blue tape spine. The cover is printed with an inverted triangle with ABRACADABRA at the top, shortened by one letter per line until only the letter A remains.

ABRACADABRA

ABRACADABR

ABRACADAB

ABRACADA

ABRACAD

ABRACA

ABRAC

ABRA

ABR

AB

A

Second printing, abridged.
IMPRINT: The Press of Kells c1936

∞

1937

∞

107.   HANDBOOK 1936-1937 OF THE WILLIAM PENN HIGH SCHOOL, THE CHERRY AND BLACK HANDBOOK
By Burr, Samuel Engle
4 1/4" X 5 1/2" 119 pages.
Red paper binding with black print. The book contains six halftone pictures and a brief history of education in New Castle, Delaware.
IMPRINT: Below the copyright, "Printed by THE PRESS OF

KELLS, Newark, Delaware."

❧

108. GENERAL PROVISIONS RESPECTING DOMESTIC AND FOREIGN CORPORATIONS CONTAINED IN THE GENERAL CORPORATION LAW OF THE STATE OF DELAWARE

By State of Delaware

The Press of Kells printed the 1937 issue. The book is yellow with the title and date printed on the spine. A different printer prints the book every year.

NOTE: Mercantile Printing Co. Wilm, De, printed the edition during Johnson's term as Secretary of State.

❧

1938
❧

109. A POSTAL HISTORY OF DELAWARE

By Bounds, Harvey Cochran

6" X 9" 121 pages.

Light blue paper binding with dark blue print.

IMPRINT: Copyright 1938 printed By Press of Kells Newark, Delaware

Unknown number printed and only thirty-eight were numbered and signed by author.

❧

110. RAPID DRILL ON FUNDAMENTALS OF FRENCH GRAMMAR

By Brinton, George Elder

4 1/2" X 11" 47 pages.

Bright blue cardboard binding held together by 3 snap-rings. The cover is printed in black with an imprint of a candle.

IMPRINT: Press of Kells Newark, Delaware 1938.

∞

III. DELAWARE TERCENTENARY ALMANACK & HISTOR-
ICAL REPOSITORY 1938 BEING A VALUABLE COMPENDIUM OF
HISTORICAL INFORMATION CONCERNING THE STATE OF DELAWARE
LAVISHLY EMBELLISHED AND ENLIVENED WITH FELICITOUS ILLUS-
TRATIONS BY THE MOST EMINENT ARTISTS AND ACCURATE MAPS
AND PLANS BY THE MOST INGENIOUS CARTOGRAPHERS, IMPRINTED
FOR AND PUBLISHED BY THE DELAWARE TERCENTENARY
COMMISSION IN THE MONTH OF DECEMBER, AD 1937 AND TO BE
SOLD BY IT AT ONE DOLLAR A COPY OF THIS, THE FIRST EDITION.
By Ward, Christopher L.
6 1/2" X 9 1/4" 56 pages.
Drawings done by Stanley M. Arthurs, Clifford W. Ashley, Albert
Kruse, Frank E. Schoonover, Andrew Wyeth and N. C. Wyeth.
On the second to the last page thanks is given to The Press of Kells for
helpful co-operation in the matter of typographical design. "This First
Edition was printed December, 1937 at The Press of Kells, Newark,
Del., on 100% rag paper made by Curtis Paper Co., also of Newark,
and bound in Lynnene book-cloth made by Joseph Bancroft & Sons Co.
of Wilmington."
The second edition has the watermarks of LINWEAVE MILANO
AMERICA (circled), with two elaborate letters, L and M entwined and
is bound in brown paper over board with a dark brown spine.
    Governor Richard C. McMullen signed a Proclamation
marking March 29, 1938 Delaware Tercentenary Day.

∞

ALPHABETICAL LISTING BY TITLE

∞

By Morris, Hugh M.

78.
AMERICA AS INTERPRETED IN THE DECLARATION OF
INDEPENDENCE, TOGETHER WITH THE PRIVILEGES AND
RESPONSIBILITIES OF CITIZENSHIP, AS SET FORTH IN CON-
STITUTION OF THE UNITED STATES.
Presented by the Service Citizens of Delaware

101.
AMERICAN LEGION AND AMERICAN LEGION AUXILIARY
OF KENNETT SQUARE, PENNSYLVANIA PRESENTS HIS-
TORIC DELAWARE / PRODUCED BY JOHN T. HALL; DIA-
LOGUE AND CONTINUITY WRITTEN BY JOHN T. HALL;
OUTLINE BY CHRISTIAN C. SANDERSON; INCIDENTAL
MUSIC BY CHRISTIAN C. SANDERSON AND HIS POCOPSON
VALLEY BOYS; MUSIC BY GEORGE MADDEN AND HIS
ORCHESTRA, THE

71.
AN AMERICAN LOOKS AT HIS WORLD:
By Glenn Frank.

40.
ANNUAL BANQUET OF THE ALUMNI OF DELAWARE COL-
LEGE

45.
BLUE AND GOLD 1919, THE

46.
BLUE AND GOLD 1920

64.
BLUE AND GOLD 1922, THE

55.
BLUE HEN'S CHICKS IN CARICATURE, THE

By Gee Tee Maxwell

56.
BLUE KETTLE, THE
By Women's College staff and students

100.
BRANDYWINE BULLETIN
Editor Otteni, Ernest

2.
CALENDARS

35.
CHRONICLE OF 1918

104.
COLLECTION OF RECIPES, A
By du Pont, Irene S.

89.
COLONIAL FINANCES IN DELAWARE
By Rodney, Richard Seymour 1882-1963

32.
COMMENCEMENT DELAWARE COLLEGE JUNE TENTH TO JUNE THIRTEENTH NINE HUNDRED AND SEVENTEEN.

102. COMMENCEMENT EXERCISES OF THE UNIVERSITY OF DELAWARE, PROGRAM OF THE. (1935)

51.
CONVENTION of the AMERICAN ROADBUILDERS ASSOCIATION

27.
CREED AND DEED
By Hugo, Victor

29.
CULTURAL-PRACTICAL COLLEGE EDUCATION FOR WOMEN, A
By Women's College of Delaware

26.
DANCE PROGRAM FOR THE JUNIOR PROM

103.
D'ANDELOT AND BELIN FAMILIES
By Laird, Mary A. B. Du Pont

76.
DECLARATION OF INDEPENDENCE AND CONSTITUTION OF THE UNITED STATES OF AMERICA

84.
DELAWARE. (1926)
Published by the Bureau of Markets of the State Board of Agriculture State of Delaware.

98.
DELAWARE. (1932)
Published by the Bureau of Markets of the State board of agriculture, state of Delaware.

85.
DELAWARE ALUMNI NEWS
Published by the Executive Committee of the Alumni Association at Newark, Delaware.

73.
DELAWARE BULLETIN, THE
By the Alumni Association of Delaware College of the University of Delaware.

10.
DELAWARE COLLEGE in the SERVICE of THE NATION

6.
DELAWARE COLLEGE REVIEW
By Delaware College staff and students.

7.
DELAWARE FARMER, THE

43.
DELAWARE MAGAZINE
Published monthly by Delaware Magazine Publishing Co., at Newark, Delaware.

88.
DELAWARE NOTES

21.
DELAWARE SONG ALMA MATER

41.
DELAWARE STATE HIGHWAYS; THE STORY OF ROADS IN DELAWARE FROM THE DAYS OF THE "BEASTS OF *BUR-THEN"--TO THE ROAD TO TO-MORROW". By Delaware State Highway Dept.

111.
DELAWARE TERCENTENARY ALMANACK & HISTORICAL REPOSITORY 1938 By Ward, Christopher L.

65.
DELAWARE, ANNUAL OUTING OF THE SONS OF DELAWARE OF PHILADELPHIA

30.
MOTTO CARD

58.
DREAMS AND OBSERVATIONS BEING VERSES OF FANCY
AND FACT
By Benson, Alden Richardson 1860-1927

97.
DRY LAW, FACTS NOT FICTION 1890
By Wilson, Harold David (Three Gun)

99.
DU PONT DE NEMOURS, 1739-1817
By Du Pont, B. G.

54.
ENGLISH BIBLE: BEING A BOOK OF SELECTIONS FROM THE
KING JAMES VERSION, THE
Edited by Sypherd, Wilbur Owen

17.
ENGLISH COMPOSITION FOR COLLEGE FRESHMEN
By Sypherd, Wilbur Owen and Dutton, George Elliott.

47.
FIFTY YEARS OF DELAWARE COLLEGE 1870-1920
By Vallandigham Edward Noble 1854-1930

90.
Flag of Delaware, Official

108.
GENERAL PROVISIONS RESPECTING DOMESTIC AND FOR-
EIGN CORPORATIONS CONTAINED IN THE GENERAL COR-
PORATION LAW OF THE STATE OF DELAWARE
By State of Delaware

49.
Good Attendance Award

36.
GOSPEL ACCORDING TO SAINT JOHN AS FOUND IN THE
KING JAMES VERSION, THE

107.
HANDBOOK 1936-1937 of the WILLIAM PENN HIGH SCHOOL
By Burr, Samuel Engle

50.
THE INAUGURAL ADDRESS OF GOVERNOR DENNEY,
DELIVERED AT DOVER ON JANUARY THE EIGHTEENTH,
NINETEEN TWENTY-ONE, THE
By Denney, William D.

59.
JANUARY SUMMER, A
By Sharp, Dallas Lore, 1870-1929

74.
KAPPA ALPHA DANCE PROGRAM

52.
KELLS-THE STORY OF THE VISIT OF A VAGABOND PRINT-
ER TO THE SHOP WHERE MASTER CRAFTSMEN STUDY
AND WORK AT THE ART OF PRINTING.
By Vagabond Printer, [John Schultz]

75.
LECTURES ON HISTORY AND GOVERNMENT: SERIES ONE,
1923-1924
University of Delaware with an introduction by G. H. Ryden.

62.
LIBRARY AND WAR MEMORIAL CAMPAIGN, UNIVERSITY
OF DELAWARE 1922

63.
LIBRARY AND WAR MEMORIAL FOR THE STATE OF

DELAWARE, A

67.
LIFE OF ELEUTHERE IRENEE DUPONT, FROM CONTEMPO-
RARY CORRESPONDENCE 1792-1794 11 VOLUMES.
By du Pont, B. G.

77.
LINCOLN ON THE CONSTITUTION

105.
LITTLE KNOWN HISTORY OF NEWARK, DELAWARE AND
ITS ENVIRONS
By Cooch, Francis Allyn with introduction by Ryden, George H.

94.
LIVES OF VICTOR AND JOSEPHINE DU PONT
By Du Pont, B. G.

53.
LOG IN THE DAM, THE
By Johnson, Everett C.

9.
LOUISE HOMER CONCERT PROGRAM

14.
A little magazine from a neighboring town which "promises to
become a monthly affair"

82.
MEMORIAL BOOK

96.
MISCELLANEOUS SHORT ADDRESSES
By Conwell, Charles S.

42.
MOODS, A MODERN RUBAIYAT, also To The Men of Sorrows And Other Poems.
By Bell, Jerome B.

66.
NATIONAL EDUCATION IN THE UNITED STATES OF AMERICA,
By Du Pont de Nemours, Pierre Samuel, 1739-1817.

68.
NEGRO SCHOOL ATTENDANCE IN DELAWARE
By Cooper, Richard Watson and Cooper, Hermann

13.
NEWARK TRUST AND SAFE COMPANY, THE

79.
ONE-TEACHER SCHOOL IN DELAWARE, A STUDY IN ATTENDANCE, THE
By Cooper, Richard Watson and Cooper, Hermann

16.
ORDINANCES RELATING TO THE GOVERNMENT OF THE TOWN OF NEWARK DELAWARE.

86.
 PAMBO
Published by the Press Club, Women's College.

8.
PANAMA CANAL
Folder courtesy of The Farmer's Trust of Newark

83.
PARENT TEACHER ASSOCIATION POSTER
By Collins, J. Eads

57.
POEMS TO IANTHE
By Landor, Walter Savage, arranged, with an introduction and notes,
By Foster, Finley M. K.

109.
POSTAL HISTORY OF DELAWARE, A
By Bounds, Harvey Cochran

20.
PRESS OF KELLS, THE

19.
Print of Company E of Newark--Organized Militia of Delaware at
Camp Miller

72.
PRINT OF BOIS DES FOSSE'S
By Arthurs, Stanley

39.
PROGRAM AS ARRANGED by PRESIDENT MITCHELL &
MEMBERS of FACULTY of DELAWARE COLLEGE for the
ENTERTAINMENT of the DELMARVIA PRESS ASSOCIATION

80.
PROGRAM of EXERCISES of the DEDICATION of the MEMORI-
AL LIBRARY at THE UNIVERSITY OF DELAWARE at NEWARK
the TWENTY-THIRD DAY of MAY, NINETEEN HUNDRED
TWENTY-FIVE

92.
PROGRAM OF THE FIFTEENTH ANNIVERSARY OF THE
OPENING OF THE WOMEN'S COLLEGE OF THE UNIVERSITY
OF DELAWARE ON OCTOBER TENTH, NINETEEN HUN-
DRED AND TWENTY-NINE.

110.
RAPID DRILL ON FUNDAMENTALS OF FRENCH GRAMMAR
By Brinton, George Elder

81.
SENIOR CLASS of NEWARK HIGH SCHOOL PRESENTS COME
OUT of the KITCHEN, THE

24.
SHAKSPERE (Motto Card)

22.
SHAKSPERE FESTIVAL, THE

1.
SPECIMENS OF ENGLISH PROSE COMPOSITION.
By Sypherd, Wilbur Owen

12.
STATE ELECTION BALLOTS

70.
SUPPORTING AND DEFENDING THE CONSTITUTION
By Black, Henry Campbell, LL.D.

25.
TALE OF TWELFTH NIGHT or WHAT YOU WILL, THE
By Lamb, Charles and Mary

31.
THANKSGIVING PROCLAMATION 1917
By Governor John G. Townsend and Secretary of State E. C. Johnson.

60.
THIRTY HOME LESSONS FOR FOREIGN-BORN WOMEN IN
DELAWARE
By Hart, Helen

93.
TOWER HILL SCHOOL 1929-1930
By Tower Hill School.

91.
UNKNOWN SOLDIER, THE
By Dawson, Coningsby

11.
VIEWS OF DELAWARE COLLEGE
By Delaware College

48.
WHAT DELAWARE MAKES AND SPENDS
By Delaware State Program Clearing House, 1920

37.
WIN-THE-WAR CONFERENCE held under the auspices of the
STATE COUNCIL of DEFENSE for Delaware at Wilmington,
Wednesday, July 10, 1918.

38.
WIN THE WAR
By State Council of Defense

∞

ADDITIONAL PRINTINGS BY THE PRESS OF KELLS

∞

Kells performed a variety of printing jobs for a large number of businesses and organizations such as DuPont Dye Department,
Continental Fibre Co. and personal items for P.S. du Pont such as over
$2,000 worth of printing for a complimentary dinner in 1925. Work
was also preformed for most, if not all, the departments of the
Delaware College (University of Delaware) and nearly exclusively for

the Women's College and the Agricultural Department. Precious few records or work orders are now available but two such invoices found show a job for Agricultural Letters and Census Forms done on May 21, 1917 contained order number 3731. In July 16, 1918 an invoice for the Win-the-War Conference was numbered 4744. This would indicate that over one thousand jobs were performed in fourteen months. Listed below are some of the names of businesses and private persons that contracted with Kells for printing. The list is by no means complete but gives a good example of the variety of work done.

Andale Company - gummed stickers and Bulletins
Delaware P.T.A. - health bulletins
Wilmington Trust Company - financial statements
Farmers Trust Co. - protest forms
Wilmington Elec. Specialty Co. - statements
Miss Rebecca Gallagher - Christmas cards
Newark Trust Co. - general ledger forms, teller sheets, bills, certified check record
Robert Studio - Christmas cards
Edward Stern & Co. - DuPont forms
Beta Sigma Bldg. Corp.
Christiana Public School
Community Newspaper, Inc.
Newark Flower Shop
Oriole Coffee Shop
J. B. Wilson Music Co.
Chambers-Wilmington Inc.
Walker Shellender
Miss Nellie B. Wilson
D. J. Doyle
L. J. Flick
Mrs. Edgar Clark
Oldach Company
Edward Stern & Co.
U of D - letterheads and envelopes, blank applications, foreign study plan, financial reports
The Diamond Ice and Coal Co.

Three out–of–town jobs - a 100 page book, a bank
brochure, a lodge book

Items listed in the Post February 11, 1914; "A plant
Catalogue for a Kent County firm in three colors, Two fire Advertising
Brochures for a prominent Delaware Financial Institution in Three
colors, A Program for the season's greatest musical event, Two monthly publications, A Poultry Farm Catalogue, Menu's for two prominent
banquets and An Advertising booklet for a Shoe House."

For many years Kells printed Christmas Cards and would
advertise heavily in the Post. In 1917 the ad mentioned the need to
order cards early due to the lack of variety caused by the shortage of
engravers. "The Government needs copper plate engravers, and in
response to the call hundreds of operators have been released by the
commercial companies. So ordering early is the only way to assure sat-
isfaction." " Some are engraved with exquisite workmanship, some are
hand tinted, and others are attractively printed."

Only one example of the Christmas Cards has been found by
the authors and that was printed in the Post in 1925.

JANUARY 9, 1918 EFFICIENT BUSINESS METHODS,

Demand Printing---Catalogues, Booklets, Printed
Forms, Stationery, and lots of it. "Get it down in black
and white," is the slogan of the successful businessman,
and he equips his offices with the means of doing it.

What is the most annoying detail to keep track of
in your business? A printed form will help you solve
your difficulty and at the same time, by reducing the
time required to a minimum, make System your slave
rather than your master.

BUSINESS CARDS AND STATIONERY

At KELLS NEWARK, DELAWARE

Print work done on "fine Irish Linen" The Whiting
Papers Type used Old English or Cheltenham.

June 16 1926 EX LIBRIS

Character, individuality and distinction are

> acquired by your having your personal bookplate.
>
> The Craftsmen of Kells will reproduce your own
> idea or prepare an original bookplate for you.
>
> Prices range from $8 to $25 for lots of 500.

The only examples of bookplates, other than Everett's, that can be traced to Kells are those used in the Yearbooks. Some of these are printed inside the front cover and others are tipped in.

∞

BIBLIOGRAPHY APPENDIX
∞

6. 1913
DELAWARE COLLEGE REVIEW
By staff and students.

NOTE: The Review started on June 1, 1882 and continues today although it has taken the form of a campus newspaper and no longer features fine literary articles. The Star Printing Co. printed the Review prior to 1913.

∞

7. 1914
THE DELAWARE FARMER

According to History of The Delaware State Grange 1875-1975, by Joanne O. Passmore, a paper put out by the State Grange was also called *The Delaware Farmer*. She was able to locate only one copy, dated October 6, 1876 (in the Wilmington Free Library). The paper was published under that name from 1875 to 1878 and the editor in 1878 was Professor A. D. Porter of Delaware College. The State Grange again published a paper by the name of *The Delaware Farm and Home* from 1885 to 1902. Passmore makes no mention of *The Delaware Farmer* printed by Kells that can also be found in the Wilmington Free Library.

∞

10.   1914
DELAWARE COLLEGE IN THE SERVICE OF THE NATION

The text is made up of speeches by, Right Reverend Frederick J. Kinsman, D. D., Charles M. Curtis, Honorable George W. Marshall, M. D., George A. Harter, M. A., Ph. D., Victor B. Woolley, LL.D, Henry Ridgely, Esquire, Samuel Chiles Mitchell, Ph. D., George Edward Reed, Ph.D., D. D., Everett C. Johnson, Winifred J. Robinson, Ph. D., Mrs. A. D. Warner, and Mrs. Lois Kimball Matthews, Ph. D.

∞

20.   1916
THE PRESS OF KELLS

The two pages of text;

Kells was a Monastery in Ireland where in the Seventh Century, Good Monk Columba gave to the world the "Book of Kells," so perfect in design, so rich in coloring, that it is pronounced even to this day the most beautiful book in the world. In this Book of Kells, now jealously cared for at the University of Dublin, is found the Four Gospels and notes of tradition and experiences of the life around the country-side.

So our shop is called Kells. Out here in the open, with light and sunshine, we study and work at the art of printing with the peace and love that comes with work, well done.

Serious but full of fun and good cheer we believe that our Ideal represented by Head, Heart and Hand in our Imprint, is the incentive that will one day make for our Success. Spacing our type with a little thought, mixing a little brains with our ink, locking up our forms with a smile, we go to press with anxiety and eagerness of the printer born----and are enjoying the work.

Here is printed the Newark Post, where is published a part of the Truth we know.

So this is in a word the meaning of Kells. There is, in this Shop an Idea, and to make it effective in this work-a-day world is our Ideal.

THE CRAFTSMEN AT KELLS

∞

22. 1916
THE SHAKSPERE FESTIVAL

"A Community Celebration on the occasion of the three-hundredth Anniversary of the death of William Shakspere. Consisting of a pageant depicting some scenes from life and times of the Dramatist; the Performance of 'The Twelfth Night'; and an address on the Universality of his work."
"Given at Newark, Delaware on April twenty-eight and twenty-nine, nineteen hundred and sixteen. Under the direction of the Department of English of Delaware College and The Women's College of Delaware, and held on April 28 and 29."
Pageant: Frazer Field, Play: Opera House, Lecture: The Oratory

∞

27. 1916
CREED AND DEED
By Hugo, Victor
Kells description of the book:

...AT KELLS, where Craftsmen study and work at the Art of Printing, There has been printed the story of the visit of the Good old Bishop to the Conventionalist. The work has been done with care and in reverent keeping with the theme.

Set by hand in good old Bookman type, an initial letter of Cathedral suggestions, printed on Stratford paper, it touches the eye of the Book lover. Then in honor of the Bishop, it is bound in limp purple leather and stamped in Gold. One Hundred and One Copies, hand numbered completes this first edition where truly the Head, Heart and Hand of our Imprint worked to full heart's joy and content.

Aside from the story of the visit, a short description of the Bishop has been culled from the Master Creator, giving a glimpse of the Grand Good Man, at home, in his garden, at his desk, on the street--in all of which is found his philosophy of Life as he saw and lived. All of which, we have called Creed and Deed. The pleasure of doing something well--that is the reward of the Kids at Kells. It is now sent out to friends that they may share the delight of owning a beautiful book, made by honest and loving hands. As costumed with the Craftsmen of olden days, we whisper, God Speed.

∞

36. 1918
THE GOSPEL ACCORDING TO SAINT JOHN AS FOUND IN THE KING JAMES VERSION
Advertisement printed in the Newark Post February 26, 1919:

ANOTHER BOOK FROM KELLS

Once in a while, in between times, the Boys and Girls out in the Shop print a Book just as they want it done. No instructions from the customer to follow. They do it just as they see it in their mind's eye, and work at it without regard to date of delivery.

This time, it is the Gospel of St. John according to the King James Version, with the exception that it is not versed but merely paragraphed. Set in 12 point good old type Cheltenham, it makes a book of 127 pages. Initial letters and ornaments were made especially for this publication. It is printed in black, with colored initials set in gray block. The paper, heavy white antique. The binding is gray board, tipped with sheep skin and stamped in gold.

Simply and beautifully done, a book you would love. Some of our friends who buy everything we print, say it is our best. It really isn't---but you will like it.

For a present---well it is so happily different that it attracts.

The price---$2.00 while they last.

If you would like to see it, drop us a line and we will send it for your inspection.

The Scribe at Kells.

∞

52. 1921
KELLS-THE STORY OF THE VISIT OF A VAGABOND PRINTER TO THE SHOP WHERE MASTER CRAFTSMEN STUDY AND WORK AT THE ART OF PRINTING.

By Vagabond printer, [John Schultz]
NOTE: The booklet was used by way of an introduction and gives the philosophy of Kells. On the first page the following is printed in orange; "Art is the beautiful way of doing things". After the title page is; "You are welcome, worthy masters, -welcome all" -Hamlet. Next comes;

Just a Word By way of Introduction A kind, good friend whom The Old Man met out in the work-a-day world came to see us one fine day last spring. When he went home, he wrote this story and sent it back to us. Naturally we are a bit proud. He says some very good things, all of which are either true or it is our ambition so to make them.

We have other friends who have never been to see us and our Shop-but just hope to come some day. That they may catch a glimpse of the place, we are printing this story by our good friend.

He calls himself a Vagabond Printer. If like him, they are not so bad as the term is sometimes interpreted. He is a philosopher, a man of world experience, a printer, a writer and lover of Truth-and a friend.

He and our other friends are welcome, always. It is they that make Kells.

Kells is Friendship put into type.

The Craftsmen at Kells.

∞

54. 1921
THE ENGLISH BIBLE: BEING A BOOK OF SELECTIONS FROM THE KING JAMES VERSION
Edited by Wilbur Owen Sypherd
NOTE: Second Edition, printed by The Press of Kells for the University of Delaware Press, in December 28, 1923 is slightly larger than the first addition on light linen rag. The edition was 1000 copies of which 500 copies were bound and 500 were stored in sheets at Kells to be bound when needed. Published by The Craftsmen of Kells, Newark Delaware 1921. The book was used in college English Literature courses around the United States. From the Forward...The basis of selection is the relative significance of the stories, songs, essays, letters of the Bible as literature and in literature....
In 1924 Ex-Governor John G. Townsend presented a copy to every schoolroom of the State, outside of Wilmington, an inscribed copy of Sypherd's Bible.

∞

55. 1921
THE BLUE HEN'S CHICKS IN CARICATURE
By Gee Tee Maxwell
NOTE: The book was marked Volume I but a second volume has not been found. The first volume contains Caricatures of 79 men who were prominent in Delaware during the war years 1919-1921. Further volumes were planned to feature more of Delaware citizens. Gee Tee Maxwell also did several cartoons for yearbooks and the Delaware Ledger. In 1932 Maxwell produced a second book called Centennial Sketches also depicting prominent Delawareans but it was not printed by Kells.

∞

57. 1922
POEMS TO IANTHE

By Landor, Walter Savage
COLOPHON: Here endeth the Book of Ianthe written by Walter
Savage Landor and edited by Finley M. K. Foster and printed by The
Craftsmen of Kells at their Shop at Newark Delaware on the tenth day
of March in the Year of our Lord MDCCCCXXII
NOTE: Dr. Landor Ph.D. was an Associate Professor of English at the
University of Delaware.

∞

58. 1922

DREAMS AND OBSERVATIONS BEING VERSES OF FANCY
AND FACT

By Benson, Alden Richardson 1860-1927
COLOPHON:

> Here endeth the second edition of Dreams and
> Observations by Alden R. Benson. Printed in the sum-
> mer of Nineteen twenty-two at the shop called Kells
> which is on Welsh Lane in the town of Newark and the
> State of Delaware

> *To my friend*
> *Everett C. Johnson, artist, dreamer of*
> *dreams come true.*
> *Designer, craftsman, weaving the old*
> *with the new.*
> *Maker of beautiful books, the style of*
> *his work tells*
> *The "Art preservative of all arts"*
> *mastered at "Kells."*

(at the bottom is the Kells Triangle in orange.)
IMPRINT: Kells triangle on spine and "Printed at the Shop called
Kells Newark, Delaware" is printed on the title page.
NOTE: The author is a former Secretary of State from Delaware.

∞

59. 1922
A JANUARY SUMMER
By Sharp, Dallas Lore, 1870-1929
Dedication;

This charming nature story was written by Dallas Lore Sharp and the pictures were drawn by Robert Bruce Horsfall for the boys and girls of Delaware. Not for all the boys and girls of Delaware but for those who have made a worthy record in attendance at public schools. There is one man in our little state who is very anxious that all the school children shall grow up to be wise and noble men and women. To make this possible he has already given millions of dollars of money and spent days and weeks of his precious time. His name is Pierre Samuel duPont and to him this book is gratefully dedicated.

Because Delaware was the first of the colonies to sign the Constitution it is called the first state of the Union. Mr. duPont's great ambition is that Delaware also shall stand forever first among all the states in knowledge, wisdom, character and happiness. Through the Service Citizen he is trying to bring this idea to pass. No community can be at its best unless its men and women are well educated. Every extra day that a child attends school adds strength to the State and to the Nation. Every extra day spent in a classroom gives more mental and moral power to the boy or girl.

The Service Citizen is publishing this book not as a reward for good attendance but as a recognition of the fact that many pupils were wise enough to accept the privilege which the public schools offered. Each year, in Delaware, school attendance is improving and the time will soon come when every one of school age will be eager to get the full benefits of education.

Joseph H. Odell

Director, Service Citizen of Delaware.
Wilmington, Delaware
October 1, 1922.

∞

66. 1923
NATIONAL EDUCATION IN THE UNITED STATES OF AMERICA
By Du Pont de Nemours, Pierre Samuel
On the front of the dust-jacket is printed...

> This scheme for national education, written at the request of Thomas Jefferson more than a hundred and twenty years ago and never translated till now, must be of interest to all students of the science of education, especially as some of the methods suggested by Du Pont de Nemours are now being tried with apparent success in the very excellent schools of the middle west.

NOTE: The Treatise was first written in French by Pierre Samuel duPont at the request of Thomas Jefferson in 1800. The untranslated French second edition was found in the basement of the old Wilmington, Delaware Library at Eighth and Market. It was turned over to Mrs. B. G. duPont to be translated into English. 1,500 copies of the book were distributed free throughout the World at the expense of the Service Citizens. They were sent to virtually every college and university in the United States and to Congressmen, Senators and Representatives. Despite the fact that so many copies were given away the book was still able to pay for itself.

∞

68. 1923
NEGRO SCHOOL ATTENDANCE IN DELAWARE
By Cooper, Richard Watson and Cooper, Hermann
The book was published on August 3, 1923 with 1200 copies of which 1000 were sold to the Service Citizens of Delaware. The Press of Kells printed the book for the University of Delaware Press.

SUBJECT: "The problem of school attendance is here for the first time analyzed on the basis of complete records. The results are founded not only upon absence records but also upon the reason for each absence, which were carefully ascertained at the time of the absence. Educators who are concerned for their pupils in rural schools will find here an adequate summary of cause and effect."

NOTE: They were distributed free in the same manor as the "National Education" book. The book contained the following dedication: " The following pages are dedicated to the colored leaders of Delaware and to the colored fathers and mothers who care about the education of their children."

∞

71. 1923

AN AMERICAN LOOKS AT HIS WORLD: VARIATIONS ON A POINT OF VIEW / BY GLENN FRANK.

By Frank, Glenn 1887-1940.

The copyrights are 1919, 1920, 1922, and 1923 by the Century Company. 2500 copies printed and bound for the University of Delaware Press by The Craftsmen at Kells, Newark, Delaware, August, 1923. The books were paid for and distributed by the Service Citizens of Delaware.

NOTE: Glen Frank was editor of the Century Magazine and the articles in the book were also printed in the Century Magazine. The dust-jacket of one of Kells' books had the following blurb:

> The years after the war have presented more problems to thinking Americans than did the struggle itself. Mr. Frank's careful and logical analysis of these problems and his suggested solutions make the book more than a book of essays: it is a social philosophy in itself.

∞

72. 1923

PRINT OF BOIS DES FOSSES

By Arthurs, Stanley

"Interesting Work at Kells. Everyday something new,

something that challenges thought and attention. The last was a piece of Four Color work just off the Press. First a photograph of an Oil Painting, then plates made on copper. Then came the inks and blending of colors. Each form to hair register, with increasing eagerness for final results. Then the finish. There it was, a perfect blend. And still not satisfied, by experimenting we produced the effect of the brush strokes of the Artist. A perfect Gem. Even the Artist was struck with unqualified approval. A little Masterpiece--Yes. And done Here in Newark, Down at Kells, Where Master Craftsmen study and work at the Art of Printing at their Shop on Welsh Lane."

∞

75. 1924
LECTURES ON HISTORY AND GOVERNMENT: SERIES ONE, 1923-1924
University of Delaware

FOREWORD

This volume contains lectures on Government which were delivered during the years, 1923 and 1924, and is published in pursuance of the state law establishing the "State of Delaware Chair of History" and providing, among other objects, for a course of lectures to be given annually at the University of Delaware, and printed when possible.

...The University is also indebted to Mr. Everett C. Johnson, of the class of 1899, through whose generosity the publication of this book has been made possible...

∞

76. 1924
DECLARATION OF INDEPENDENCE AND CONSTITU-

TION OF THE UNITED STATES OF AMERICA

The "Fabrikoid" used ranges from light blue and tan to brown. The spine can be found in tan, reddish brown, red, brown and blue. Papers can be found with no watermark, DOUBLE ANTIQUE and DUCHESS. A copy was also bound in brown paper over board with title printed in dark brown.

The De-Luxe leather bound edition has a blind stamped cover design with ribbed spine. On the title page is "Americanization Bureau 835 Market Street Wilm, De." On the back page is the date November 1923 with the rounded Kells triangle.

The first edition was followed by an order of 2500 for Jos. Bancroft Company of Wilmington and was bound in their own book cloth to be distributed to every man, woman and child in their employ. Harry Harkins of the Hotel du Pont placed an order of a special edition and put a copy in every room in the hotel. The Waldorf in Washington D.C. and other large hotels followed with copies placed in their rooms. Orders came in from every state in the Union for business and organizations. The Continental Fibre Company had a special edition printed to be given to their customers with their compliments.

The Lions Club and The Rotary Club, both of Wilmington, secured special editions to give to each of their clubs in the United States. By 1925 the book had thirty different bindings.

What may have been the largest printing has the following on the last page: "This copy of the Declaration of Independence and the Constitution of the United States of America has been printed by The Craftsmen at Kells, at their shop in Newark, Delaware, nineteen hundred twenty-six, on the occasion of the Sesqui-Centennial Celebration marking one hundred and fifty years of American Independence." The book was designated as the official souvenir of the Exposition. This along with the deluxe edition contained a facsimile of the Declaration and a fold out of the Constitution. At lest 2600 copies were printed for the Sesqui-Centennial edition.

The binding of the book is in Colonial buff and blue, colors derived from the uniform of a Continental soldier. Plates for the facsimile of the Constitution were made from photographs of the original Constitution, taken just previous to the placing of that document in the permanent archives of the Congressional Library.

A few of the most notable differences between the two books, besides the later having the facsimiles, is the additional printing on the cover of the second book. The second printing also had a dust jacket with "Printed by The Craftsmen at Kells, Newark, Delaware U. S. A." Some pages contain minor differences in the printing.

William J. Highfield of Wilmington, Imperial Potentate of the Lu Lu Temple presented 1000 copies of the book to visiting Potentates of all Shrine templars as they gathered in Philadelphia for the Sesqui-Centennial Celebration.

In 1924 copies were given to graduates of the University of Delaware and high schools of the State of Delaware and were presented along with their diplomas. They had a tipped in plate with orange initial letter and brown type.

The Grolier Club of New York, through its Board of Censors, accepted the De Luxe edition. The De Luxe edition was bound in tooled leather complete with facsimiles. Before the mistake was discovered and corrected, page 61 under Amendment V read "...nor shall private property be taken for private use,...." The second "private" should read "public".

NOTE: The book was printed several different times, from the first edition in 1924 to the last edition printed some time after 1933. The first was due to Everett C. Johnson's inability to find a suitable copy of both in one book. The second was printed for Wilmington Trust Company Wilmington, Delaware in May 1924. A run that is dated September 1924 shows that it is the Seventh Printing. Some of the books contained a tipped in single fold leaf measuring 4" X 7" of stiff stock paper with an embossed head of Abraham Lincoln. Inside is a short speech by Lincoln about the Constitution.

P. S. du Pont purchased the Sesqui-Centennial copies that were not sold during that celebration and had them rebound in blue. A tipped in plate with "Compliments of the Association Against the Prohibition Amendment" was added and used by that association.

VARIOUS EDITIONS

Boy Scouts	$0.75 cents in brown Castilian
Popular Edition	1.00
Business Desk	2.00
Reading Table	2.50

Guest Room   4.00
Special Edition   5.00
Library (de luxe)   10.00 in Full Leather

∞

82. 1925
MEMORIAL BOOK
13" X 19"
The medal goes through the cover and the reverse can be seen on the inside. The front is the Seal of Delaware and the reverse reads;

> "IN HONOR OF THESE MAN WOMAN FROM
> DELAWARE WHO LOST THEIR LIVES IN THE
> WORLD WAR THIS MEDAL IS STRUCK BY PER-
> MISSION OF ACT OF THE GENERAL ASSEMBLY
> 1925"

The same medal, in sterling silver, was given to Delaware veterans who served in the First World War.

Only one book was produced and it is located on display at the University of Delaware Memorial Hall. The book has the name of each Delaware veteran who was killed during World War I. Each page has one name hand printed.

84. 1926
DELAWARE.
By State of Delaware. Published by the Bureau of Markets of the State Board of Agriculture State of Delaware.
The Legislature authorized the printing of 13,000 copies to be distributed through State offices, the Chamber of Commerce, the Service Clubs of the State and the Bureau of Markets.

The Cape Henlopen Light at Lewes fell into the sea just months before the printing of the book, after being undermined by the action of the waves in the almost two centuries it was in use as a beacon for mariners.

The book contains several photographs of scenes around Delaware, such as manufacturing plants, shipyards, various schools, old churches, bridges, roads, etc. Royden L. Hammond, of the State Board of Agriculture took most of the photographs.

An article in the Morning News praised the book stating that, "...is one of the most artistic in production as well as interesting in reading matter, that has ever been issued by the State. It contains an immense quantity of information concerning Delaware and its history."

∞

86. 1928
PAMBO

Published by the Press Club, Women's College.

The Christmas Issue 1935 carried an editorial titled The Craftsmen which begins "We felt like a classic example of the "Bagholder" this September when we returned to college and realized that the publication of PAMBO was to be our privilege-a privilege for which we were very grateful, but one about which we felt we knew so little. Our knowledge of publication hitherto had been a confused jumble of terms—galley sheets, the dummy, proofreading—and a not very certain knowledge of which of the terms came at the beginning of the process and which came at the end of it. We have groped around, made frantic trips to Kells with questions which we later blushingly realized were silly, and we say now, modestly, that we think we have learned something of this business of publication...."

∞

88. 1928
DELAWARE NOTES

Delaware Notes were printed one series a year from 1923 to 1961 with 33 series printed. The printing was done entirely by contract. The only series printed by Kells were the Fifth Series, 1928 and the Sixth Series, 1930.

In Hullihen papers box 317 1925-27 page 117 in a letter to Professor F.K.W. Drury of Brown Univ. Providence, Rhode Island dated Sept. 25, 1925 states the printing of *Delaware Notes* is let out entirely by contract.

The Delaware Notes were first printed in 1923 and were designed to encourage publication of original works. Prior to the

Delaware Notes, faculty writings would appear in a series called *Delaware College Bulletins* dating back to the 1890's. The most popular volumes were those containing the history of the university and became widely available in scholarly libraries. Those interested in specific articles could obtain an offprint, which meant that anyone published in the *Delaware Notes* would be more widely read.

The editor Ezra B. Crooks, a professor of philosophy and social science, continued to be editor until his retirement in 1942.

∞

96. 1931
MISCELLANEOUS SHORT ADDRESSES
By Conwell, Charles S.

EXPLANATORY NOTE

The enormous costs of the World War brought many nations to a condition approaching financial chaos. The United States, too, incurred a debt of many billions and consequent economic disturbance. Soon after the war, as an aid to the recovery of normal financial conditions, the Federal Government, co-operating with the banks of the State, launched thrift propaganda. Mr. John S. Rossell, Wilmington, Delaware, who was, at that time, president of the State Bankers' Association of Delaware, appointed the writer chairman of the Committee on Thrift and Savings of the Association; and in that connection the first three of the following addresses were delivered before the bankers. The others, selected from a large number, were delivered in churches, before women's clubs and county granges, and the Legislature. Many of them are extracts from longer addresses.

C. S. Conwell,
Camden, Delaware
May, 1931.

∞

100. 1934
BRANDYWINE BULLETIN

Editor Otteni, Ernest

The Brandywine Bulletin, formerly the *Brandywine News*, started in January 1934 under the ownership and management of the Brandywine Business Men's Association. The business manager Rodmond S. Mahaffy was also connected with the Press of Kells. Kells continued to print the newspaper up until December 10, 1935. On that date a section of a headline article read, "...The BRANDYWINE BULLETIN appears today under new management. The previous publisher, Rodmond S. Mahaffy, because of stress of private business and consequent inability to longer give the publication his personal attention has severed all connection with it...."

ILLUSTRATIONS

∞

INDEX

∞

Numbers in *italic* refer to illustrations

Of course you have not read this
far, and probably only
the beginning, so
here's the
end.

Thank you as usual.
Yours very truly,
Everett Johnson